The Slight Edge

The Slight Edge

Getting from Average to Advantage

LEO A. WEIDNER

with ROBERT L. WRIGHT

LEOWEIDNER.COM

CFI
Springville, Utah

The views expressed within this work are the sole responsibility of the author and do not necessarily reflect the position of Cedar Fort, Inc., or any other entity. Permission for the use of sources, graphics, and photos is also solely the responsibility of the author.

ISBN 978-1-59955-164-7

Published by CFI, an imprint of Cedar Fort, Inc., 2373 W. 700 S., Springville, UT 84663
Distributed by Cedar Fort, Inc., www.cedarfort.com

LIBRARY OF CONGRESS CATALOGING-IN-PUBLICATION DATA

Weidner, Leo A., 1934-
   The slight edge : getting from average to advantage / Leo A. Weidner with Robert L. Wright.
      p. cm.
   ISBN 978-1-59955-164-7
   1. Success—Psychological aspects. 2. Self-actualization (Psychology) I.
Wright, Robert L. II. Title.

   BF637.S8W347 2008
   158.1—dc22

                        2008010675

Cover design by Jen Boss
Cover design © 2008 by Lyle Mortimer
Edited and typeset by Melissa J. Caldwell

Printed in the United States of America

10 9 8 7 6 5 4 3 2 1

Printed on acid-free paper

I dedicate this book first to my sweetheart, Shirley, without whose guidance and support I could never have been anywhere close to putting all this together.

Next my fabulous parents, who for sixty-nine years were sweethearts until my dad passed away at age ninety-four. Their foundation of love and their believing I could do anything gave me the self-confidence to embark on this fabulous journey of life that I love.

Next the over 2,000 clients without whose feedback, trial and error, and suggestions, I could never have fine-tuned this work. My one-on-one experience with them gives this book credibility.

Of course, without my faith and belief in my Heavenly Father and His Son, Jesus Christ, I could never have done this for sure.

Table of Contents

The Ultimate LifeBalance Tool—Your LifeCreed

Helping Others Gain the Slight Edge

Introduction
What Keeps Us from Becoming All We Dream of Being?

As a LifeBalance Coach, my occupation for the last forty years, I speak with people every day, most of them on the phone, who have dreams and desires for themselves. Typically they don't speak of their dreams without some prompting, but they all have them. We all do. When we allow ourselves to do so, we see ourselves accomplishing so much more, of being so much more. Unfortunately for most of us, these moments are short-lived and do not propel us to greater heights, and in fact, they do the opposite. They create great pain and frustration and lead us to the conclusion that it's just too hard, too frustrating, or too disappointing, so it's best not to bother. We begin to be satisfied with what we have and to settle in where we are.

Yet some accomplish so much more. We occasionally meet someone who has obviously figured out how to turn these dreams into reality, to accomplish the impossible. Is it because they are never frustrated or don't have the challenges we face? Or do they have something more?

As you read this book, I will share with you an incredible journey. It's a journey that I have taken and one that I have led thousands through, one-on-one. It is a journey filled with adventure and excitement, and with incredible hope! Whether you see yourself with a better job, being more productive in your work, having a more fulfilling occupation or family life, having more successful children, or dream of an ideal relationship with your spouse, I'll help you build it, with a proven step-by-step implementation plan. As you begin to see this wonderful future opening up to you, not only will you accomplish all the things you have dreamed for yourself, you will also begin to dream even bigger, more fulfilling dreams and take those you love on this amazing journey.

So once again, I ask you, "What keeps us from becoming all we dream of being?" And I'll answer you, with absolute conviction—nothing. You just need to understand the little things, the step-by-step process you can do each day, and understand how to tap into the fuel that these emotional experiences can give us. You just need a slight edge. You don't need to start over, and you don't need to beat yourself up or everyone around you—you just need the Slight Edge. And I'll show you how to get it. It's worked for thousands of others. In fact, I can promise you that it has worked for everyone who has ever put these principles to work. It will work for you.

So hold on, it's going to be an exciting ride.

The Journey Begins

I had just finished a wonderful LifeBalance coaching session with one of my clients when the phone rang.

With my headset still in place, I hit the button and said, "Hi, this is Leo."

The voice on the other end began, "Leo, my name is John Reese. I was referred to you by two of your clients. I've seen what your program has done for them, and I want to know more."

After sharing some personal information and background with each other, John related the following:

"I was in the airport yesterday on my way to a business meeting. I had a few minutes before my plane boarded, so I browsed the bookstore. I thumbed through the latest self-help book and it was the same old story—lots of great ideas, in fact too many, but no simple way to implement them. I thought to myself, 'I can barely keep up with the stuff I have to do now. How in the world will I ever find the time to do this?' I knew the book would just end up on the shelf like all the others, so I put it back and walked out.

"Leo, your brochure talks about getting rid of stress, making more money in less time, improving marriage and family life, getting in shape, and even overcoming bad habits and addictions—and doing all that with some simple daily tools that really don't take that much time. It sounds too good to be true! How do you do it, and can you help me?"

Perhaps you can relate to this individual's frustrations. If so, you're not alone. Over the last forty years I have received literally thousands of calls like this one from a variety of wonderful people—stressed out entrepreneurs, executives, salespeople, and business owners wanting to make more money while balancing their work and family and personal lives; overwhelmed physicians, nurses, police officers, military personnel, and other emergency professionals coping with incredibly demanding careers while trying to nurture their relationships at home and maintain their own health and well-being; everyday people with goals and aspirations who believe they can be and do so much more, but they just don't know how to organize their lives to achieve their dreams.

Do you want to get rid of stress and enjoy more of the journey? Do you want to make more money while working fewer hours? Do you desire greater success and fulfillment in your career? Would you like to improve your marriage and family relationships? Do you want to lose weight or get in better shape? How about overcoming a nagging bad habit or addiction? Do you have unrealized goals that just never seem to work out? Whatever your dreams or desires may be, you *can* make them a reality, and the remarkable thing is, you don't have to make major changes in your life or spend great amounts of time to do it! You can achieve all the success you desire by doing a few easy, simple things each day—by gaining the Slight Edge in your work, family, and personal life. This book describes, in detail, the step-by-step process you need to follow that is tailored to your personality.

Dr. Napoleon Hill Issues a Challenge

We all have dreams of being more successful in our careers, families, and personal lives. But somehow in the immediacy of life, the vision of our ideal future gets put off and pushed back. Feeling overwhelmed by goals and changes that seem too big to manage, or by self-improvement programs with too many tips and techniques and not enough simple "how-tos" is nothing new. Back in the 1960s, I had the privilege of working closely with Dr. Napoleon Hill, founder of the modern self-improvement movement and author of the mega best-seller *Think and Grow Rich*. One day Dr. Hill turned to me and declared:

"I spent over twenty years interviewing and analyzing America's most successful people, individuals like Henry Ford, Charles Schwab, Teddy Roosevelt, Wilbur Wright, Tom Edison, Alexander Graham Bell, and so many others—five hundred in all! I identified the keys to their success and I've spent all these years teaching others what I uncovered. But the thing I haven't been able to do is put all of this into one easy, simple system that people can use to actually implement these things into their daily lives. Leo, how do we do that?"

From that day forward it became my life's work to develop and teach simple tools that would allow *everyone* to enjoy the benefits of the success principles employed by the five hundred prominent Americans Dr. Hill had interviewed. I spent several years helping this master of success and motivation create and operate the Napoleon Hill Academy. I then worked with Success Motivation Institute (SMI) in Texas for five years. I dedicated the next five years to further development and testing of these simple tools while helping major corporations assemble and train their national sales and management teams. Finally, for the last twenty-plus years, in a role I created known as LifeBalance Coach, I have continually expanded and perfected my implementation system while working one-on-one with over two thousand individuals—men and women from a variety of professions and backgrounds.

Finally, after forty years of what I consider a "labor of love," I can say with great joy and satisfaction, and complete confidence, "I have fulfilled the challenge given me by my beloved friend and mentor, Dr. Napoleon Hill." The simple implementation system he longed for is a reality. It is called *The LifeBalance System* and includes very simple and easy-to-use LifeBalance Tools.

The LifeBalance System

You may be wondering where the term *Slight Edge* came from. In my one-on-one work with so many wonderful individuals over the years, two simple principles have always held true:

1) People are extremely busy and occupied with everyday life. Any self-improvement program that is too complex, contains too many components, or requires too much time is successfully implemented by very few.

2) The gap between being average and incredible is far more narrow than most people realize. It's the little things that separate the highly successful from the mediocre.

How many times have you optimistically declared a New Year's resolution, enthusiastically scribbled down a lofty goal, or after reading a great self-improvement book declared, "I'm going to do that right now!" only to find that your goal is just too much, existing habits are too hard to break, your time is too limited, or your plan is not effective? Eventually the whole idea just fades away into nothing. When I first met my clients, many of them felt the same way. Many of their goals were unmet and their dreams unfulfilled. But they still had hope—a hope that my LifeBalance Tools would give them the slight edge they were searching for. After using my tools, I am happy to say they weren't disappointed!

You don't have to make radical changes to your life. It isn't necessary to overcome your bad habits all at once. You don't have to master dozens of techniques or carve out hours of your hectic schedule. If you can learn how to use a few of my very simple LifeBalance Tools in your daily life and relationships; if you can find just a few minutes in your busy schedule;

if you can be just a little better today than you were yesterday—you will succeed with this program. I GUARANTEE IT! The LifeBalance System is not a theory, a clever marketing ploy, or another collection of good ideas. It is the direct result of forty years of testing and proving with over two thousand people, one at a time—it's how-to and it's real life. Thousands have used it to achieve great success and so will you!

Get ready to begin an exciting journey—one of tremendous hope where there has been doubt or despair; one of great success where mediocrity or failure once stood; one where peace of mind replaces stress; one of health, prosperity, and flourishing relationships. Come with me now and learn how to implement my simple LifeBalance Tools that will give you the Slight Edge and lead to the realization of your highest goals and aspirations.

The following quote encapsulates the essence of my lifetime focus and goal in writing this book and LifeBalance coaching:

RADIATING GREATNESS COMES FROM WITHIN

There is one responsibility which no man can evade; that responsiblity is his personal influence. Man's unconscious influence is the silent, subtle radiation of personality and the effect of his words and actions on others. This radiation is tremendous. Every moment of life man is changing, to a degree, the life of the whole world.

Every man has an atmosphere, which is affecting every other man. He cannot escape for one moment from this radiation of his character, this constant weakening or strengthening of others. Man cannot evade the responsibility by merely saying it is an unconscious influence.

Man can select the qualities he would permit to be radiated. He can cultivate sweetness, calmness, trust, truth, justice, loyalty, nobility and make the vitally active in his character. And, by these qualities, he will constantly affect the world.

This radiation, to which I refer, comes from what a person really is, not from what he pretends to be. Every man, by his mere living is radiating, either sympathy, sorrow, morbidness, cynicism, or happiness and hope or any other of a hundred qualities.

Life is a state of radiation and absorption. To exist is to radiate; to exist is to be the recipient of radiation.[1]

Note
1. David O. McKay, "The Mission of Brigham Young University," 27 April, 1948, given at BYU.

Prelude

The Bunker Bean Effect—Discovering and Reaching Your Full Potential

In casual conversation with adult family members, friends, or colleagues, how many times have you heard someone say, "I'm still trying to figure out what I want to do when I grow up"? Some of the first questions for new clients are: "What is your vision of your ideal life—what does it look like?" "If you won the lottery tomorrow and money was no longer an issue, how would you spend your time?" The most common responses are "I'm not sure," or "I've never really thought about it."

It is easy to place limitations on yourself based on what you believe you can or can't do. You may also allow family, friends, peers, and associates to define you based on who they think you are and what they believe you should be or do. Who are you really? What can you accomplish? What is your ideal self and ideal life?

Over the years, many of my clients have received great inspiration from the following story known as *The Bunker Bean Effect*. It is a wonderful parable about the greatness within each one of us.

The Bunker Bean Effect

Harry Leon Wilson, who in 1912 penned the novel *Bunker Bean*, says it all started when Bunker Bean became an orphan as a small child. Alone and poor, always dressed in ragged clothes that hung loosely from his small frame, he was mocked and taunted by cruel, merciless children. Fear greeted him when he awoke in the morning and remained his constant companion until sleep put it to rest. He was afraid of everything: elevators, dogs, children, grown-ups, policemen, the future, life—even himself.

One fateful day a mystic moved into the cheap, rat-infested boarding house and rented the room next to Bunker Bean. A friendship developed during the next few weeks. The mystic's preoccupation with a book on reincarnation captured Bunker's imagination. He learned that his new friend believed all people have had previous lives as someone else before being born into their present lives.

The more Bunker Bean thought about this new idea, the more he believed it. One evening after dinner the mystic proclaimed that he, and he alone, could see into the past and could tell who Bunker Bean was in his past lives. A small pittance of money, which Bunker could ill afford, was delivered to the mystic for the declaration. Bunker followed the mystic to his room and after a few minutes of incantations and trance-producing gyrations, his friend loudly proclaimed: "Bunker Bean!" The mystic spoke with authority. "You are the reincarnated Napoleon Bonaparte, conqueror of the world!" Bunker Bean stood in amazement. Timidly he asked, "How could I, who am afraid even of my own shadow, have been the feared and courageous Napoleon?"

The mystic explained that life goes in cycles. "Sometimes you are born during the upper part of the cycle and sometimes during the lower part. Napoleon lived on the upper part when he exhibited the qualities of courage, initiative, strength, determination, and power." Bunker Bean then learned that his present life was the result of being born during the lower part of the cycle.

Depressed, he turned to leave, but the mystic yelled in a high-pitched voice, "Bunker, the lower part of the cycle is almost completed! You are now reentering the upper part, the same part you were in when you were Napoleon!" The mystic assured Bunker that it would not be many days before he would feel a change taking place and know the prediction was true. "Even as we speak, you are on your way to becoming courageous, determined, strong, self-reliant, fearless, successful," whispered the mystic.

The very thought that he was once Napoleon caused Bunker Bean to stand a little straighter. By the end of the first day he could even detect hints of the promised change. Now that he thought about it, there was a certain majesty in his look; he began to take on a certain warrior air. When he thought of his "true" identity—Napoleon—he vibrated with a strange new power and determination.

Bunker Bean spent every spare moment reading books about Napoleon. He hung the great general's pictures in the little dirty attic room where he could feast his mind upon his former self. He tried standing, thinking, and acting like Napoleon. The image never left his mind. Even when he was confronted with fear he merely thought, "How would Napoleon feel and what would he do?" and the fear vanished.

He discovered that Napoleon was a master strategist, winning his battles in his tent. Bunker decided he, too, would plan, organize, and think out problems before facing them. He thought of every obstacle, challenge, and danger he might face during the day and determined how Napoleon would react. Like Napoleon he made sure nothing was left to chance.

The large, colored picture of Napoleon was a constant reminder to Bunker of the great power and strength hidden in his breast. He visualized himself leading and directing vast armies. He vividly imagined the smell of gunpowder, smoke, and blood.

Something strange began to happen to Bunker Bean. He started acting like Napoleon. He forgot his timidity, his fears, and his meager existence. Each challenge was faced with, "How would Napoleon handle it?" He began applying the same principles that made Napoleon great. His fellow workers and employer were amazed at the change in his personality. His boss gave him a more responsible position. Bunker Bean began to feel and be successful.

Not only did Bunker Bean change, but he was amazed at the way people reacted to him. They wanted to be near him and even followed him as they would a leader. Seeing the changes in these people suggested to him that they might know his real identity.

Years went by and Bunker Bean continued his rise in life and fortune. But one day, when he was pondering over his greatness as Napoleon, he thought, "Before Napoleon who was I?" He searched for and found his old friend and inquired of him. "That will cost you greatly!" said the mystic. "Money is no problem now; just tell me," said Bunker Bean.

The answer he received did not disappoint him. Before he was Napoleon, he was the greatest ruler the world had ever known. He was

Ramses, the mighty Egyptian pharaoh. Bunker learned that Ramses was tall, handsome, and dressed meticulously. Bunker hired a professional tailor to fit him in such a way as to enhance his physical characteristics. His new clothes made him feel like a king, so he began acting like a king. He stood tall, expanded his chest, drew in his waist, and stood erect. He worked to develop the physical and mental discipline of Ramses. He had already discovered that it takes a vivid mental image along with the matching behavior to bring to the present the great qualities of the past. He was a king and must, therefore, do as kings do. Money, for example, was not an issue, because kings always have as much as they want. Bunker knew that when money was needed it would be available, and it was. He was becoming a wealthy man. Bunker Bean was invited to direct large organizations. He was a leader because he thought like a leader and acted like a leader. Never again would he be afraid of life. He was the mighty pharaoh of Egypt. He was born to be a king. His destiny was to rule and so he would do those things that characterized greatness.

The mental image grew stronger with each passing day and in direct proportion, strength, vitality, and excitement for life surged through his veins. Not only had he been the courageous, mighty Napoleon, but also the strong, calm, and powerful Ramses. He was a combination of them both. He thought courage at night and awoke in the morning with a giant's strength. His visualization poured the necessities into his personality to mold and fashion a king and a conqueror.

But one morning tragedy entered Bunker Bean's life—tragedy that neither Napoleon nor Ramses could combat. He discovered that his mystic friend was a fake, a con artist. There really was no such thing as reincarnation. He really hadn't been Napoleon or Ramses. He really was nothing more than his weak, timid, fearful, insignificant self.

Bunker Bean was a beaten man for a few moments. Then, as if by revelation, he thought, "When I believed myself to be a king, others reacted as if I were a king. When I believed myself to be weak and timid, others reacted as if I were weak and timid."

A new and inspiring truth now dawned upon him. "I can be anything I can imagine and visualize in my mind." During the years he had believed himself to be the reincarnated Napoleon and Ramses, he had accumulated great wealth and position, yet no one had known about his belief except his mystic friend. He had gained all by believing that he could do it. He believed in himself and his dreams. Ramses and Napoleon were only crude bits of scaffolding on which he had climbed to success.

As you begin applying the LifeBalance principles in your daily life, don't sell yourself short when it comes to identifying your ideal self and ideal life. Like Bunker Bean, believe in these great truths:

Everyone is born a king.
Everyone is born to riches.
Everyone is born to greatness.

1

Harness Your Brain's Natural Built-In Power!

A NUMBER OF YEARS AGO one of my LifeBalance coaching clients, professional golfer Keith Clearwater, received $90,000 for taking first place in a popular tournament. On the final hole, in a four-way tie for first place, Keith sank the winning putt. Sharing second place, the other three competitors earned $20,000 each. Since Keith pocketed four-times the money, simple logic would suggest he was four-times better than his competition, right? No, just one golf stroke better.

Every four years I look forward with great anticipation to the glorious Summer Olympics, the world's greatest athletes converging in one place to compete for the elusive gold medal. One of the most exhilarating events is the race to determine the world's fastest man—the 100-meter dash. I recall one year when the medal ceremony made an unusual impression on me. The Olympic medalists stood on the three-tiered platform, the gold-medal winner atop the highest level, flanked by the silver and bronze holders below. I suddenly realized that although glorious, those fleeting moments in the spotlight would pass quickly for the silver and bronze winners, but not for the one who held the gold. Product endorsements, TV commercials, talk shows and movie contracts, and books and articles would likely make this athlete wealthy overnight. All this attention would suggest that he was overwhelmingly better than his second- and third-place competitors. According to the race clock, the difference was 11/1000 of a second!

Over the last forty years, I have worked one-on-one with my clients, each possessing his or her own unique gifts and talents, and each harboring desires to achieve greater success in some aspect of their lives. Early in my LifeBalance coaching career I often asked myself, "Why is it that an elite few manage to consistently achieve their highest goals, while the majority seem to struggle or even flounder?"

In nearly every case, it wasn't anything big that separated the successful from the rest. Like competing athletes, the difference between those who were achieving their career, marriage, and health goals, and those who were not was minimal—akin to a single golf stroke or a thousandth-of-a-second—nothing more than a slight edge. In fact, remarkably, those who struggled most typically shared one common flaw—they tried to do too much all at once or they focused all their attention on one part of their life. They did not know how to harness this desire or to formulate a plan that would allow them to accomplish their dream.

Through the years I have worked with people who had great plans for their life. They had the genuine and sincere desire to improve their lives. They would lay awake at night wishing for things to be better. And periodically they would grit their teeth, clench their fists, and determine to do better. They reasoned that their past failures were caused by lack of willpower, and they decided to strike out on this new path. Unfortunately, more often than not, their own mental models (habits of thinking) would catch up with them, and they would become exhausted with the effort of working against their existing habits.

The Enormous Power of Habits

Have you ever observed children as they go through the wondrous and often frustrating process of learning their first simple skills? Tiny fingers awkwardly struggle to tie that first shoelace bow. A nervous hand laboriously scrawls a barely legible name. At first these simple tasks can be excruciatingly difficult and time consuming. But with each repetition the task grows progressively easier until something magical happens—you don't have to think about it anymore. It becomes automatic; you have created a habit.

The remarkable power of habit-formation is built-in to the very fabric of your brain and the rest of your nervous system. Habit formation is your brain's number one priority. Why? Because the brain's watchword is *efficiency*. Since the moment you were born your brain has focused intensely on being efficient. And the most effective way to be efficient is through the formation of habits. This is what your brain seeks—to focus its energy and attention on mastering a skill as quickly as possible—to make it a habit. Your brain can then move on to direct its efforts at learning and mastering the next skill. This is how you continually grow and progress.

While your brain's habit-formation power is a remarkable gift, it can also work directly against you when you attempt to implement new ideas or change past behaviors. Once your brain expends the time and energy to develop a habit, whether it's good or bad, it doesn't want to give it up! Imagine what would happen if each time you tried to walk, speak, tie your shoes, or engage in any other already learned skill, you had to master it all over again? What if every time you got in your car, you had to stop and think about what the pedals do and what the knobs and buttons for? Were it not for the power of habits, you wouldn't get very far in life. Once a habit is in place, your brain stamps it with "mission accomplished" and vigilantly guards what it has worked so hard to create. In essence, your brain builds a twenty-foot-high, thirty thousand volt, razor-wired, super-security fence to protect all your hard-earned habits, boldly displaying the warning sign "KEEP OUT!" This fence not only keeps new ideas out but also becomes a cage that severely limits your ability to change and build new habits that could benefit you.

Imagine what happens when you discover an exciting idea or new goal and enthusiastically declare, "I want to start doing that right away!" With great zeal you write it down, paste it on your bathroom mirror or refrigerator, or put it in your calendar or PDA. But then, more often than not, the same scenario unfolds. In spite of your best intentions, in the busyness and immediacy of everyday life, the great idea, firm commitment, or new goal fades away and is forgotten, almost as if you had never considered it. What happened?

Would the idea, commitment, or goal have made a positive difference in your life? Did you have a desire to follow through and do it? Then what was the problem? Consider the situation based on your brain's dominant priority of *efficiency*. You get excited about a new idea or goal. You make a commitment to yourself to start doing it right now. But your brain responds: "Hold on just a minute! Let me get this straight. Just because you're all pumped up about some self-improvement book you read, you expect me to abandon years of energy and effort and simply jettison all the precious habits I've worked so hard to build? I don't think so—it wouldn't be efficient!"

For additional information on mental models, please refer to Appendix C in this book; I also highly recommend the book *The Power of Impossible Thinking* from the Wharton School of Business (Wind, Crook, and Gunther).

What we see is what we think. We usually trust what we see with our own eyes or perceive with our other senses. But research shows that we often use little of the sensory information we take in from the outside world—most of it is discarded. Though we experience the process as "seeing the external world," what the incoming stream of images actually evokes other experiences from our internal world. In short, we see the external world through the filter created by our internal models. These filters, these existing mental models, determine how we see the world and, more important, what we feel about it. The brain makes no distinction from the things we actually see and physically experience, the gaps we fill in based on our previous experiences, or the filter we saw them through.

The most exciting aspect is that we can change our entire past, and our future, by changing the filter we see the world through. While we cannot change the actual experiences we have had, we can change the framework that our brain uses to interpret them. When we change our mental models, we change our past. But more important, we change our future. This is the power of mental models, and this is at the heart of the tools I have developed.

Additional Insight

In describing the brain's habit-building process, many neuroscientists refer to the formation of **mental models**. Your brain has an amazing built-in process that takes everything you experience and stores it as part of a specific mental model. For example, as a child learns to tie his shoes, his brain begins piecing together a mental model with all of the components and connections necessary for that activity. Each time the child ties his shoes, the mental model becomes more solidly connected and deeply rutted, until eventually it becomes dominant—the brain's preferred model for that activity—in other words, a habit. Then in the future, when the child expresses the thought or intention "tie my shoes," his brain immediately searches throughout its data banks to find the mental model that can accomplish the task in the most efficient way possible.

Mental models are not limited to simple physical tasks, but are the filters or glasses through which you make sense of the world. Your brain interprets and reacts to everyone and everything around you based on your past experiences—your mental models. You don't see the world as it is, but rather as you trained yourself to see it (according to your unique mental models). When a mental model becomes dominant (a habit), it directly controls how you think, feel, and behave in any given moment, and has enormous impact on the success or failure in every part of your life. *Your* mental models (not theirs) fully determine your attitude and how you perceive, feel, and respond toward your spouse, children, friends, co-workers, and every person around you. If you want to change your life or relationships in any way, you can only do it by changing your mental models, which is what the LifeBalance System and this book are all about. *Change your mental models—change your life!*

Stop Fighting Against What Your Brain Does Naturally

We live in the greatest information age in history. For example, it has been estimated that between 1999 and 2003 the amount of new information available in the world more than tripled! Amidst this deluge, people keep looking for that new magical self-improvement book or technique that will finally help them succeed.

We don't need more information. What we need is a simple way to start implementing what we already know. After a lifetime of learning what helps people succeed, I can tell you that the key is to stop fighting against what your brain does naturally!

Many people approach personal change and achievement like the man on the first floor of a shopping mall with a goal of getting to the second floor. He faces two escalators. Both reach the next floor, but one has motorized stairs moving upward, while the other travels down. Considering both options he concludes, "The up-escalator is moving awfully slow and it's full of people. I'll bet I can get there quicker if I run up the down-escalator that is empty." So off he goes. Fueled by spontaneous enthusiasm and determination, he initially makes impressive progress. But soon he begins struggling and losing ground. He can see his goal, he really wants to get there, he's trying hard, but trudging up the downward-moving stairs begins taking its toll. Eventually, exhausted and deeply disappointed, he finds himself standing once again at the bottom of the escalators. Resolved to his fate, he sighs, "I don't need to go up there anyway. I can get whatever I need down here." Loyal to his old habit (dominant mental model), he turns and walks off to begin his efficient and familiar first-floor shopping routine.

How often are you like this man—a grandiose New Year's resolution, an excited determination to implement *all* seven newly-discovered techniques, an easy method to fix your marriage *right now*, and a guaranteed way to double your income this month? Whenever we try to "do it all at once" we set ourselves up for failure and disappointment. Like the man who grits his teeth and charges up the down-escalator, we fight against the natural current of the brain and quite frankly it rebels! Instead, why not "go with the flow" and harness the power of your brain's marvelous habit-formation tendency? Don't fight it—embrace it, work *with* it.

Don't Take Shortcuts

If you will simply follow the LifeBalance Tools laid out in this book, your success is guaranteed. However, please be aware that you will be tempted to take shortcuts. Remember, by its very nature, your brain seeks the path of least resistance and keeps things the way they are. In order to override this tendency, you need to prepare to read this book differently than other self-improvement books you have read in the past.

This is a workbook; it is not designed to be skimmed over, quickly reviewed, or rapidly read in a few sittings. You cannot do this and expect to change your mental models at the same time. If you stop to ponder each key concept, consider every insight, and complete all of the exercises, it will take you several weeks to finish the book, but in doing so your life will be changed forever. Take your time, be patient, and do the work. The LifeBalance System is very simple, and my tools are very easy to use. Once you learn them, you will possess the skills to take you wherever you want to go in life. It has taken you a lifetime to create the dominant mental models that are keeping you from all the happiness and success you desire and deserve. Certainly you can invest a few weeks to start down the path to your exciting new future!

Having a Strong Motive Is the Key to Change

The stories you'll read in the next few pages show how important it is to have a motive. Without motive, there is very little desire to change. Having a strong motive is the key to change.

——————— I Must Dance with Sophia! ———————

I have a client in his late fifties who was diagnosed with a serious heart problem. The doctor counseled him to make some radical changes to his diet. Being raised in an Italian family, he loves rich food. He said, "What if I just eat what I want and die when I'm sixty-five? At least I'll die happy." Obviously I needed to help him find a powerful motive for changing his eating habits (food mental models).

After much discussion and Feelings Journaling (a Slight Edge Tool you will learn to use in chapter 3), he discovered it. He has a two-year-old granddaughter, Sophia, whom he absolutely adores. He has a clear vision of dancing with her at her wedding. With the "power of his heart" fueling the process, and using the Slight Edge Tools, he began changing his mental models and his diet because he just has to dance with Sophia at her wedding! This motive is so powerful that every time he thinks about it he gets choked up.

—————

What Would You Do?

How many times have we heard a new idea, seen something we'd like to include in our life, or felt genuinely compelled to make a change? We have that rush of excitement, and for a moment, believe we can accomplish it. We set out with determination and conviction to become what we dream of being. While initially it sounds like a good idea, we soon tired of the work involved, and decide to settle. We have all been in situations where the reward just didn't seem worth the effort. Does that mean our initial excitement was not genuine or that the goal wasn't worthwhile? No, it just means we allowed our existing habits to determine our path. We convince ourselves that it's just too hard or that we're "just made that way." But settling is denying who we really are and what we are really capable of. We simply need to have a mechanism that allows us to harness our initial motive and to bring it back, on demand, to fuel our change.

Imagine you're standing outside a burning building, and someone excitedly tells you he left his wallet on the counter inside. What would your reaction be? You would probably say, "That's too bad." If this same person said there was a painting worth one million dollars hanging in the building, there might be some willing to attempt to salvage it, but most of us would not consider it worth the risk or the effort. But if we knew our child or loved one was trapped in the building, we would do whatever it took to rescue them. What's the difference? Motive—the emotional fuel that propels us to action. Motive is what allows us to overcome the power of habit, create new habits, and achieve our dreams. Motive, when tied to a plan, turns dreams into reality.

The Volkswagen Bug

I had a client who desperately desired to lose fifty pounds. As part of her motive, she visualized herself walking down the beach in a bikini and all the guys turning to look at her. She described in written detail how she felt experiencing this. It seemed to be a very powerful motive. But after only a few weeks, she was not making much progress.

After pondering and Feelings Journaling, she finally came up with a different motive. It seems that weeks before, she and some fellow student leaders at her college had planned to travel to a meeting in a Volkswagen Bug. She remembered how humiliated she felt when, due to her overweight condition, she couldn't fit into the back seat. What made it even worse was that a male student leader she was attracted to had already climbed into the backseat. She later found out that he wasn't interested in her, primarily because of her weight.

For her new motive, this young woman visualized herself at her desired weight, easily and gracefully sliding in to the back seat of the Bug. She could clearly see the amazed look on her friends' faces, especially on the face of the young man as she motioned him into the back seat to sit next to her. This scene set the tone for a new motive that she simply plugged into her daily Slight Edge Tools. She immediately got back on track and was able to overcome the obstacles, stick to her plan, and fulfill the dream of her ideal weight.

And now, to borrow from Paul Harvey, here is the "rest of the story." Some months later this woman and this man got married. Today, twenty years later, she's still slender and very attractive. And him? Let's just say he's aged a little. She still loves him to pieces.

The tools I have developed over the last forty years all center on clearly identifying a motive and using its power to keep us on the path. I can provide the tools that will lead you to your dreams, but you must provide the motive. If you ever feel yourself slipping back into old habits, or doubting the value of your dreams, look closely at your motive. If it's not propelling you to change, it's not a powerful enough motive. Motives that are emotional, that move us to tears, or raise goose bumps are the kind of motives we're looking for. Only you can know what motive works for you—it's individual and personal. That's where its power lies.

Highlight and Make Notes as You Go

While reading books in the past, you may have seen an idea jump off the page. Or your heart was touched as you pondered a story or related an experience to your own life. Perhaps you have experienced strong emotions like compassion, love, anger, humility, and regret. Maybe you've received sudden bursts of inspiration or solutions to problems. I believe inspiration can reach us at many different times and in a variety of ways, especially when we are reading truth. Unfortunately, many of these experiences, while powerful at the time, fade away as we put the book down and return to the busyness of life.

I highly recommend you read this book with a highlighter and a regular pen at hand. Highlight ideas or sections that stand out, and make notes in the margins about *why* you feel impressed and how you can use it. If you need more space to write, go to the blank *Important Ideas & Insights* pages at the end of each chapter. When you create your LifeCreed in chapter 9, the notes you have recorded throughout the book will be invaluable.

A Simple and Easy Way

While highlighting and taking notes will help you form new mental models, progress can easily come to a halt when notes are stored away on a shelf and forgotten. One of the easiest and most effective methods I know for taking advantage of your notes is to simply record them in your own voice on a tape recorder or computer. Then, while driving in your car, walking, jogging, or bicycling, you can listen to it over and over again.

This is a simple way to begin your ideal life. Because you have taken notes with a special emphasis on your emotions and feelings, each time you listen to your recording your own unique and powerful motives will be reinforced over and over again. As you listen and ponder, your awareness will be raised to a higher level. Every time you listen to the recording you will be practicing—creating repetition. It's important to always ask yourself *why* and journal about the *why* when you listen to the recording or read this book.

Now, let's get started with the simple, easy how-to system that will help achieve all of the success you've been dreaming of. In the next chapter you will learn how to use a powerful LifeBalance Tool that will produce immediate positive results in whatever area of life or relationships you want to focus on first.

NOTE: *As you consider the principles taught in this chapter, you may want to review the concept of Mindbody Science and how it affects habit formation. Appendix C is included at the back of this book with detailed information.*

Important Ideas & Insights

_____
_____
_____
_____
_____
_____
_____
_____
_____
_____
_____
_____
_____
_____
_____
_____
_____
_____
_____
_____
_____
_____

Two Simple LifeBalance Tools That Will Give You Success—

Right Now!

2

The Byte—Instant On-the-Spot Success

I RECALL A NUMBER OF years ago reading the results of a scientific experiment involving a hungry barracuda. The scientist began with a long water-filled aquarium divided into two equal sections with a removable "invisible" glass wall. On one side he placed a barracuda that had not eaten for many days. On the other, a small school of mouth-watering minnows. The instant the bite-sized fish were placed in the tank, the barracuda darted toward them and collided head-on with the glass wall. Repeated attempts produced the same result. Finally, battered and exhausted, the big fish gave up. Then the scientist lifted the glass wall. Predictably, the vulnerable minnows huddled at the farthest end of the tank. But, surprisingly, the famished predator made no attempt at his easy prey! Conditioned by repetitive collisions with the barrier, the powerful fish almost starved to death with food a few feet away.

Old habits and attitudes, repeated failures and disappointments, even the rut of daily routines, can raise "invisible" barriers in our personal lives, relationships, and careers. Clouded by our past experiences (mental models), we continue swimming in one end of the tank while success and happiness are within easy reach. Herb Otto, a national expert on human potential, made an interesting observation. He claimed that only one out of every 110 people focus on the way things *can* be done. The other 109 (or over 99 person of us) tended to focus on the way things *can't* be done. Most of us become preoccupied with what does not go well rather than what does go well!

In the early years of my LifeBalance Coaching, I quickly discovered that while people were looking for overall success in their lives, there was always one or two particular areas—the glass wall—that was impeding their progress. When there's a camel in the middle of the tent, it can be difficult to focus on anything else. I developed the Life-Balance Tool known as **the Byte** for the specific purpose of helping individuals experience immediate success with the most pressing problem, challenge, need, or issue in their lives. The earliest development and testing of the Byte concept was for my own situation as a young father. I was struggling to recover from a very bitter divorce where my ex-wife abandoned our family and left me devastated and alone. I am happy to say that using the tools described in this book I grew from that experience. I now have a wonderful life with my sweetheart Shirley with whom I've been happily married for more than thirty years.

If there is one thing you could choose to improve in your life right now, what would it be? Perhaps it's something in your personal life—a bad habit; phobia or compulsion; an unrealized goal; a health, weight, or fitness issue. Maybe it's connected to a challenge in your most important relationships—your marriage, a child, extended family, a friend, or a colleague. It might be related to your career or financial situation. Whatever it is, I guarantee the Byte will help you begin making progress today!

The Power of Mental Models

As we discussed in chapter 1, memories of everything you have ever experienced have been stored in your brain as specific mental models. These mental models are the filters or pair of glasses through which you see and interpret everyone and everything around you. You see the world not as it is, but rather as you are (according to your mental models). To get an idea of just how powerful mental models can be, consider a real-life experience.

─────────── **Is It Real or Is It 3-D?** ───────────

One of my colleagues related his experience with mental models at Disney World:

A few years ago I took my family to Disney World. One of the attractions was a 3-D movie. While waiting in line, TV monitors entertained us with information and previews about the show. Finally as we all filed into the theater, we received our colored 3-D glasses. Even though we were excited to see the movie, everyone was fully aware it would be an optical illusion created by camera angles and the multi-colored glasses. Once the show began I was particularly tickled by my smaller children as they stretched out their hands to touch the 3-D characters or sunk back in their chairs trying to avoid the scary parts. I thought to myself, "Wouldn't it be great to be a kid again and be fooled by all of this?" A moment later a little robot character in a hover-craft suddenly darted toward the audience and shattered a neon sign that sent an explosion of glass shards hurling directly at our faces. Instantly I closed my eyes and threw my head back, almost breaking the nose of the poor man sitting behind me! Coming to my senses and totally embarrassed, I looked around and was relieved that my wife and children hadn't seen my silly reaction. Wondering if the guy behind me had noticed, I glanced his way as we exited. As our eyes connected, he gave me a big smile and winked. It was great to feel like a kid again!

How is it possible that a grown man, intelligent, experienced, and *knowing* it was all fake, could respond this way? Let's track what happened: Seeing the image of the shattering glass, his brain immediately searched its data banks looking for the mental model that could most effectively answer the questions "What does this mean?" and "What should I do?" It just so happens that as a child, my colleague had several close calls with shattering glass. Add to these experiences every thought he had entertained over his lifetime related to the dangers of shattering glass and you have hundreds or even thousands of repetitions. When the 3-D image activated his "shattering glass mental model," did he stop to consciously reason about the reality of the situation? No! He reacted *instantly*.

This story illustrates several key concepts that will help you understand why the Byte is so remarkably effective:

Key Concepts ✆➔

1. When the emotion or meaning of a mental model is powerful, your brain does not distinguish between what is real and what is imagined—it simply takes action! With the Byte you can use this to your advantage. For example, although overcoming a particular habit, improving certain relationship, or

achieving a specific goal may appear out-of-reach or unrealistic, with the Byte you can create a mental model with such powerful emotion and meaning that your brain will assume it's "real" and respond accordingly.

2. Each time a mental model is activated it grows larger and more dominant, until it becomes automatic. By using the Byte you will easily create the daily repetition necessary to build any dominant mental model and habit you desire, and change any aspect of your life for the better.

Your Instant "Mental Model Switcher"

You may be wondering how the term *the Byte* originated. In computer language, a byte is a small unit of information that gives the computer a command to do something specific. In the LifeBalance System, the Byte is designed to give your brain a specific command that instantly generates an enormous amount of mental force, switching to the mental model you desire, on the spot.

The power of the Byte resides in the fact that your mind cannot focus on two dissimilar thoughts at one time; it can't access two opposing mental models at once. When you find your mind dominated by thoughts that are not in harmony with your goals and desires, you can use the Byte to dispel and replace these thoughts by "switching" to the mental model of your choosing. Never underestimate the incredible force of mental models, the awesome power of your thoughts—"As a man thinketh . . . so is he." I love the words of the great James Allen in his timeless best seller *As a Man Thinketh*:

> As the plant springs from, and could not be without, the seed, so every act of a man springs from the hidden seeds of thought, and could not have appeared without them. . . .
>
> Man is made or unmade by himself; in the armory of thoughts he forges the weapons by which he destroys himself; he also fashions the tools with which he builds for himself heavenly mansions of joy and strength and peace. . . .
>
> All that a man achieves and all that he fails to achieve is the direct result of his own thoughts.[1]

In my own words: *Change Your Mental Models (thoughts)—Change Your Life!* There is no more simple and effective way to do this than with the Byte. It's time to move forward and create your first one.

Create Your First Byte

In all my years of LifeBalance Coaching, I have yet to find a client who did not have an important relationship they wanted to improve. And in every case, doing so had a positive and even profound effect on many aspects of their personal lives and careers. To meet this need I created a simple form of the Byte. It is designed to greatly improve any relationship you have—spouse, child, parent, sibling, co-worker, and so forth. To give you a glimpse of the power of the Byte, here's one client success story:

——————— Hey Marine—Take Out the Trash! ———————

Sometimes mental model change in a relationship is gradual and incremental. Other times, it's like a light suddenly turning on in a dark room. That's what happened to one Marine who was allowing a small irritation to disrupt an otherwise wonderful marriage. During a LifeBalance training session with the US Marine Corps at Camp LeJeune, we asked participants to think of an important relationship they would like to improve.

A hand went up. It was Anthony, a big, lean, rugged man, just what you would likely picture when you think of the Few, the Proud, the Marines. "Yeah, I'll tell you something that needs to change in my marriage—the trash!" he blurted out. Puzzled, the whole group waited for an explanation. "The trash! My wife is always naggin' on me to get the trash out the night before pick-up. What's the big deal? I always get it out in the morning in time for the trash collectors. What does it matter when I do it, so long as I do it? Why does she have to have it out the night before? It drives me crazy! We've been fighting about this our whole marriage."

The LifeBalance trainers and the other Marines spent twenty minutes trying to reason with Anthony about how it was such a small thing, that he should just let his wife have her way. But he wouldn't budge. He just couldn't get out of his dominant mental model regarding the trash—he kept automatically selecting that mental model over and over again. During the break I sat with Anthony and suggested he create a Relationship Byte for the situation. I asked him to write down his feelings about all the wonderful qualities he admired in his wife; why he loved her; what motivated him to marry her in the first place. I asked him to remember an experience when his love, admiration, and respect for her were deeper than ever. He spent the break writing all these feelings out.

After the break we listened to a special music set. Then it was time to close for the day. Suddenly Anthony asked if he could say something to the group. This big, tough Marine stood up and with a slight quiver in his voice said, "I can't believe what a jerk I've been! How could I have been so stubborn about a stupid little thing like the trash? What was I thinking? My wife is a queen. I should be washing her feet when I come home from work."

The room was silent. We all just sat there, our mouths wide open, staring at Anthony. Suddenly the entire group broke out in applause! We all had witnessed the power of the Byte to generate mental force and switch Anthony to a completely different mental model. I asked him to summarize all those notes he had just written and put them on a card or sheet of paper. I told him to read that Byte whenever he started to think something negative about his wife.

FOLLOW THESE FOUR SIMPLE STEPS TO CREATE YOUR FIRST BYTE

Step 1: Name the Individual You Want to Focus On

On a sheet of paper write the name of the individual with whom you want to improve your relationship. It could be your spouse, child, co-worker, and so forth.

Step 2: Connect to Deep Emotions and Meaning

Like advertisers and Hollywood, you want the descriptions in your Byte to activate mental models that are filled with powerful memories, emotions, feeling, and meaning. When you review or think about your Byte it should immediately take over the stage of your conscious mind. If reading your Byte sends chills up your spine, makes your hair stand up on end, brings you to tears, or fills you with an uplifting spirit or inspiration, then your Byte is constructed properly. To achieve **maximum motive power** proceed as follows:

- Write down the most positive qualities, attributes, gift, and talents you admire in the individual you have selected. If it's your spouse, think about what it was that originally attracted you to him or her—why you fell in love.

- Think back to the most positive or inspirational experience you've had with this individual. Describe it in detail with special emphasis on "your feelings toward him or her" at the time.

Step 3: Make It Portable

Transfer what you have written to a index card. Carry this with you in your pocket or purse.

Step 4: Awareness and Practice

Throughout the day and evening, *be aware* of when you are thinking about the individual. The instant you have thoughts about him or her, immediately take out your Relationship Byte and review it. As you do, focus on what you have written. Allow all of the positive feelings and emotions to wash over you—immerse yourself in the moment—and fully enjoy the wonderful mental model you have activated. Remember, each time you practice and access this new mental model, it grows stronger and more dominant. The next time will be easier and the next easier still until, just as you learned to tie your shoes and ride a bike, your new way of thinking about your spouse, child, or co-worker will become automatic, a habit.

There you have it—the Byte. Simple, easy, and instantly accessible. As you consistently use this LifeBalance Tool as described, *I promise you* that your mental models will change and so will your relationships—in ways that will astound you. Later on in the book you will learn about creating your LifeCreed. Adding a Byte or Bytes to your Creed will allow your Byte to have a greater, more consistent impact in your life.

Additional Insight

In my LifeBalance coaching I often come across people who mercilessly beat themselves up over the mistakes they've made in their relationships—especially with their spouse and children. While it's not intended as an excuse, understanding the powerful role that mental models play in the way we interact in our families can help us be a little more gentle, more forgiving of ourselves and others, and give us the hope to move forward in a positive direction.

I've often heard parents declare in frustration, "I sound just like my mother!" or "I can't believe I just did that—that's exactly how my father behaved!" My response is "Duh!" Of course you have a tendency to talk, react, and behave the way your parents did. Think about the mental models you formed as a child.

- Recent studies conducted by Stanford University have revealed that what we watch *does* have an effect on our imaginations, our learning patterns, and our behaviors. First we are exposed to new behaviors and characters. Next we learn or acquire these new behaviors. The last and most crucial step occurs when we adopt these new behaviors as our own.

- One of the most critical aspects of human development that we need to understand is the influence of repeated viewing and repeated verbalizing in shaping our future. The information goes in almost unnoticed on a daily basis, but we don't react to it until later, when we aren't able to realize the basis for our reactions. Our value system is being formed without any conscious awareness on our part of what is happening.

You observed your parents thousands of times in all kinds of situations. Combine this incessant repetition with the powerful emotions and feelings that only a family environment can create, and you have *dominant* mental model/ habit formation at the highest level imaginable!

Is it any wonder, then, that in similar circumstances in your marriage and family life these mental models are triggered and you sometimes behave the same way your parents did? Your brain is doing exactly what it does best— being habitual and efficient.

The good news is you can change these mental models by applying the same process that formed them in the first place—strong emotion and meaning coupled with practice and repetition. So stop beating yourself up and starting using the Relationship Byte. Remember: baby steps. Be just a little better today than you were yesterday—that's the Slight Edge. After just a few days of using the Byte, you'll be amazed at how your mental models are beginning to change. *You choose* which family traditions to carry on and jettison the ones that are counterproductive.

Here's another amazing example of how one of my clients used the Byte to achieve remarkable results:

The Byte Saved Her Marriage

Several years ago a client's husband had committed a serious betrayal in their marriage, causing her severe mental and emotional anguish. She harbored enormous hurt and resentment, but her husband was humble and apologetic.

She was willing to see if the relationship could be saved. She worked on focusing on "Jack #2," the repentant and striving man she is married to now, rather than "Jack #1," the man who had betrayed her. It was difficult at first, but eventually with my coaching, she was able to see all of her husband's good qualities—the things she admired most in him when they first fell in love. She made a list of Jack's finest qualities. As she worked on this, she remembered a time when they were on vacation in South America and Jack was interacting with some of the local people. She recalls, "As I watched I was amazed at his compassion, inspiring words, and the way he uplifted and loved those people. I was so proud of him and my heart was filled with so much love for him."

She took that experience and wrote about it in as much detail as she could, with full emotion, and in the present tense as if she were there observing it all over again. Whenever she found her mind dominated by thoughts of Jack's betrayal, she would take out the list of his qualities and the written description of her experience with him in South America and read it. Each time it would fill her heart and mind with wonderful feelings. She visualized herself observing Jack and allowed all the emotions of love and appreciation to wash over her. Through her Relationship Byte a miracle began to unfold: Her attitude and feelings toward Jack began to change and soften. Today she and Jack have one of the most beautiful love affairs I know of. Every day Jack serves her and their love only gets deeper and stronger. They turned a horrible adversity into a fabulous blessing. As Napoleon Hill taught me—every adversity and every defeat carries within it the seed of an equivalent or greater benefit, *if you look for it!*

Transference of Thought

In numerous studies over the last several decades, scientists have clearly shown that *thoughts are things*. In other words, the thoughts you allow on the stage of your mind create energy and messages that are transferred to people around you. This process operates the same for negative and positive thoughts. As a relationship deteriorates, the minds of the individuals involved become increasingly dominated by negative thoughts. After awhile, others can feel the negative energy and sense the negative thoughts without any words being spoken. In fact, these negative thoughts can be transferred over great distances.

The same holds true for positive thoughts about other people. The energy and message of positive thoughts are transferred without any words expressed. Consider this example:

When Gandhi was asked how he was able to lead India to independence from the British Empire, he indicated it was not what they said, although that was important, nor what they did, but is was their "being-ness"—their "collective intent" that brought about such a miraculous result.

Many of my clients have tested and proven this with their Relationship Byte. After twenty years of marriage, one man was having serious marital problems. He created a Byte consisting of:

1. A list of his wife's great qualities, the things he loves and admires most, the reasons he married her in the first place.

2. A detailed description of his most cherished experience with his wife, a time when he felt the greatest amount of love, admiration, appreciation, and closeness.

He said nothing about the Byte to his wife. Whenever unflattering thoughts about his wife came into his mind, he took out his Byte, reviewed it, and pondered on it. As his thoughts became more positive, his attitude toward his wife began to change. Over time, his wife began to be influenced by his positive attitude, and her demeanor and attitudes also began to change. Their marriage improved significantly.

Whether you're at home, at work, or across the globe, focusing on your Relationship Byte will generate a powerful energy that will be transmitted to those you care about most. A great book that describes how we transfer our energy, positive or negative, to others is *The Hidden Messages in Water* by Masaru Emoto, a world famous scientist. Don't let the title fool you! This is a great book on how our thoughts affect others miles away.

Dr. Emoto has provided such great insight into how energy is transferred between human beings. He states that we as human beings are composed of approximately 70 percent water. His book describes over twenty years of research and experimentation on water crystals.

For instance, he describes taking two pitchers of water and placing them in separate rooms. One pitcher is exposed to beautiful music like Bach and Mozart. The other is exposed to Acid Rock. He describes other experiments where he talks to one beaker of water lovingly and to another harshly.

In both of the above examples, the soft music and loving words produce beautiful crystals, and the hard music and bad words produce ugly crystals. You have to see the pictures in his book to appreciate what happened.

This book describes in such beautiful detail the effect of positive thoughts and words on others. It also vividly describes the affect negative and ugly words or thoughts have.

I teach my clients that negative words or actions depress the immune system and make the body vulnerable to all kinds of health problems. This book provides the scientific evidence to support this teaching in a clear and graphic format. I highly encourage you to buy Dr. Emoto's book.

The Submariner and the Watch

Years ago when I was serving in the US Navy, I had an experience with thought transfer that has stuck with me. I use it frequently when teaching someone how our thoughts are transferred, not just across the room or across town, but across the world!

In 1954, I was serving aboard a US Submarine. We had sailed across the Atlantic and our first port of call was Gibraltar (the Rock). When we were tied up, the representative of the Omega Watch Company from Switzerland came aboard and was showing us the fabulous watches we could buy at a deep discount.

One watch caught my eye. It was a solid gold Omega Officially Certified Chronometer that sold at the time in New York City for $500 (a lot of money in 1954). The watch salesman was offering it for $132. He indicated he would bring our watches to us when we tied up in Marseille, France, a few weeks later.

I really wanted that watch. I had the money in savings at home in Portland, Oregon, but I had no way of contacting anyone to get the money to me. I figured I could borrow the money from some of my shipmates, but no one offered to help. We left Gibraltar and were out in the middle of the Mediterranean Sea. I was on lookout one day, really thinking about the watch that I wanted to have. I know it sounds silly, but I yelled out "Mom, I need $100!" Since she was a few thousand miles away, I doubt she heard me.

A few weeks later we pulled into Marseilles. The mailman came aboard the boat with our mail, and there was a letter from my mother. I opened it to find a cashier's check for $100! Her note said: "I had a feeling you might need this." That watch is still on my wrist fifty years later and running as good as new.

Some would call it coincidence, but I've had far too many experiences like that to doubt the absolute reality of thought-transference.

Many Uses for the Byte

Now back to the Byte. The Byte is a wonderful tool to restore love and harmony to a marital relationship. The Byte can also be used to restore any important relationship. For example:

- Negative feelings toward a teenage child who has rebelled and caused the family pain and disruption.
- Resentment toward a parent who caused you pain as a child.
- Bitter feelings for a brother or sister, or for extended family members.
- Bad feelings for a boss, colleague, or co-worker.
- Negative feelings toward yourself for past mistakes or failures.

Follow the Four Simple Steps and create a Relationship Byte for any relationship you desire to improve. Through simple and consistent practice, your mental models will change, and you will see the improvements you are longing for.

THE BYTE HAS UNIVERSAL APPLICATION

In addition to improving relationships, there are many applications for the Byte. You can use the Byte to change mental models and develop new habits in *any area* of your life. The Byte is a universal change mechanism. As you ponder the Byte applications below, stop and create a simple Byte for your own unique situation. It won't take long and the rewards will be tremendous—it's the little things you consistently do each day that steadily move you toward the realization of your dreams.

The Byte in Business

I have a client in the insurance business that hated to talk with people on the phone, but he loved working with people face-to-face. Whenever he had to make sales or client follow-up calls on the telephone, his mind would fill with negative thoughts and fears.

To begin the Byte creation process, I asked him to make a list of all the gifts and talents that made him so effective when he was face-to-face with people. I also had him describe the reasons why he loved meeting with people, the unique services he provided to them, and why they appreciated him so much. All together this formed his "Success-on-the-Phone Byte."

Before each phone calling session, he reviewed, visualized, and experienced the feelings and emotions of his Byte. He made all his calls one day each week. After six weeks he called me and said, "Leo, I woke up this morning and realized I'm really excited about talking with people on the phone! I can't believe I'm saying this but it's how I feel."

Key Concept &—¬ ─────────────────────────

When my client told me how excited he was I immediately responded, "Write down exactly what you're feeling. Capture the excitement of this experience right now." "Why?" he asked. "Because down the road you're going to have an off-day when some of your negative feelings about the phone return. By capturing the full emotion of your excitement and adding it to your Byte, you'll rid yourself of the negative thoughts when they come."

Over time his mental model and the meaning of the telephone changed from "I hate to talk to people on the phone" to "I have a powerful motive for talking with people on the phone and I love it!"

─────────

The Byte for a Presentation, Speech, or Performance

Competitive athletes use a similar process to the Byte. As they prepare for an event, they visualize their performance in their mind over and over again. They see and feel themselves crossing the finish line first, giving a perfect 10 performance, or scoring the winning goal. They literally experience the emotions of standing on the podium, receiving the gold medal, and holding up the trophy to the cheer of the crowd. Whenever doubts, fear, or discouragement enter their mind, they dispel and replace them by mentally rehearsing their Byte.

The great golfer Johnny Miller described how before every swing he would visualize the perfect outcome he desired: the ball leaving his club; the trajectory the ball would follow; and the exact spot where it would land. His enormous success using his own version of the Byte speaks for itself.

You can do the same thing when preparing for an important presentation, speech, or interview. See yourself doing it perfectly. Write down the feelings you have as everyone claps, congratulates you, awards you the sale, or gives you the job. As you prepare, read and visualize this Byte over and over again. Any time doubts or fears arise, dispel and replace them with your Byte.

A Byte for Compulsive Behaviors and Addictions

Growing numbers of people suffer from compulsive behaviors and addictions. They describe a wave or overwhelming urge that suddenly washes over them to indulge in their addictive behavior. Once this urge hits, tying to control it can be extremely difficult or virtually impossible. If this describes your situation, create a Byte. Do it when you are under control and free of the urge to act out your addiction. Your Byte could be a list of all the positive benefits you would have in your life if you were free of your addiction. It could be a letter to yourself giving you words of encouragement or a powerful message to change your mental model and thought pattern. Consider some real-life examples from among my clients and the Bytes they created. I will teach you later about the **5-Step Discovery Process** that will give you even more ability to perform.

I Promise You

I have a client who had a drinking problem. He tried time and time again to stop without success. I suggested he create a Byte. What would activate feelings and emotions, a motive, so powerful that it would override his craving for alcohol and shift him to a new mental model?

First, I suggested he promise his wife that he would quit. He indicated he had done that many times and it had failed. I asked him, "Do you really want to stop?" "Yes," he insisted. In our past conversations, I had discovered he had an extremely close relationship with his sixteen-year-old son. I suggested he promise his son that he had seen his dad drink for the last time. I suggested he take a photograph of his son and on the bottom of it write the words, "I promise you." He was to put this photo in his wallet so that if he went to the liquor store to buy a bottle, he would see the photo when getting out his money.

He was stunned by this suggestion. He was so angry at me for making it that he didn't speak to me for ten days (now that's powerful meaning!). But he came back and agreed to use the photo and promise to his son as his Byte. In addition to the Byte, he had a statement regarding his alcoholism in his LifeCreed, and he wrote in his Feelings Journal about it regularly (you will earn about these LifeBalance Tools in later chapters). From that point forward he remained alcohol-free. I recently received a card from him. In part it read:

I have six and a half years of sobriety. Thanks! I am now four years a consecutive Top of the Table qualifier, six years Court of the Table, and fourteen years MDRT member. (These are very prestigious awards/positions in the insurance business.) Thanks! I am in good shape—I run a 5K every single night. Thanks! Annie still loves me and is the center of my world. Thanks! Robbie is my close and wonderful son. Thanks! I am alive. Thanks! P.S. You still aggravate me. Thanks!

I Am a Non-Smoker

During a LifeBalance Institute weekend retreat, we were training the audience in the use of the Byte. One participant, Patty, had been a smoker for over twenty-two years. She had tried to quit many times without any lasting success. Patty created a Byte to counter her craving for cigarettes.

She understood the principle about mental models—when mental models containing forceful emotions are activated the brain does not distinguish between what is real and imagined. Patty then constructed her Byte with the following elements:

1. It began with the statement "I am a non-smoker," as if it were already true.

2. It contained an instruction for her to clearly and vividly visualize her lungs as completely clean and vibrant as she repeated the word *breathe.*

3. It included a detailed description of her vision of a long and healthy life, enjoying her children and her future grandchildren.

4. It also contained her commitment to her children to be a non-smoker and a vivid description of the admiration on their smiling faces as they congratulated her for being free of her addiction.

From that weekend forward, Patty has not smoked another cigarette! Never doubt the power of motive in changing mental models and even lifelong habits!

The grand key to the Byte is that it can instantly create a motive stronger than the negative thought, desire, or compulsion you're trying to dispel and replace. Use the Byte to overcome a particular negative thought pattern, behavior, or habit that is disrupting your life. Be sure to repeat the Byte every day or have it available if you start to falter.

NOTE: *The Byte does not replace professional therapy, recovery programs, support groups, or other interventions that are so crucial to those suffering from addictions and other serious disorders. The Byte is intended to be a support and additional tool that can be used in conjunction with these essential resources.*

Mother Teresa said, "We can all do a small thing with great love." The Byte, by definition, is a small thing, a small thing that will create a big difference in your life. Through the years some of the most heartwarming experiences I have shared with my clients have involved their successes with the Byte. This pocket-sized tool for improving relationships and changing habits will bring positive change to you as it has for me and many of my clients, family members, and friends.

NOTE

1. James Allen, *As a Man Thinketh* (New York: Fall River Press, 1992), 11, 13, 43.

Important Ideas & Insights

_____
_____
_____
_____
_____
_____
_____
_____
_____
_____
_____
_____
_____

3

The Miracle of Feelings Journaling

YEARS AGO, I WAS on the freeway during rush hour in a large city. There was nothing unusual about the experience—just a typical day in traffic—except that I found myself in a particularly deep state of contemplation. It suddenly seemed to me that we were all on a giant conveyor belt, each car on autopilot, systematically moving forward, slowing, stopping, and moving again—a mechanized symphony directed by some master computer program. Most of the faces I observed were expressionless, almost robot-like in their appearance. Then it hit me: "This is how we live a significant portion of our lives—on autopilot, like robots going through the motions, unaware of our deepest feelings, dreams, and potentials and those of the people around us!" Though it was a kind of surreal *Twilight Zone* experience, the more I thought about it, the more I realized it represented what our brains do naturally.

In chapter 1 you learned about your brain's number one priority—*efficiency*—meaning that your brain seeks to turn everything you do into a habit as quickly as possible. While habits can give us the opportunity to continually learn and master new things, this natural built-in tendency can also put our lives and relationships in a rut where we get so stuck in our ways that we retard or even shut down our own progress. In essence, we go on autopilot and live ever-greater portions of our lives at very low levels of *awareness*, where we repress or avoid dealing with our feelings, and spend very little time proactively directing the conscious stages of our minds. In fact, many times we're so locked on autopilot, we're not even aware of what we are feeling.

And if this tendency to go on autopilot isn't enough, we also live in the dizzying blur of a science-fiction-come-true world where virtually everywhere we turn there is something to grab and occupy our minds—multi-media cell phones, the Internet, 250-channel cable TV, virtual realty video games, and pocket-sized DVD players. Add our mile-a-second-paced lives, where we attempt to juggle and balance an array of items, and it can be all too easy to simply go into survival mode. We can lose sight of our dreams and aspirations, our relationships with those that matter most to us, our own feelings and emotions, the simple pleasures and joys of life, and the many blessings of life we take for granted. We just keep pushing robotically forward.

How do you switch off your autopilot and begin enjoying the success and fulfillment that comes from being more aware of, harnessing and directing, your deepest thoughts and feelings? The simplest and most powerful method you will ever use is the LifeBalance Tool known as **Feelings Journaling**. Of all the tools I teach, this one is the most important.

What Is Feelings Journaling?

When people first hear the term *Feelings Journaling,* some (especially men, who tend to have the hardest time with and greatest misconceptions about this tool) respond like this: "Oh great, you want me to get all mushy and write down my 'feelings' in a diary, right? Does it have a pink cover with a pretty floral design and a delicate locking gold clasp and matching key?" Others, while completely comfortable talking in general terms about feelings—"I hate broccoli" or "I love that song"—panic when asked to write down their innermost feelings. For these people, writing their feelings can be awkward and uncomfortable. To avoid the difficulty of the exercise or potential pain, they convince themselves that some things are better left buried and forgotten.

Feelings Journaling is not a diary. Nor is it a simple daily log of "I came, I saw, I went, I did." It is, as the latest neuropsychological studies show, one of the most powerfully productive and positive processes you can experience—accessing and expressing in writing your deepest feelings. Feelings Journaling will take you to places within yourself that you have probably not visited recently, or perhaps ever. It is a simple exercise that takes only minutes to complete. At the most basic level, Feelings Journaling consists of the following easy steps:

1. Be completely open, honest, and unrestricted. Write whatever you are feeling—positive or negative. Be totally honest and unrestricted. Don't worry about spelling, grammar, or sentence structure—just let it flow onto the paper or computer screen, uninterrupted. You can feel completely at ease writing this way because your Feelings Journal is for you.

2. It's for your eyes only. If you have the slightest suspicion that someone could somehow get hold of your journal and read it, you will probably not allow yourself to write in a completely open, honest, and uncensored manner. Don't allow anyone to have access to your Feelings Journal without your permission. Develop appropriate security measures so you will feel more at ease. If you keep a handwritten journal, *do not use a bound book*. Keep your journal in a three-ring binder so you can add pages as needed or take out those you don't want anyone to read.

3. Destroy negative entries. If you write something that you would not want anyone else to read, when you are finished, delete it from your computer or destroy the handwritten pages.

4. Write in the same place and same time. The quality of your life today is a direct result of the habits you have formed over time. The key is to form specific habits that lead to what you want most in life. Developing a daily Feelings Journaling routine is one of the most important habits you can acquire. To do this, set a regular time (preferably first thing in the morning, before everyone is up) in a quiet, private place where you can look out the window, ponder, think, and record whatever is on your mind. Doing this at the same time and place every day will quickly establish a new mental model.

Some people have a tough time finding peace and quiet at home for Feelings Journaling. Over the years, my LifeBalance clients have used a variety of approaches to remedy this problem. Some pull into a parking lot on the way to work and journal. Others stop by a coffee shop and sit in their usual spot. And some simply close their office door and take a few minutes to Feelings Journal before starting their work day. For over twenty years I have sat in my La-Z-Boy chair almost every day, looking out the same window and writing in my journal.

Key Concept 8̶—̶
───

Feelings Journaling will become an appointment with the most important person in your life—you! If you "try to find the time," you'll likely never do it. Make this appointment a major priority in your life. Be sure to develop a powerful motive to do this, or you won't. The remarkable benefits in every aspect of your life will amaze you.

───────────────────

5. Develop your skills over time: Feelings Journaling does not come easily or naturally to most people—especially men. In the beginning it can be difficult, but with practice and time, you'll become progressively more comfortable and skilled at it. It's like learning to play the piano or some other musical instrument: at first your fingers feel awkward and uncoordinated, but in time you begin playing beautiful music. Be patient, start out slowly—only five to ten minutes a day—and build up from there. Use your **Feelings Journal Checklist** (see below) to stimulate thoughts about what you should write. Stick with it and Feelings Journaling will become one of the most productive and fulfilling daily activities in your life!

YOUR FEELINGS JOURNAL CHECKLIST

When beginning the journaling process, many people complain, "I just can't think of anything to write." To help you overcome this obstacle, develop a **Feelings Journal Checklist.** As you sit down to write and review this list, certain items will ignite feelings within you and start you writing. To construct your first checklist, make a list of the things in your life you are most concerned about, most desirous to achieve, or most grateful for. You may want to start with the **Six Key Relationships** (see chapter 4) in your life and create a checklist something like this:

Spiritual
How is my relationship with God?
What can I do to improve it?
Is there a recent—or not so recent—spiritual experience I should record?
What blessings have I received from God?

Emotional/Intellectual

What am I feeling today? Why?

What is really important in my life? Why?

Where am I improving in my life?

What area in my life needs more attention? Why?

What am I most excited about? Why?

What am I most discouraged about? Why?

What am I most grateful for? Why?

Physical

How do I feel physically? What can I do to improve?

What is most discouraging about my physical condition? Why?

How is my diet? What can I do to improve it? How would this benefit me?

How do I feel about my fitness level and exercise? What can I do to improve? How would this make a difference in my life?

What am I most grateful for with regard to my physical body, health, or abilities?

Family

How has _____(name of spouse) blessed my life?

What are _____'s (name of spouse) strengths?

How have each of my children blessed my life? (List each child separately.) What are each of their strengths?

What complaints or disappointments do I have?

Are there any areas of concern I should focus on?

Social

How can I improve my interaction with people?

Which of my friends needs some special attention? Why? What can I do to help?

How has someone among my friends, neighbors, or colleagues blessed my life?

Financial

What am I working toward in my career? Why?

What am I most concerned about? Why?

What do I find most exciting about my work? Why is this exciting?

What do I find most discouraging? Why?

How have I been blessed financially?

Make Your Own Custom Checklist

The questions above are just a sample of what could be on your checklist. Make your own list according to what's going on in your life. List any topic that you need to explore your feelings about, such as a specific person, task, goal, talent, or concern. Add new items at any time and remove others when you have exhausted all thoughts about the topic. After you create your LifeCreed (see chapter 9) you may choose to add items from it to your checklist. Obviously, you don't write about every item on the checklist at once. Place the checklist next to your keyboard or writing pad to stimulate your feelings and help you start writing.

Take the Feelings Journal Challenge

For six of the next seven days, spend at least 5 minutes each morning, journaling your feelings. You will notice a real difference in your life!

I started journaling years ago quite by accident. As I was going through my divorce, my ex-wife was telling my wonderful kids all kinds of bad stuff about me that was not true. I refused to get into a spitting contest and tell them bad things about their mom. I decided I'd write down what was happening to me, and if and when the kids wanted to read my side, there it was.

I really had no idea what I was doing. During the divorce some friends who knew what I was going through asked me how I was able to be upbeat with all that was happening to me. I said I didn't know. I didn't realize until years later the cathartic benefit of writing down what I was feeling and what was happening to me, what I now call Feelings Journaling.

Although you may not fully realize it, there are aspects of your personal life, relationships, and career where you react or respond out of habit or autopilot mode. In many of these areas, developing a greater level of awareness and connection to your deepest feelings would greatly improve your success, happiness, and sense of fulfillment. One of the amazing attributes of Feelings Journaling is that it is a universal tool—it can be applied to any area of your life you wish to improve. In addition, simplicity, ease of use, and immediate access at any time or place make Feelings Journaling a remarkable tool. As with the Byte, all that is needed to get results is a very small amount of time and effort on a consistent daily basis.

There are virtually unlimited daily applications for Feelings Journaling. Here are the top eight benefits and applications my clients and I have enjoyed and used over the years. I highly recommend you implement these applications in your own life. You'll be astonished by the results!

THE TOP EIGHT DAILY APPLICATIONS AND BENEFITS

OF

FEELINGS JOURNALING

I. Crystallize Thoughts, Work through Problems, and Release Stress

Have you ever been burdened with a problem, challenge, or worry that you can't find a solution to, one you can't get out of your head? Are their times when you feel bored, lonely, stressed out, angry, depressed, or anxious? On occasion, is your mind overwhelmed with thoughts and activity, so much so that you can't concentrate? You may even have trouble sleeping. The tendency is to put your head down on your pillow and just keep pushing forward, or give up all together.

The reality is, no matter how much you attempt to bury your feelings and stop thinking about your problems, they will manifest themselves in one form or another—your mind and body will find a way to release. For example, chronic stress, which has been called America's number one health problem, is not something to take lightly—it can have profound effects on your immune system and your overall health. On March 22, 2005, *USA Today* cited research placing stress-related illness as the cause of up to 90 percent of all primary care physician visits! Another excellent article that confirms these findings can be found in the *Bottom Line/Personal* Magazine (May 15, 2008). It's entitled, "Stress is Behind 90% of All Visits to Primary Care Physicians" by Dr. Kathleen Hall, PhD. It reports what stress can do to a person, including in a variety of health problems such as heart disease, cancer, diabetes, memory problems, and weakened immune system. I encourage you to read this article. One of the greatest stress relievers is Feelings Journaling.

Sometimes life can become overwhelming; your mind like a glass is filled to capacity and spilling over. Feelings Journaling allows you to confront pressing issues, address them, and then move on, clearing out your mind and making room for other things.

One client writes, "Whenever I'm confronted with any challenge, problem, or emotion I can't work out, I immediately go and Feelings Journal. By the time I'm done journaling I find that one of two things has happened. I have the solution or I realize that what was weighing me down is no big deal. Either way, I'm free of the problem or burden, and I feel peace. Instead of obsessing and laboring over it like I used to, I can journal and then move on. The amazing thing to me is that my Feelings Journal is always available to me, anytime and anyplace. All I need is a pen and something to write on. Who would've thought something so powerful could be so simple?"

A very simple and easy method for working through problems, clearing out persistent thoughts, and finding solutions is through a Feelings Journaling application known as the **5-Step Discovery Process.**

THE 5-STEP DISCOVERY PROCESS TO RELIEVE STRESS, RESOLVE A CONCERN, AND FIND A SOLUTION

Often there is a major concern or stress that can dominate our thoughts and feelings, diminishing our ability to fully focus and enjoy the journey. Basic Feelings Journaling will help you identify this concern, but you will need more to resolve it. The following 5-Step Discovery Process is a powerful advanced application of Feelings Journaling that will provide you with the mental clarity to either eliminate the concern or formulate a specific plan to deal with it positively and effectively.

STEP 1: What?

Write down as much as you can in answer to the question, "What is concerning me or stressing me out?" To help you be more specific, answer the question, "What do I mean by that?"

STEP 2: Why?

Answer as thoroughly as possible the question, "Why is this concerning me or stressing me out?"

STEP 3: How?

Write down everything that comes to your mind in response to the inquiry, "How can I resolve this concern or stress—what are the potential solutions?"

STEP 4: Obstacles?

Ask yourself, "What will keep me from implementing these solutions?" Then write down all of the potential obstacles you can think of. Next to each obstacle write down how you can overcome it. Add these to the solutions you identified under Step 3.

STEP 5: Motive?

Clearly imagine in your mind that the concern or stress has been resolved or greatly reduced. Describe in detail how your life is better and *how you feel* as a result.

————— I Can't Breathe and I Can't Sleep! —————

A dramatic example of the power of the 5-Step Discovery Process to resolve concerns is how one of my clients used it to alleviate anxiety attacks and insomnia.

Things were progressing nicely in Mark's personal life, family relationships, and career. Imagine his surprise when for no apparent reason he began having trouble sleeping at night. When he lay down, his heart and mind raced. He felt a darkness settle over him, a fear and foreboding that something was wrong, that something terrible was going to happen. He felt a restriction in his chest making it difficult to breathe. He thought it might all be related to a heart or lung problem. But extensive testing showed everything as normal. To his shock, the diagnosis came back as anxiety attacks!

Not wanting to get trapped in the "sleep medication cycle," Mark sought other remedies. Having experienced many years of great success with Feelings Journaling and the Byte, he applied these tools, but the symptoms continued. Then he began asking himself, "What is at the root of all this—what is the cause?" In a conversation with a dear friend, he was reminded how financial stress and worry had been his nemesis since childhood. He journaled about this and came to the conclusion that he did have some deeply buried financial fears.

At night, whenever he found himself lying awake with mind racing and heart palpitating, he got up and went through the 5-Step Discovery Process. This is the format he used:

1. What?—I have financial worries.

2. Why?—Why do I have these concerns?

3. How?—How can I resolve these worries? What can I do tomorrow to improve my financial situation? What are the specific actions steps I can take? Who and what do I know that will help me?

4. Obstacles?—What are the obstacles standing in my way and how can I get over them?

5. Motive?—As I clearly imagine my life with all of the financial abundance I desire, what is my life like and how does it feel?

Using this simple process, Mark discovered that miraculously his mind and body became calm and he was able to go to sleep and rest peacefully! He had confronted his fears directly and worked logically through the problem, mapping out a solution and envisioning the success that would surely come. With all of this accomplished, he was at peace and his mind could rest for the night.

Once you have applied the 5-Step Discovery Process, you can use what you have written out of step 5 to create a Byte as an additional tool to help you find relief from a pressing worry, concern, or problem. For example, in Mark's case, he took what he had written in step five (Motive) and transferred it to a index card. Whenever he sensed feelings of anxiety beginning to surface, he pulled out his Byte and reviewed it. This helped in switching his thoughts away from fear and worry to solutions and the positive expectation of a wonderful outcome.

Remember, the mind is remarkably powerful. Whatever you allow to consistently play on the stage of your mind becomes a self-fulfilling prophecy—you get what you think about!

THE 5-STEP DISCOVERY PROCESS FOR A MAJOR GOAL

Have you ever optimistically set a new goal only to find after a few days or weeks the initial enthusiasm for the goal fizzles out? Usually this happens because the initial goal-setting process is missing some critically important elements. Without these elements, the goal is really nothing more than a wish. Use the 5-Step Discovery Process to clearly articulate in writing each critical step of the goal-formation process.

STEP 1: What?

What is your goal? What is the ideal situation you hope to create? Be specific—keep asking and answering the question, "What do I mean by that?"

STEP 2: Why?

Why do you want this? Be specific—keep asking and answering the question, "What do I mean by that?"

STEP 3: How?

How can you make your goal a reality? Write down the individual steps of your action plan—be as specific and complete as possible.

STEP 4: Obstacles?

What are the obstacles that may get in your way? Be specific. Next to each obstacle, identify a solution for overcoming it. Add these to the action plan you created under Step 3.

STEP 5: Motive?

Imagine it's the future and you have achieved your goal. Describe *in detail* how you feel and what your life is like.

II. Purge Negative Feelings

Through your Feelings Journal, you can uncover and expel negative thoughts, feelings, and memories about certain people, places, or events that have been festering inside you for years—even from childhood. For reasons science is just discovering, when you take the time to write out worries, negative thoughts, and emotions, they begin to lose their power over you. As negativity loosens its choke-hold on you, you are able to see objectively and discard the concerns that drag you down, focusing instead on the positive. With this baggage cleared out, your health, success, attitude, energy, and relationships substantially improve. When new problems and negative thoughts arise, Feelings Journaling will help you resolve them and move on. To get rid of these negative feelings about people, places or events, my good friend Gary Lundberg, a marriage and family counselor, recommends the following ten steps:

> **1. Give yourself permission to be completely free** and open in your writing, holding nothing back—no words or descriptions are prohibited—and just get it on the paper.

2. Have two pens (no pencils), a large amount of paper, and unlimited time.

3. Go to a quiet place where you can be undisturbed and uninterrupted—no cell phones allowed!

4. Never direct your writing toward yourself, such as, "I'm such a stupid person," or "I really messed up when I . . ." Don't include any direct references, accusations, or statements about yourself when expressing your negative feelings.

5. Write about a person or situation associated with a lot of negative emotions.

6. Address the person however you feel about them: "Dear so-and-so," or "You dirty, no good . . ."

7. Write as fast as you can and don't worry about handwriting, spelling, grammar, punctuation, language, or flow of thoughts. Just let it all gush out onto the paper.

8. If you're in the middle of writing something and a new thought or feeling comes, start writing about that—write with total abandon.

9. Write until one of three things happens:
- You become so emotional you must stop yourself.
- You run out of things to write.
- You run out of time (hopefully not this one).

10. When one of these three things happens, take all the pages you've written and seal them in an envelope. Immediately go to a location (fireplace, incinerator, or even a freshly dug hole in the ground) where you can safely burn the envelope containing all the pages.

IMPORTANT: *Never re-read a single written word. Simply set fire to the envelope. Imagine the powerful meaning this has as you see the negative words, feelings, and memories consumed by the flames. Watch as the ashes float up into the air and disappear. Many of my clients have described this feeling as a great burden being lifted from their shoulders. With the words destroyed, no one will ever read them again, not even you.*

Example of Real-Life Applications: One client had recently experienced a bitter divorce. He was filled with anger and resentment, and these feelings were negatively impacting every aspect of his life. Incredibly, he Feelings Journaled 142 pages! It required journaling on separate days to get it all out. He took a large wooden toy sailboat, cut off the top and filled it with all 142 pages. Setting the boat on fire, he floated it out onto a lake near his home. He watched the pages and the boat burn and eventually sink out of sight. He said the burden lifted from him that day was nothing short of miraculous. He was able to resume his life, free of the destructive feelings and debilitative emotions.

A client tells of the power of Feelings Journaling in assisting him in getting rid of dark childhood memories:

I had a really traumatic childhood filled with emotional and physical abuse. I carried a lot of this baggage into my adult life, and it was causing problems in my marriage and my relationships with my kids. I learned how to journal my feelings. One Saturday afternoon I spent several hours getting it all out, all the dark, terrible memories, all the anger, all the fear and shame. I held nothing back, not even profanity. My writing took up many pages. When I was finally done I took all the pages and sealed them in an envelope. I took the envelope into my backyard and I lit it on fire. I stood and watched the pages burn and the smoke rise up into the air and disappear. I can't explain it, but as that smoke floated up, I felt a huge burden lift off of my mind and my shoulders. When all that was left were ashes I felt a deep sense of peace. That experience put me on a path to amazing accomplishments in my career, my marriage, and my family life.

III. Prepare to Communicate

By crystallizing your thoughts and working through any negatives, journaling lets you uncover feelings for the people you care about. This advance preparation allows for far more healthy and open communication. In addition, Feelings Journaling can help you prepare for important meetings, presentations, and speeches. Consider the following examples:

- You've had an argument with your spouse and you're still angry. As you journal your angry feelings, you gain perspective on the situation and your anger fades away. You perhaps begin to see where you were at fault. In effect, yelling at your spouse on the pages feels almost as good as doing it in person—and then it's out of your system and gone. (Following the ten steps for getting rid of negative feelings is very helpful). As you Feelings Journal you talk about how and what you can say to reconcile with your spouse. Later when you discuss the matter with your spouse, you find to your amazement that you're able to speak clearly and calmly, your words unfolding exactly as you journaled beforehand.

- A very successful client had an important business presentation he needed to make to his partners. Nervous and not sure how to put the presentation together, he put himself in the place of his partners and journaled about their concerns, feelings, and desired outcomes. This exercise crystallized his thoughts and showed him exactly how to structure the information he wanted to communicate. After the presentation his partners commented about how incredibly well prepared he was and how he hit their key points right on the mark.

- You have an interview scheduled with one of your employees and are not sure what to say. You decide to journal about all the talents, qualities, and positives this employee demonstrates. During the interview you express appreciation and praise for all of these things. When you have a few suggestions for improvement, they are extremely well received by the employee, and you both leave the interview feeling understood, uplifted, and motivated. For weeks afterward you notice your relationship with the employee has greatly improved.

- A successful public speaker uses the Feelings Journal to prepare for his presentations. He visualizes his audience and then writes about their needs, how he can best serve them, and how he feels about them as his brothers and sisters. Based on these things, he sketches an outline of his presentation. He envisions himself making the presentation, sees the smiling faces and nods of approval from the audience, hears their applause at the end, and sees himself interacting and answering their questions afterward. With this vision in mind, he writes about how blessed and fulfilled he feels. He often comments how amazed he is that such a simple exercise could have such a powerfully positive effect on his presentations.

IV. Improve Family Relationships

It's easy to focus on the negative characteristics and flaws of our spouse, children, and others close to us. Over the years this focus leads to the formation of dominant negative mental models, fault-finding, sarcasm, nagging, and a drifting apart in our closest relationships. Feelings Journaling is a powerful tool for turning our hearts and minds to focus on the positive attributes, gifts, and talents of our loved ones while preventing the negative from poisoning and destroying these relationships.

One client is a dedicated athlete. He keeps himself in top physical condition. Several years ago, in the midst of raising a large family, his wife began to put on weight and to get out of shape.

He said, "At first I started thinking negative thoughts whenever I looked at her. Then I found myself making critical comments about her weight and appearance. It really hurt her feelings and became a serious wedge in our relationship. Then I started journaling every morning about why I loved her so much. What was it about her that attracted me when we were first dating? What were her outstanding qualities, talents, and gifts? How had she blessed my life and our children's lives? From the very first journaling session I started to feel different. I found that the weight issue was a tiny matter compared to all of the wonderful things about her. After a week or so of journaling it just wasn't a big deal any more. My thoughts and feelings about her turned to total love, appreciation, and acceptance."

Another client resisted the idea of journaling feelings. He said, "That's just not my thing." I asked, "How much time do you spend telling your wife how you feel about her, like you did when you were first courting?" He responded, "I tell her I love her once in awhile." "How much time do you spend with each of your children affirming their unique gifts and talents and building them up?" I inquired. He admitted not much. In fact, he never really thought much about it.

Like most guys, after the children starting arriving, John focused on working to provide for his family. He worked hard, and at night, like most men, he looked forward to coming home to escape in front of the TV or to his workshop. He tried to spend time with his kids, but the thought of consciously focusing on their talents had never crossed his mind. When asked about his wife's unique talents, he mumbled something about her "being a good cook."

He was encouraged to start Feelings Journaling about each member of his family, their unique talents and charateristics, why he loved and appreciated them, and how he could help each one and make life better for them. He even started asking his wife and children how he could be a better husband and father. At first they were shocked, but soon they began offering him a few suggestions that he journaled about.

It's been three years since John started on his Feelings Journaling adventure. He is amazed at the thoughts and feelings he expresses to his children. His wife feels loved and nurtured. Instead of the occasional offhand "I love you," he shares his feelings of admiration, appreciation, and love with her because he has been Feelings Journaling about them first.

He observed that a side benefit to all of this is how it has improved his productivity as a salesman. In the last three years, he has more than doubled his income and has personally related to his clients far better than ever before. John observed, "I never knew how much of my life I was missing out on by not being in touch with and expressing my feelings." He is committed to Feelings Journaling for the rest of his life.

V. Receive Inspiration

As you write in your Feelings Journal, amazing ideas and insights about all aspects of life will come to mind. You'll ask yourself, "Where did that answer come from?" Your Feelings Journal will act as a conduit for continual inspiration and as a written record of that inspiration, and it's never forgotten and can be retrieved and acted upon at any time in the future.

I believe there is an energy, a spiritual power all around us. It is there for us to tap into and receive knowledge, guidance, and insight. But we can only do this when we take time to shut out the noise and distractions of the world. One of the most effective tools you will ever use to accomplish this is your Feelings Journal.

VI. Increase Creativity

After Feelings Journaling for several months, you will have opened up extensive neural pathways to the right side, the creative side, of your brain. As a result, you will find significant increases in your intuition, not only during your journaling but at many other times during the day and night. This increase will usually be noticed more by men, as women typically possess a ready-made intuition as a result of their unique female brain structure. Whether you are a man or a woman, you will see increases in your overall insight and creativity.

One client tells of how he was working on an important project and hit an impasse—he just couldn't figure out the solution. While Feelings Journaling, a picture of the solution came into his mind and he furiously jotted down the details. Remarkably, the problem was solved and he was able to proceed.

VII. Capture Special Moments

Can you remember special times in your life when you felt over-whelmed by the emotions, feelings, or spirit of the experience? Perhaps it was your wedding day, the birth of your first child, an incredible family vacation, a tender moment with your spouse or a child, the death of a loved one, or an inspiring sermon. There are many moments like these when your perspective is clear; the feelings of your heart are rich and deep. These experiences are precious treasures. Sadly, many of these special moments dim over time until they become a faint memory.

The Funeral

Recently I attended the funeral of an extended family member. Among the attendees I noticed the ex-husband of the deceased. He was a crusty old trucker, very macho in appearance and demeanor, and as expected, showed no emotion. But then, as they prepared to close the casket, I noticed his expression began to soften. He looked on his ex-wife for the last time and then turned his gaze toward his son and grandchildren. Tears began running down his cheeks. I thought to myself, "He's having a **Special Moment**! What is he thinking about?" Perhaps he was wishing he had worked things out and avoided the divorce all those years ago. Maybe he was thinking he should have spent more time with her. Perhaps he was observing his son and remembering all the times he wasn't there for him. And very likely, he was tenderly considering the sweet faces of his young grandchildren and making a commitment that he would not allow any more precious time and opportunities to be lost.

As the funeral ended, I watched him get into his big rig, the tears gone and his face expressionless, and drive away. I knew that most likely within a few days, back on the road and back in his old environ-ment, habits, and mind-set, his special moment would begin to fade, eventually leaving only a faint memory. Gone would be his clarity, his regret, his determination, and inner commitment to make a change.

How often have you experienced Special Moments? When have you tapped into clarity, inspiration, or a spiritual state, and then let them slip away? Don't allow this to ever happen again. The information you receive in these moments can't be found in any self-improvement book, audio program, or seminar. You, your situation, and your needs are unique. Through these special experiences you will find answers for you and your family. When they come to you, you must have a way to capture and hold onto to them, so you can revisit, ponder, nurture, and develop these answers over time. Don't let these sacred moments slip away—they have great power to relieve your stress and concerns, improve your relationships, and bring you the success and happiness you're searching for.

Keep a Special Moments Notepad

Keep a small pad of paper with you (or use your PDA). When you find yourself in the midst of one of these sacred experiences, make a note about your feelings as soon as possible. That evening, or the next morning, review your notes and then write in your Feelings Journal about the experience in detail. When you're feeling down or in need of inspiration, or require a push to recommit to promises you've made to yourself and others, you can go back and relive these experiences as you read your Feelings Journal entries. In chapter 9 you will learn how to reference these notes as you prepare to create and record your **LifeCreed**. Through your LifeCreed you can take your insights from these special moments and start doing something about them on a daily basis.

VIII. Write Your Life Story

As we look back on our lives, we cannot number or recall all of the important experiences, insights, lessons, and events. Some we remember with vivid clarity, others are dim and faded, and many are forgotten altogether. By making note of your Special Moments and then writing in your Feelings Journal, you are compiling a record of your feelings and insights during your engagement, your marriage, honeymoon, the birth of each child, your career experiences, the trials, joys, challenges, and triumphs that are part of your life story. Imagine being able to give excerpts from this record as a gift to your spouse, children, parents, siblings, and others at key times in their lives.

One of the most valuable and underutilized treasures is the knowledge and wisdom possessed by preceding generations—people who have been through the school of hard knocks, who have learned valuable lessons and gained Solomon-like wisdom. This precious gift should be shared and passed on to those coming up through the ranks. Yet many have no method for passing this legacy on other than talking from their memories, which significantly fade with time. And many don't like talking about themselves or aren't very good at telling stories or sharing feelings. If you are such a person, you can use excerpts from your Feelings Journal to create your own life story to give to family members.

The Feelings Journal is a simple and easy-to-use tool through which you can reflect on and appreciate your life, mentor your children and grandchildren, and pass on a precious legacy that will benefit generations to come.

Jim, a client, occasionally gives selected journal entries as gifts to family members on special occasions. On his twenty-fifth wedding anniversary, Jim gave his wife a beautiful leather-bound book containing journal entries from their wedding day, the birth of each of their children, and numerous entries containing expressions of his love, gratitude, and admiration for his wife. She will treasure that gift always. When each of his children leave home for college or get married, he gives them special journal entries from the time of their birth to the present. Think of what this does for each child's self-esteem and the bond of love with their father, as they read about his thoughts and feelings for them!

What Clients Say about Feelings Journaling

Over the years, thousands of clients have received incredible benefits in every aspect of their lives as a result of Feelings Journaling. Consider these insights from some of my clients:

"I love to journal because it frees my mind from the information that bombards me from different directions. I receive so much information that I need to take a step back and reflect on what information is important to me so I can live a fulfilled life. I write in my journal to express my views and organize my thoughts. Writing about my feelings helps me to focus on the goals that are important to me and my family. Also, journaling helps me to sort out my problems. I feel that journaling is talking to my best friend, which is *me*."

"I am much more creative since I started to keep a Feelings Journal. Journaling challenges my brain to write something each day that is meaningful. It was difficult to write one paragraph a day when I first started. After one year, I don't have any problem writing one page. My goal is to write two pages per day if time permits. Writing the extra page forces my mind to be creative and it forces me to delve into my feelings about the topic I have chosen to write for the day's entry. As a result, I am developing the creative right side of my brain."

"After I journal I find my brain is thinking about what I wrote as I go through the day. My brain, unconscious to me, is thinking about solutions to problems or mulling my feelings so I can come to some conclusion when I'm least expecting it. I find thoughts coming to my mind about problems I wrote about a month ago that just seem to pop into my mind at the appropriate time."

"I have discovered that the words will flow effortlessly from my mouth if I journal about my feelings. For example, I journaled about returning to my former profession a couple of weeks before I had an interview for a position. I wrote my thoughts about the job and my feelings about how I would approach the job. At the interview I thought I had not prepared for it very well. However, the words flowed effortlessly from my mouth and it was one of the best interviews I have ever had. Journaling helped me to prepare for the interview, because I was able to sort my feelings about the job, before I went to the interview."

"Journaling has improved my spiritual life. I write about my feelings about my faith in God and Jesus Christ. Writing about God increases my faith because I am imprinting my thoughts in my mind as I write them on paper. I write about Bible passages that really affect me and these thoughts will come to my mind at the right time when I'm faced with a situation that calls for God's guidance."

"Writing in my Feelings Journal forces my mind to think differently than when I talk. I am able to remain more focused on what I want to accomplish today than I was one year ago because of writing my feelings in my journal. I am always happier and my day feels more fulfilled when I make time to journal because I am taking time away from my busy life to be with myself. As a result, I am better at discovering who I am and identifying what is really important to me."

Important Ideas & Insights

The Slight Edge
In Your Career

4

Is Your Life Dying from Making a Living?

WE LIVE IN A society that places tremendous focus and value on making money. Of all the activities in our lives, we devote the lion's share of time, energy, and attention to obtaining money. Many keep score by how much they earn or have, the size of their house, or the make and model of their car. Others, in contrast, struggle just to keep their heads above water.

Regardless of their level of income, in our money-centered society many find they are "dying from making a living." Their marriages, relationships with their children, health, spirituality, and overall love of life are dying. The associated stress is killing them. It doesn't matter whether a person makes thirty thousand dollars or one million dollars a year, because the components of happiness aren't found in money. In fact, many who achieve the highest monetary success often sacrifice success in their personal and family lives. Though more than capable of giving and serving in their marriages, families, and society, people miss out on these potentials because making money takes so much of their time and energy.

I recently read an article about a medical doctor who conducted a survey of twelve hundred people with highly successful careers. His survey revolved around two major topics: 1) Did the professionals enjoy their personal/family life? and 2) Did they enjoy their work?

The responses were very telling: 80 percent enjoyed their work but did not enjoy their personal/family life, while 15 percent enjoyed their personal life but not their business life. Only 5 percent enjoyed both their personal/family life and their work.

In 1966, 42 percent of UCLA's freshman class said they thought it was essential or very important to be "very well off financially." Now, nearly three-quarters of UCLA freshman said being affluent is very important to them. A Pew Research Center poll mirrored those results. It found that among 18- to 25-year-olds in the United States, 80 percent see getting rich as a top goal for their generation. Based on my experience coaching clients, this is no surprise. Often, the measure of our success in life is tied to our success in the workplace—not in successful families, not in a good relationship with a spouse. There is a feeling that to have a successful career, we have to put it ahead of relationships in our life. My experience proves something else completely.

LifeBalance = More Financial Success, Less Stress, and Better Relationships

Almost all of my clients first hired me as a LifeBalance Coach because they heard I could show them how to make more money and be more productive in their business. Had I initially told them, "I will help improve your health, marriage, and relationships with children, as well as lower your stress and attain LifeBalance," many would've fired me. They would have said, "I'm not looking for a marriage counselor or fitness trainer—I just want to make more money!" But once they began implementing the system, all came to understand that the most effective way to make more money is through achieving balance in the things that really matter most in life.

The key to financial success is creating an environment in your everyday life that allows you to truly *focus* your attention. When your life is in balance, your mind is clear and at peace—you are productive. Conversely, when you are constantly preoccupied with worries and stress about money, your marriage, children, health, bills, and your ability to focus and to be productive are greatly diminished.

Have you ever tried to carry on a conversation with someone who was preoccupied or whose focus was somewhere else? Have you ever been interrupted while concentrating on a project and found it difficult to get back in the mood and establish your focus all over again? Have you ever gotten into an argument with your spouse, child, co-worker, or boss, and then tried to concentrate on your work? Or have you ever been troubled by a major worry, only to find that it dominates your thoughts day and night? *The mind cannot focus on two dissimilar things at once.* If you are preoccupied with stress and worry, your productivity and ability to succeed, financially or otherwise, is limited.

Many Feel the Stress and Do It Anyway

On considering these concepts, many respond, "I have stress every day—it's just the way it is. I just deal with it and push myself forward." Some even insist they manage just fine financially while dealing with stress and worry at the same time. In limited cases, this may be true, but at what cost?

Years ago when I lived in Oregon, I would occasionally sit and watch the tugboats pushing giant, heavy-laden barges up the Willamette River. Even though the tugs were outfitted with massive diesel engines, the forward progress of the barges was slow and cumbersome, requiring massive amounts of horsepower and fuel to propel them up the river. It seemed as if the tugs and barges were laboring through thick sludge rather than cool, clear water. Yet had the same tugboat engine been strapped to the hull of a sleek speedboat, the result would've been much different. Are you a tired tugboat struggling to force a stress-filled barge upstream? Or are you a streamlined, power-packed craft roaring upriver heedless of the current?

One of my clients tells the story of a hike he went on as a teen:

I was with a group of friends on a fifty mile hike in the High Sierras. Several in the group decided to play a joke on me. During our breaks, they put rocks in my backpack—a few at a time. As the day went on, my pack felt heavier and heavier. I assumed it was because I was growing progressively tired with the miles. Then in the mid-afternoon, I discovered the rocks and removed them. I was amazed at the difference in my backpack—it was so light! I immediately went to the front of the group and hiked easily until sunset.

How many of us are weighed down with heavy burdens, pressures, stresses, and worries, but, like the hiker, expend tremendous energy trudging ahead anyway? We push on, but at what cost? Years of "feeling the stress and doing it anyway" can exact a heavy toll on marriages, families, and physical and mental health. If we take steps to rid ourselves of these burdens, how much more effective can we be?

Do Not Accept Bad Advice

What about those who advise, "Focus on making money and that will relieve most of your personal pressures"? The traditional philosophy that tells us to work hard and focus on making money is alive and well. When you eliminate all the jargon and fluff, this philosophy is really saying, "Put making money first in your life, and everything else will work out."

In his book *The 7 Habits of Highly Effective People*, my friend Stephen Covey talks about the need for a healthy balance between the goose (production capability) and the golden eggs (production). If the goose is neglected, overworked, and driven to produce even more precious eggs, production may go up temporarily, but in the long run, you kill the goose!

Think of yourself as the goose and the money you earn as golden eggs. Push yourself, work long hours, sacrifice nutrition and exercise, neglect your marriage and children, carry heavy burdens of stress and worry—all in the name of more golden eggs—and eventually you'll end up losing what matters most and killing the goose in the process.

Often when my clients begin to get their lives in balance, they look back and say, "Leo, my life was dying from making a living and I didn't even know it. My total focus was on money, and I was missing out on all the really meaningful things in my life." One client told me, "I'd go to the office with my guts in a knot from an argument with my wife; I was stressed out about my teenage son failing school; I was overweight and out of shape; I was self-medicating with caffeine, food, TV, and a lot of other escapes. I was making good money, but my life was a mess. After applying my LifeBalance tools it was amazing how different I felt with just a few minor changes."

Wrap Your Career Around Your Personal Life, Not Your Personal Life Around Your Career

An anonymous writer once penned: "Don't ever let what you do for a living become what your are." In today's hectic, push-and-shove, bottom-line-focused business world, that's hard to do. Indeed, most people wrap their personal lives around their businesses or careers.

Take both of your hands and stretch them out in front of you, palms up. Now, form your right hand into a fist. This represents your business or career, while your left hand represents your personal and family life. Now take your open hand and wrap it around your fist. What is at the center or core? The answer is your business or career. With this typical approach, most people end up neglecting what matters most in their lives.

Rather than taking this all-too-common approach, I teach my clients to wrap their businesses or careers around their personal lives, placing what matters most to them at the center. As a result of this small yet pivotal adjustment in priority, the reduction of stress and the spike in productivity and personal income are nothing short of astounding.

You may think, "I spend this much time with my family and this much with work, therefore I'm balanced." But balance is not about time. It's about having the peace of mind knowing you are putting what matters most in your life first. When you can describe your life with phrases such as "I exercise, I eat right, I spend quality and quantity time with my spouse and children, I nourish my spiritual nature, I have hobbies I really enjoy, I love my work, and I serve and give to others," then you can with credibility say, "My life is in balance."

When you wrap your business or career around your personal and family life, you tap into hidden stores of energy and lift your attitude at work. Knowing you're taking care of what matters most sets your mind at ease; you are at peace. You're able to concentrate on your work. Creativity soars. Your communication and relationships with colleagues, employees, and clients improve markedly. Everything in your business or career improves because you have achieved true LifeBalance—you have attained the **Slight Edge.**

——————— Portrait: Finding a Balanced Life ———————

I recently received a testimonial letter from one of my clients. It illustrates the importance of achieving LifeBalance:

When I first began working with Leo I really didn't know how out of balance my life was. I just figured I was like everyone else—working long hours, stressed, problems at home, out of shape and overweight, just trying to stay on top. Isn't that the norm? Leo tried to show me where I was out of balance, but I didn't want to see it; I didn't want to admit it. However, when I started keeping my Feelings Journal and listening to my LifeCreed, I discovered my life was out of balance in a lot of ways.

So I decided to start using Leo's system of putting myself, my God, and my family first. And as I did, amazing things started happening with my business. It's hard to explain, but I think it comes down to this: When you put the people that really matter most first in your life, you transfer energy and thoughts that say to your clients, employees, and co-workers, "I'm a person of integrity and inner strength who really cares about others and not just using them to get power or money—because I put those who matter most first in my life."

To put it bluntly, you're free from the stress of a wife who thinks you're a jerk, from kids who are out of control and hardly know their dad, and from lousy health. When your personal and family life is in order, you can fully focus without distraction on your business. As a result, you start to care about others more and treat and communicate with them better. You feel better about yourself and your life, and you become more effective in business. My income went way up and at the same time I was able to spend more time on personal pursuits and my family. I never thought I could do both of these at the same time.

Do you place what matters most at the center of your life? How do you achieve this thing called LifeBalance?

True LifeBalance Is All about Relationship

If you truly desire to make more money, reduce stress, and increase balance in your life, the grand key is the quality of your relationships. If you truly want to place what matters most at the center, begin focusing on your relationships. I've heard it said, "Whatever issue you're struggling with, it can always be traced back to a relationship." I promise that if you take care of the key relationships in your life, everything else will fall into place.

In an effort to illustrate the importance of key relationships and their order of priority, I have developed the **Relationship Pyramid** (see next page).

Building from the base up, each relationship offers foundational strength and power to those above it. Only with each level of the pyramid built upon the other, in order, can you reach the top—the realization of your ideal self and your ideal life. If you try to take shortcuts or only partially construct the lower levels (putting the financial relationship first or giving it the major focus), the resulting pyramid is skewed, off-kilter, and will eventually collapse.

Let's briefly examine the building blocks of the Relationship Pyramid.

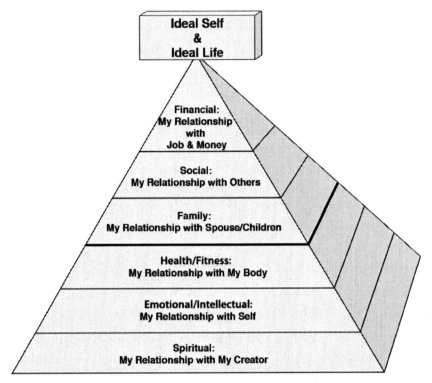

Spiritual—My Relationship with My Creator: This relationship needs to come before all others. When you are spiritually in-tune, balanced and connected, you possess an inner peace and strength that ripples through all other relationships and circumstances in your life. When you establish a strong relationship with things spiritual, everything else in your life falls into place.

Emotional/Intellectual—My Relationship with Self: Under the time constraints of job, family, and myriad other commitments, many of us find it easy to neglect our relationship with self, which comprises strengthening and increasing our emotional and intellectual capacities. One of the most powerful concepts covered in this book is best conveyed by the statement, "As a man thinketh, so is he."

Your thoughts, feelings, and especially self-talk at any given moment govern how much success you experience in business, marriage, and family. In other words, your inner world dictates your outer world. Like many people, you can simply be reactive, allowing your thoughts and emotions to be dictated by the current dominant circumstance or situation, which in turn will dictate the quality of your life and relationships. Or conversely, you can learn how to be proactive, purposefully directing your thoughts and emotions exactly as you choose in any given situation to produce the specific results you want most. Feelings Journaling facilitates this.

Health/Fitness—My Relationship with My Body: In our hectic lives, one of the first relationships we neglect or abuse is the relationship we have with our bodies. Exhausted from long hours at work, family pressures, and the overall stress of life, exercise is often the last thing on our priority list. We often procrastinate, or bypass it altogether. After a long day it's hard to get oneself motivated for five sets each of ab crunches, pull-ups, and push-ups. And we don't have time to jog in the morning because "I have so much to do today." Armed with so many excuses, at the end of the day we often just fall on the couch and vegetate in front of the TV.

Likewise, our fast-paced society makes us prone to reach for fast food rather than seeking out fresh, nutritional alternatives. In social settings, we eat what others are having. And at night, while crashed on the couch, we consume more junk food. Such abuse seriously weakens our bodies, saps our energy, dampens our attitude, and generally erodes our health and well-being. If your relationship with your body isn't right, it will have an adverse effect on virtually every other area of your life, including your ability to be successful in your business or career.

You Must Serve Yourself First

I've used a bold line on the pyramid to separate the first three rela-tionships: Spiritual, Emotional/Intellectual, and Health/Fitness, from the other three. The quality of the first three relationships is essential to your success in every other relationship and aspect of your life. In order to achieve the highest level of success in your marriage, family, social life, and career, *you must serve yourself first.*

Family—My Relationship with My Spouse and Children: A great man once said: "No success [no matter how great] can compensate for failure in the home." We live in a society where the earnest pursuit of wealth frequently takes precedence over marriage; the thirst for recognition overshadows family. Most husbands and wives don't get up in the morning and say to themselves, "Today I'm going to neglect my spouse and children." People just get so caught up in the busyness of life that, by default, they end up neglecting those they care most about.

I believe we were created to derive our greatest joy from serving first our spouse, then our children. I believe the greatest gift we can give our children is allowing them to observe us loving and serving our mate. Unfortunately, in the rush of building a career, we can miss out on those opportunities to experience this remarkable joy.

Social—My Relationship with Others: As you place the first four relationships first in your life, you will find a dramatic improvement in your relationships with everyone else. Your attitude will change for the better. You will find it easier to be warm, friendly, and enthusiastic. Others will sense your positive aura, feel your energy, and be drawn to you. You will develop greater richness in your relationships with employees, co-workers, colleagues, clients, friends, extended family— everyone you meet.

Financial—My Relationship with My Career and Money: If you will take care of—in order of priority—the five key relationships listed above, I promise your relationship with money and your job will be enhanced in ways that will astound you. Like so many of my clients, you will evolve to the point where you can double (or more) your income while reducing your work hours by one-third, if you are in an entrepreneurial environment. If you earn a salary or wage, you will find yourself gaining remarkable opportunities for growth and advancement. I'm not suggesting you won't have to work at it. But if you will attend to the other five key relationships in the pyramid, your overall effectiveness and performance in your career will significantly increase. You will do more, do it more effectively, and do it in less time. Your ability to deal with the challenges and difficult issues spawned by the business world will be strengthened while your worries and stress will fade away.

Important Ideas & Insights

_____

_____

_____

_____

_____

The Slight Edge
In Your Personal Life

5

Put the Most Important Person in Your Life First—YOU!

As you learned in chapter 4, the bold line on the Relationship Pyramid separates the first three relationships (Spiritual, Emotional/Intellectual, and Health/Fitness) from the other three. The quality of the first three relationships is essential to your success in every other relationship and aspect of your life. In order to achieve the highest level of success in your marriage, family, social life, and career, *you must serve yourself first*. Many have conditioned themselves to believe they don't have time or it's not a top priority to worry about spirituality, emotional/intellectual recharging, or fitness and nutrition. Others genuinely try to undertake these priorities, but do so sporadically. Choosing any of these approaches will only end up costing them in the end. Some may neglect these critical relationships and still manage to make lots of money, but again, at what cost?

The LifeBalance Daily Self-Care Routine

Many have asked, "How do I find the time to focus on my spiritual, emotional, and physical health?" After testing and proving my LifeBalance System with thousands of individuals, I have found one tool that virtually guarantees you will take care of these priorities every day. It is known as the **Daily Self-Care Routine**. Follow these simple steps to implement this powerful tool:

1. Set a specific appointment with yourself at the same time every day. First thing in the morning is best, when your mind and body are rested, relaxed, and open. Your morning routine will energize every part of your body, attitude, and outlook, setting you up for success in everything you do that day.

2. Believe that this is the most important appointment of your entire day. Nothing takes priority over this time. Instruct your family, secretary, partners, manager, and boss that you are not to be disturbed during this time. If you don't take this approach, things inevitably will come up to take priority. If you have trouble creating a strong enough motive to do this, I suggest using the 5-Step Discovery Process to develop a motive or a Byte.

THE DAILY SELF-CARE ROUTINE: At least five out of every seven mornings each week, set an appointment with the most important person in your life—yourself! During this time focus on improving your spiritual, emotional, and physical health—strengthening yourself against the challenges and trials of the day ahead:

1. Spiritual: *Spend at least 15 minutes* cultivating a spiritual connection—whatever that means to you: prayer, inspirational literature, scripture reading, meditation, and so forth.

2. Emotional: *Spend at least 5 minutes* writing in your Feelings Journal. The emotions you keep bottled up inside will find ways to manifest themselves one way or another. You can choose the time and place to get them out as you write in your Feelings Journal, or you can wait for your pent-up emotions to express themselves in anger, stress, depression, illness, a heart attack, or addiction. The Feelings Journal will improve your emotional, mental, and physical health in ways you never imagined!

3. Physical: The good news is that taking care of your physical health is not that difficult or complicated. It only requires a few simple steps each day. The first is a mere *twenty minutes* or more of physical exercise each morning as part of your Self-Care Routine. Experience has shown that several key elements will increase the likelihood that you will continue with consistent, daily exercise:

- **Clearly identify your motive:** Before you begin your exercise program, take the time to write down why you want to do it. This could include things like a description of what you will look and feel like ninety days from now, finishing your first marathon, being able to play basketball with your son, and so forth. Your motive must be clear, powerful, and reviewed often. Use the 5-Step Discovery Process to accomplish this.

- **Do it in the morning:** Studies have shown that of those who exercise in the morning, 75 percent keep it up long-term. Of the afternoon exercisers, 50 percent continue on, and the evening exercisers come in last place with only 25 percent staying with it. In addition, exercise in the morning speeds up your metabolism so that you become a "fat-burning machine" all day long. If at all possible, exercise early in the day. If you cannot, choose another time and stick with it!

- **Do something you enjoy:** If your exercise routine or activity is drudgery and torture, it is very unlikely you will stick with it. Choose something you really enjoy. This can be anything from the lifting weights, jogging, and aerobics classes to racquetball, tennis, swimming, basketball, cycling, or walking. If possible, you may want to hire a trainer to get started.

- **Make it convenient:** If you have to travel thirty minutes each way, go through elaborate rituals to get ready, or in some other way be inconvenienced, you'll likely give it up after awhile. Try to make your morning exercise as convenient as possible. Some prefer to have weights or a treadmill at home. Others join a health club that is only a few minutes from home. Still others simply ride a bike, jog, or walk. You can also add simple fitness activities to your day by parking your car farther away and walking, taking the stairs instead of the elevator, or taking a break to do some sit-ups or push-ups on your office floor.

- **Team up with a partner or group:** We all need outside motivation and support from time to time. Many people find that teaming up with a workout, aerobics, jogging, walking, cycling, or exercise buddy is a big help. If you have committed to another person to be somewhere or start with them at a certain time, you are more likely to honor that commitment even when you don't feel like getting up to exercise. On the days when you excited about exercising, you can motivate your partner, and on your down days your partner can do the same for you. Make it fun. Enjoy each other's company. Bring a little competition or goal setting into the routine. Have fun!

- **Don't overdo it:** The tendency for many who suffer with addictions is to have an all-or-nothing attitude. Some may think, "Every single morning of my life I am going to run three miles, lift weights for an hour, and swim a mile!" Of course, this kind of zealous excess cannot be maintained for very long. The individual quickly burns out and abandons exercise altogether. Studies clearly show that short, consistent exercise is dramatically more productive than sporadic week-end warrior type efforts. Thirty minutes a day, four or five days a week will produce remarkable results! The key is *consistency*.

The entire self-care routine need not take more than *forty minutes* to start. Quantity of time is not the issue—quality is the key. This simple Daily Self-Care Routine has produced tremendous results for thousands of people.

Additional Insight

Engaging in a Daily Self-Care Routine each morning may be new for you, and it may be a struggle to consistently implement. To create your greatest chance for success, remember these important points:

- Whenever you begin developing a new habit or mental model, the old mental model resists because it wants to stick with its existing routine, whatever that might be. So start out with small steps, something you can succeed with. Remember, the more you do something, even a little bit, the more you can and will do it—this is the way your brain is designed. Your entire morning only needs to be 40 minutes in the beginning. As you see the positive results this simple activity makes in your life and relationships, you will be motivated to lengthen the time. Be patient and make steady progress.

- As you become more comfortable with your Daily Self-Care Routine, and begin to experience the incredible benefits, you will be motivated to continue and even increase the amount of time and effort you spend. Simply allow the process to naturally evolve over time, and don't stop prematurely before your new mental models have a chance to develop and become automatic.

Important Ideas & Insights

6

Discover and Attain Your White-Hot Imperative

Most of us are so focused on doing what is important, productive, or immediate—job, health, family, service, or church—that rarely do we take time to sit and contemplate, let alone work on what is really exciting to us. The project that makes us really excited is what I call our **White-Hot Imperative (WHI)**. While many of the goals or objectives you have may take months, or in some cases, years to achieve, your WHI is exciting and can be realized in a relatively short period of time. In effect, your WHI is the most exciting but not necessarily most important thing you would like to do, achieve, or acquire right now.

Why should you identify and pursue your White-Hot Imperative? If you are involved in achieving the most *exciting* thing in your life, it generates an energy and power that drives everything else in your life. There can be dozens of goals or ideals you have in mind for the future. For some people, just thinking about this big chunk of goals can be overwhelming, even a little discouraging. In contrast, your WHI allows you to pursue the most exciting thing in your life right now, while still working on your long-term objectives.

Achieving your WHI is fun, stimulating, and rewarding. It provides you with an immediate and exciting victory, and builds belief and expectation. In essence, you're using success to build upon success. When one WHI is achieved, you can begin pursuing another.

The WHI is one of the most powerful LifeBalance tools you will ever use. Your brain can stand almost anything but boredom. Our lives, careers, and relationships can become mundane, routine, and boring.

Pursuing the most exciting thing in your life will fuel your drive to achieve everything else you desire and add a wonderful dose of fun to your existence! Pursuing and achieving your WHI makes you more enthusiastic, optimistic, and positive. You will broadcast a positive energy and aura to everyone around you. Your whole outlook on life changes for the better.

What is Your White-Hot Imperative?

Of the thousands of people who have implemented the LifeBalance System in their lives, most could not come up with their White-Hot Imperative right away. They could name many things that were important, urgent, worthwhile, or socially responsible, but isolating the most *exciting* thing in their lives was a real challenge. In many cases their WHI was a dream that had always been in the back of their minds, but they pushed it aside, considering it foolish, unrealistic, not a priority, or not achievable.

One client finally realized that the most exciting thing he could imagine was earning $200,000, something he'd had previously rejected as unrealistic. Once he allowed himself to make it his WHI, it became a reality.

Another client discovered he had a passion for driving construction equipment. The huge engine, the feeling of control—it was his secret fantasy. He established this as his WHI and ended up going to Wyoming and operating heavy equipment on an oil rig. He was in heaven! In the past he'd dismissed thoughts of doing such a silly thing. He thought, "How could a professional with a master's degree want to do that? I don't have time for such frivolous things. I wouldn't even know where to go; I wouldn't know where to start." A few years after his Wyoming experience, this man launched a very successful business and later got involved in driving race cars.

Consider some other examples of White-Hot Imperatives:

- The president and co-founder of a large medical lab discovered she wanted to paint wildflowers. Today, in addition to running her successful business, she is a well-known watercolor artist.

- A couple with nine children set out to build their dream home, a home that today is spacious, beautiful, and functional.

- A prominent financial advisor envisioned starting up a band that played songs from the '50s and '60s. Today he and his buddies are booked months in advance.

- A successful author and speaker grew up in southern California and always wanted to learn to surf, but had never gotten around to it. At age forty-five, he identified this desire as his WHI, took a vacation to the coast, and learned to do it. He was thrilled.

Virtually all of these individuals, and hundreds of others like them, had spent their lives focusing only on what was important, urgent, responsible, expected, or realistic. When they identified their specific WHI and made it a reality, every other part of their lives was supercharged! All subsequently went on to identify and work toward achieving other WHIs.

Use the following exercises to stimulate your thoughts and feelings to discover your first WHI. Once you discover and achieve one WHI, use these exercises to identify the next one:

1. You've won the lottery: Imagine you've just won the lottery. What's the most exciting thing you want to buy, place you want to go, thing you want to do or experience? This could very well be your WHI.

2. Imagine you have one year to live: Imagine you've just been told you have one year to live. List three things you still want to accomplish. Now assume that eleven months have passed and you have only thirty days left. You haven't done any of the three things you listed. Now you can only do two of them. What are those two? Now imagine there's only one week left in your life and you have only enough time to do one. What will it be? This could be your WHI.

3. When you were a kid: Think back to when you were a child or a teenager. What was one thing you always dreamed of doing but never got the chance? This could be your WHI.

The WHI Plan

Once you have identified your WHI, the next step is to create a plan to make it a reality. This plan consists of six simple steps. Once you have obtained your WHI or are well on your way toward it, you can choose a new WHI and form a new plan to achieve it.

Six Steps of the WHI Plan

1. Describe your WHI clearly and completely: The more specific you are with your WHI, the more readily it will be programmed into your brain and the more quickly it will be realized. Remember to state everything in first person, present tense. For example, let's assume your WHI is *I've always wanted to see Paris.* A more detailed WHI might look like this: *John and I are spending two romantic weeks immersed in the wonders of Paris.*

2. Motive: A powerful motive, or why, accesses and builds a powerful mental model in your brain. The more powerful the motive, the more powerful the resulting mental model will be as well as the thoughts, actions, and habits that flow from it. Your motive can be identified and clearly articulated using two exercises:

- **Why do you want your WHI?** By answering this question you can more clearly define your motive. You can also ask yourself: "Why am I so excited about this goal? Why is it my passion and obsession?" Remember to state everything in the present tense.

- **How do you feel?** Visualize yourself already in possession of your WHI—literally see and feel yourself experiencing it. How exactly do you feel having obtained it? Describe your feelings in vivid detail and in the present tense.

Continuing with the example of the Paris WHI, the following is just a brief sample of how to articulate your motive: *Going to Paris fulfills a dream I have had since I was a child. I see myself there and it is the most beautiful, romantic, and exciting place in the whole world! John and I walk arm in arm down the beautiful streets. We are at the top of the Eiffel Tower, and the view is breathtaking! The sights, sounds, and smells—it's all a wonderful fantasy come true! I will treasure this experience for the rest of my life.*

3. Identify the obstacles: Many of us set goals and then abandon them when overpowered by the obstacles. To achieve your WHI, you need to identify potential obstacles up front. To do this, complete the following exercise.

Make a list of the reasons why you don't already have the WHI you have chosen, or state what could keep you from achieving it. List in detail every obstacle or problem you may face in reaching your goal. Using our example of the Paris WHI, the obstacles could include:

- We don't have the money.

- We can't get the time off work.

- What will we do with the children for two weeks?

- It's a frivolous idea. The money would be better spent on something more practical.

Overcoming these obstacles will be part of the price you must pay in order to achieve your WHI.

4. Weigh price against motive: Before you begin your journey to the realization of your WHI, you must weigh the price you will have to pay against your motives. If your why or motive isn't stronger than the obstacles you will face, then the chances of attaining your WHI are slim to none.

Imagine a set of old-fashioned scales. On one side place your motives or why; then, one by one, place each possible obstacle on the other side of the scale. See yourself facing the obstacle. Is your motive strong enough to overcome it? If the answer is "no" or "I'm not sure," you need to go back to Step 2 and expand on your motives so they have more clarity, detail, and meaning—more powerful emotion attached to them. It may even be necessary to identify a different, more powerful motive that is strong enough to overcome the obstacles.

5. What and When: Your plan should contain specific action steps or benchmarks—*what* you will do and a timeline, and *when* you will do it.

The famous adage asks, "How do you eat an elephant?" The answer: "One piece at a time." As you look at your WHI as a whole, it may seem impossible or overwhelming. You may be asking, "How can I ever do it?" You can do it one piece at a time.

Let's continue with our Paris WHI: *John and I are spending two romantic weeks immersed in the wonders of Paris.* With this desired end in mind, establish a timeline with incremental action steps or benchmarks to get there. This may be done as follows:

- **Choose a completion date:** Your brain responds better when given a specific deadline. We will assume today is January 1 and you set the dates for your Paris trip as September 1 through September 15, eight months from now.

- **Create a timeline with action steps or benchmarks.** Try to address each of your obstacles in the process. For example:

On September 1, John and I fly to Paris and begin our two-week fantasy-come-true. Starting with our paychecks on January 15, we each set aside $187.50 every two weeks from now until September 1. This gives us the $6,000 cash we need to pay for our fabulous Paris excursion. (Note how this addresses obstacle 1.)

On Monday of next week, John and I both put in our request for vacation time for September 1–15. It's so exciting to actually make it formal—we're really going! (This addresses obstacle 2 and adds to the motive.)

On Sunday I call my mother and make arrangements for her to be here in our home to watch the children from September 1–7. I call my sister and arrange for the children to stay at her place from September 8–15 (obstacle 3).

John and I have discussed it and we both agree that spending the money on Paris is one of the best investments we will ever make in our marriage relationship. Besides, it will be one of the most incredibly exciting and forever memorable experiences of our lives! (This addresses obstacle 4 and adds to the motive.)

NOTE: *Put each of these action steps on your calendar and track your progress.*

6. Create a Byte for Your WHI: Taking the content from all five steps, combine it to create a Byte. This might fit on a index card or, if you need more room, you can record it in your day planner or onto your PDA. Review it daily as a reminder of what you are accomplishing. To increase the power of this Byte to its maximum, record it in your own voice and then listen to it as you commute, exercise, and so forth. Make sure you are positive and up-beat when you record it. Leave a 4–5 second gap between each main point, so you can really focus and visualize.

Using the example we have been working with, below is a sample of a completed WHI ready to create a Byte:

On September 1, John and I fly to Paris and begin our two-week fantasy-come-true. Going to Paris fulfills a dream I have had since I was a child. I see myself there and it is the most beautiful, romantic, and exciting place in the whole world! John and I walk arm in arm down the beautiful streets. We are at the top of the Eiffel Tower, and the view is breathtaking! The sights, sounds and smells—it's all a wonderful dream come true! I will treasure this experience for the rest of my life.

Starting with our paychecks on January 15, we each set aside $187.50 every two weeks from now until September 1. This gives us the $6,000 cash we need to pay for our fabulous Paris excursion.

On Monday of next week, John and I both put in our request for vacation time for September 1–15. It's so exciting to actually make it formal— we're really going!

On Sunday I call my mother and make arrangements for her to be here in our home to watch the children from September 1–7. I call my sister and arrange for the children to stay at her place from September 8–15.

These parts come out of the Byte when they are finished, and others are added as needed.

John and I have discussed it and we both agree that spending the money on Paris is one of the best investments we will ever make in our marriage relationship and our personal lives. Besides, being in Paris for two whole weeks is one of the most incredibly exciting and forever memorable experiences of our lives!

Through the power of the Byte and the WHI, you'll be amazed at how easily you will achieve the most exciting goal in your life. Once you're nearing completion of one WHI, identify and plan your next one. Always have a WHI in process to keep the fire of excitement constantly burning, which will positively impact every other aspect of your life.

As you use the tools in the LifeBalance System, having a WHI creates excitement and energy that will propel you through some of the challenges you may face. Like how the weighted flywheel in an engine generates more power with less gasoline usage, so will the WHI empower you to have a more exciting, fulfilling life.

Important Ideas & Insights

_____

_____

_____

_____

_____

_____

_____

_____

_____

_____

_____

_____

_____

_____

_____

_____

_____

_____

_____

_____

_____

_____

_____

_____

_____

_____

_____

_____

_____

_____

_____

_____

_____

The Slight Edge
In Your Family Relationships

7

Develop a Continually Growing Love Affair with Your Spouse

Most married couples can vividly recall their engagement and courtship, wedding, honeymoon, and the months that followed immediately after. These were days filled with romance, communication, and closeness. But as the years go by, things can change. College and work, long hours spent climbing the corporate ladder or building a business, full-time nurturing and raising of children, the overall busy routine of life—all of these can take precedence, and too often romance wanes, communication breaks down, and couples drift apart. They become what I describe as **married singles**.

Married Singles

If you have ever found yourself a married single, and most couples do, you know that it has a far-reaching effect on every aspect of your life: your attitude, your stress level, your ability to focus at work, your relationship with your children, your health, and the level of peace and happiness in your life. It's just a fact—if your marriage isn't right, everything else begins to drift, and your life falls out of balance.

So many marriages end up where couples are living together as married singles. The spark of excitement that was there earlier has now become hardly a flicker. Couples create separate lives for themselves while remaining married. Successful people have the resources and excuses to perpetuate this condition. Since they can afford to maintain two lives—separate hobbies, activities, and even vacations—the drive to resolve the situation, one way or another, is minimized. They lose the excitement of the relationship and replace it with excitement for something else.

Are you and your spouse living together as married singles? Has one or both of you emotionally divorced the other?

If there is room for improvement in your marriage, or even if you feel like you are on, or have already crossed over, the brink of emotional divorce, don't despair—there is great hope! It is normal for a marriage relationship to experience some level of emotional divorce from time to time. Recognizing the signs of emotional divorce, either in yourself or in your spouse, is often the beginning of **emotional remarriage**. You can survive the temporary state of emotional divorce and keep it from becoming a permanent divorce. You can leave the world of married singles and once again become a united, loving married couple—a wonderful partnership!

I have always been so concerned about why so many marriages head into the married singles routine after the first couple of years. Recent studies have provided me with some answers that have helped many of my clients understand what's happening in their relationship and to take steps to avoid the miserable condition of married singles. These recent studies have opened my eyes to why marriages start to drift apart.

It starts when couples first marry. The man is so excited to find the woman of his dreams, and he just cannot get enough of her. My friend Napoleon Hill called it sexual transmutation. That means men will do anything they can think of to get their sweethearts to respond in a loving way toward them. The smiling, giggles, and expressions of love a wife expresses fills a husband's heart. Men also value physical intimacy with their spouses. For them, it is a natural way to express their love. Most women don't understand that men need this intimacy on a regular basis. It has a major influence on the man being more loving and attentive and keeping his stress level down. Some women think their husbands are overly aggressive because he wants to make love on a regular basis. That may be true in some cases, but studies have shown that most men need intimacy to maintain balance in their life.

Women are designed to think differently. When they find the one of their dreams, hormones and endorphins are released when she is touched, hugged, and looked at lovingly by him. Even just being with her man can release these endorphins and hormones. I love seeing young married women, or engaged women, glow when they look at their men. It's like the hormones and endorphins are rockets going off in their body.

Then the baby comes along. Women are designed by our Creator to nurture babies. Their motherly instincts take over, and their hormones and endorphins are released by holding, nurturing, nursing, and taking care of their precious babes.

A husband understands that the baby needs the mother's attention and that he has to play second fiddle for a while. So what does he do? He turns to his work, friends, and other activities for his satisfaction and fulfillment. All is well for him as long as he is intimate with his wife on a regular basis.

The husband begins to take his wife for granted, and the wife is involved with the baby (in many cases babies) as time passes. The situation is further compounded because most men have no knowledge of how to build a loving relationship with a woman. So how can a husband and wife avoid becoming married singles?

The answer is, I believe, that man is designed by our Creator to derive joy from serving his wife and putting her first in his life. He did this when he courted her and when they were first married. The answer for women is to remember her husband needs attention, nurturing, and appreciation for the many ways he is serving her.

From my personal experience I know that less than 5 percent of marriages have a relationship where both spouses feel their marriage is above an eight on a ten-point scale (with ten being the best). Spouses need to show in words and actions that their mate is truly first in their life and in their thoughts. During the first years of marriage, this showing of love is a daily occurrence. It is sad to see marriages that started out so well fall into married singles or end up in divorce.

It does not have to happen if couples will follow the simple advice and steps given in this book. They need to realize that the thoughts and feelings of a man and a woman are very different from each other.

Men—put your wife first! Women—put your husband first! That is a major part of the answer to a loving, secure, and nurturing relationship.

As has been proven with many of my clients, when a man has a loving and nurturing relationship with his sweetheart in his home, he has reduced stress in his life and is much more productive and successful in his work.

The Key to a Successful Marriage

In the sections that follow you will learn how to use simple, powerful tools that will assist you in building a wonderfully fulfilling marriage relationship. Thousands of couples have used these tools to rekindle the spark of romance, reopen the lines of healthy communication, and literally save their marriages. At the core of all of these tools and at the heart of any lasting and growing success in marriage, there is one grand key—**selfless service**. Every failed marriage can be traced back to one overriding cause: one (or both) of the spouses was selfish or self-centered, and not really realizing what was happening, the couple focused elsewhere.

I believe that our Creator designed us to derive our greatest joy from serving our spouse. If both husband and wife will each place the other's needs first, without condition, and focus on selflessly serving one another, their marriage relationship will be the crown jewel of their lives. Even if only one spouse practices selfless service unconditionally, it eventually creates an environment where the other spouse can't help but soften. Of course in some cases, the served spouse may be emotionally unstable and unable to accept service, let alone give it. Without outside professional help and cooperation on the part of the unstable spouse, separation and divorce are very likely.

Remember, giving love unconditionally is the key. True joy comes from giving, not receiving, which is a concept so contrary to the "what's in it for me" instant gratification society we live in. I am not suggesting that one spouse become a slave to the other. It is each spouse's responsibility to reciprocate and not become spoiled. Giving unconditional love virtually always wins the day, and even the most aloof and disgruntled spouses eventually come around.

Many intellectualize about unconditional love and preach its merits, but few actually understand and live it. The all-too-common attitude of "Why should I keep giving when I don't get anything in return?" is the norm. This statement, however, is an attitude of *conditional* love and is the root cause of many problems in marriage, families, and society as a whole. I have received hundreds of testimonials from LifeBalance clients who have discovered the joy of serving their mate. One successful executive who had been married for over thirty years declared:

I can't believe what has happened since I started really focusing on serving my wife! I finally realize that it's all about giving and not about getting.

I can't believe what this simple change in my focus has done for my business, my stress level, and the love and romance in my marriage. This is the greatest time of my life!

Mental Models

After years of marriage it's so easy for negative feelings, resentments, and frustrations to creep into the relationship. Over time, nagging, arguing, contention, silence, and boredom can become the norm. In this environment, the brain builds mental models that link all of these negative emotions and memories to the face and voice of our mate, so that after awhile, just seeing or hearing our spouse can ignite a negative response. Left unchecked, this negative mental model can become deeply rutted and dominant. After a number of years, it will eventually lead a couple to despise each other.

The true power of my relationship tools is that they can reverse this negative process in marriage. Every time you use one of these tools you are creating new mental models—new neural connections in your brain and new meaning. Over time, the face, voice, and presence of your spouse comes to mean something different to you. Soon the sound of her voice or the look in his eyes begins to elicit feelings of tenderness, romance, caring, unconditional love, passion, gratitude, and a host of other powerfully positive emotions. You are literally building new mental models, shrinking old negative ones, reprogramming your brain, and redesigning your marriage. The commitment and excitement of your courtship and early marriage are rekindled, and a deeper love and closer relationship than ever before begin to unfold.

By using these tools, you bring specific aspects of your marriage relationship off of autopilot and "above the surface," where you can work on them and build your ideal relationship together.

NOTE: *The greatest gift a husband and wife can give as parents is honoring and loving each other in the presence of their children. Through his direct example, a father teaches his son how to love and honor his mother and his future wife. He teaches his daughter how she should expect to be treated while dating and by her future husband. Through her direct example, a mother teaches her children how to love and honor their father. It is easy to teach children by example in this way when a husband and wife focus on serving each other.*

Key Concept ⌖

A happy marriage can help mend physical wounds and ease the negative health impact of a stressful job.

As you begin learning about the LifeBalance marriage relationship tools, you should take special note of a recent study that gives a whole new perspective to the benefits of a happy marriage:

Marilyn Elias, *USA TODAY,* VANCOUVER, B.C.—A happy marriage apparently is good medicine, but hostile spouses may be harmful to one another's health. Couples in conflict-ridden marriages take longer than the happily married to heal from all kinds of [physical] wounds, from minor scrapes or athletic injuries to major surgery, suggests a study out over the weekend. And the health toll taken by a stressful job seems to be eased when the worker has a pleasurable home life.

"Even a simple discussion of a disagreement slows wound healing," says psychologist Janice Kiecolt-Glaser, who did the study with co-author Ronald Glaser of Ohio State University College of Medicine. Overall, couples took longer to heal when asked to thrash out points of conflict than neutral issues. Hostile couples — peppering both discussions with criticism, sarcasm, and put-downs — healed the slowest. It took them 40% longer, or two more days, to heal, and they also produced less of the proteins linked to healing. These are minor wounds and brief, restrained encounters. Real-life marital conflict probably has a worse impact, Kiecolt-Glaser adds. "Such stress before surgery matters greatly," she says, "and the effect could apply to healing from any injury."

On the upside, good marriages may buffer couples against the stress of demanding jobs in which the worker has little control. In a study with 201 married adults, those in high-strain jobs had higher blood pressure at the start, says University of Toronto psychiatrist Brian Baker. A year later, though, spouses in pleasurable marriages actually improved a couple of points in diastolic (bottom) blood pressure readings, despite their rough jobs. Meanwhile, those who seldom enjoyed talking or activities with their spouses had about a three point rise in blood pressure after coping with stressful jobs for a year.

"You may not be able to get away from the job stress," says Baker, "but a good marriage soothes people, minimizing bad effects from the job." (April 2006)

LifeBalance Relationship

Tools

Warm Fuzzies

This oddly named tool is extremely powerful in restoring and building communication and closeness in a marriage. Most of us are pretty good at remembering the big events, the major holidays, the birthdays, the anniversaries—usually, that is. On such occasions we give expressions of love or **Warm Fuzzies** to our spouse. But what about all the other days of the year? Research has found that in happy, healthy marriages, there is a 5:1 ratio of positive emotion to negative emotion. In marriages that are dysfunctional and doomed, there is a 1:1 ratio of positive to negative emotion. How often do we get so caught up in the immediacy of life that we don't stop to show the little courtesies and kindnesses? We need to make small deposits into our spouse's "emotional bank account" that over time add up to a substantial positive balance.

Finding little ways to let your spouse know how much he or she is loved is one of the essential ingredients in keeping romance alive in a marriage. One "I love you" or thoughtful gesture that says, "I care," may not mean much by itself; it's like a single drop in a bucket. But as a few more drops are added, soon there is enough to swish around, then enough for a drink, and so on.

Warm Fuzzies are the same way. If enough are given, they eventually fill the bucket so full your spouse is immersed in them! The secret is to keep the bucket full! In this way, if your spouse feels hurt or unappreciated on account of some careless or unknowing action or word on your part, he or she can reach into the full bucket and draw from the reserve of the past love and support you have deposited. Your spouse remains secure in the knowledge that you really do love and care for him or her. Without this reserve to draw on, little misunderstandings, disagreements, or insensitivities can pile up, eventually destroying the relationship. Here are six different Warm Fuzzy gifts you can give your spouse each day:

The Warm Fuzzy Gifts

1. I Love You: Always tell her at least three times a day, "I love you."

2. I Appreciate You: Every day look for something to appreciate—something she has done for you, the kids, or others. Express your appreciation by telling her or writing a little note.

3. Affirm Her Gifts: Make a list of her gifts or talents and every day try to mention how she has impressed you with at least one of her gifts or talents.

4. Recognize Her: Every day try to recognize something about her that stands out. "You look great" is okay, but it's too general. Be more specific: "You're hair looks really nice" or "You have beautiful eyes" or "That dress looks great on you!"

5. Serve Her: Look for some way to serve her—wash the dishes, run an errand, fill her glass with water—anything to show her you're thinking of her and want to make life easier for her.

6. A Love Note: Jotting down some tender feelings about your spouse and leaving a note where she will find it later is magical.

As you are considering the Warm Fuzzies that you will give, reflect on the positive qualities of your spouse. Spend time thinking about the things you appreciate about them. Here are some from my clients to get you started:

Husband's Qualities to Be Admired

Hard worker	Has confidence in others
Eternal optimist	Has confidence in himself
Life of the party	Makes others feel important
Conservative spender	Supports my decisions
Sharp dresser	Shares responsibilities
Level-headed	Likes kids and plays with them
Generous	Loves God
Source of strength	Great problem-solver
Doesn't give up	Doesn't nag about housekeeping
Likes people	Shares wisdom with others
Helps others succeed	Intelligent, wise, and gentle

Wife's Qualities to Be Admired

Peaceful to be around	Appreciative
Fastidious	Frugal

Sensible	Always sees the best in situations
Nurturer	Looks for good in others
Practical	Intelligent, wise, and gentle
Persistent	Appreciative
Mentor	Takes good care of self
Unselfish	Good conversationalist
Confident	Trusting
Cheerful	Makes others feel good about themselves

Give at Least Two Warm Fuzzies Every Day

With Warm Fuzzies, *consistency* is the key. It's easy in the busyness, demands, and distractions of life to lose track of these little acts of love, kindness, and appreciation. As a reminder, make a note on your daily calendar that simple says, "Warm Fuzzies." Then, sometime during the day, take a few moments to give your spouse a Warm Fuzzy. I recommend you give a variety of Warm Fuzzies, and do it at least twice each day. This will help keep your relationship fresh, exciting, and always growing. For example:

- As you leave for the day, or when you arrive home, hold your spouse in your arms, look directly into his or her eyes, and say, "I love you and appreciate you so much."

- Just before you leave for work, place a note on the bathroom mirror or kitchen counter.

- Write a special letter and leave it on your spouse's pillow, or send it in the mail.

- *Without being asked,* help your spouse in the kitchen, clean up after a meal, pitch in with household chores, take the kids and let her have some private time, or do some other service. It's important to say "I love you," but showing your love through little daily acts of service demonstrates love the way our Savior did.

- Give your spouse a spontaneous back rub or foot massage.

- Praise and express appreciation for your spouse in front of your children and others.

- In the middle of the day, call your spouse: "I was thinking about you and wanted you to know how much I appreciate everything you do," or "I so appreciate everything you're doing . . ."

Combine the Byte, Feelings Journaling, and Warm Fuzzies to Yield Big Dividends in Your Marriage

I have a client named Dave who has been married for over thirty years. One day Dave's wife called to tell me she was dying from lack of intimacy—intimacy in conversation, intimacy in time together, intimacy in spiritual things, and yes, even physical intimacy. Dave, whom I have coached for over a year, had no clue there was even a problem, let alone how to solve it. In all the time I had coached him, Dave told me he and his wife were doing fine.

When I spoke with Dave about the situation, he was very frustrated. He was really trying to be a good husband. He thought he was doing everything necessary to make his wife happy. He lamented, "I bring home good money. I'm a devoted father. I'm faithful to my wife—so what's the problem?" The big realization I had to guide him to is that most men don't know how to build a long-term relationship with a woman. After the first couple years of marriage, most guys are clueless about how to continue courting their spouse. What they rarely realize is that in the period beyond their initial years together dwells a wonderful opportunity to build a truly *interdependent* loving relationship where both spouses place each other first and spend the rest of the lives loving and serving each other. While this is the ideal, in my experience and from the extensive research I have conducted, less than 5 percent of marriages have this kind of relationship. The vast majority of married couples end up as married singles. Over 50 percent get divorced and the rest just sort of co-exist.

Back to my friend and client. I told him, "Dave, perception is everything. You may think you're doing all you can to be a loving husband, but from your wife's perspective your marriage is lacking." He did admit that at home he was probably too focused on business or often just wanted to relax in front of the TV. On the verge of panic he blurted out, "Leo, I don't know what to do. I don't want to lose her!" I gently replied, "You won't. We'll start out with a few simple steps to let her know that you're focused on her. Here is what I want you to do."

1. **Make a list** of all the reasons you married your beautiful wife, including all of her gifts and talents. Duplicate this list and keep one in your office and one in your car. Any time you start thinking negatively about your wife, I want you to pull out the list and review it. (This is the Byte.)

2. On your way home from work I want you to pick out a landmark that you pass about five or ten minutes from home. When you pass that landmark start focusing on your sweetheart—think about what's on the list. When you arrive home make a dash for your sweetheart and focus your attention on her for five to ten minutes. Embrace and kiss her; tell her how much you love and appreciate her. Ask about her day and listen. Perform a small act of service like putting away the dishes, taking out the trash, and so forth. During the evening if she wants to talk with you and you're watching television or using the computer, shut it off. It's important she knows she is first in your life at all times. These are small things, but they will begin to have a powerfully positive effect on her that will surprise and thrill you.

I also instructed Dave that during his Daily Self-Care Routine to Feelings Journal about why he loves and appreciates his wife. This prepared him to communicate with her in ways he had never done before.

Dave was relieved to understand the few simple steps he could implement to move his marriage to a higher level. He said, "Leo, initially when I learned about my wife's dissatisfaction, I felt completely overwhelmed and confused about what to do. Now I'm so excited because I know exactly what to do and it's really not that big of a deal."

Right now, put down this book and give your spouse a Warm Fuzzy— in person, by phone, in a letter or note, or through some act of service. DO IT NOW!

During your Daily Self-Care Routine, journal your feelings about *why* you want to give your spouse Warm Fuzzies every day—how will it make him or her feel? How will it make you feel? What will it do for your marriage? Put this notation where you can review it regularly, like on your calendar. Now, take out your calendar and make the notation *Warm Fuzzy* every day for the next thirty days. Give your spouse at least two Warm Fuzzies each day and watch the magic unfold! Especially with those you love the most.

Being a Friend

As you consider your relationship with your spouse, consider this information from relationship experts Drs. Les and Leslie Parrott of the Center for Relationship Development at Seattle Pacific University. They have created a list of traits to look for in enduring friendships:

1. Makes time
2. Keeps a secret
3. Cares deeply
4. Provides space
5. Speaks the truth
6. Forgives faults
7. Remains faithful
8. Laughs easily
9. Celebrates your success
10. Connects strongly

These traits are equally as important in building strong marital relationships. After all, who should be a better friend? Dale Carnegie advised that people can find more friends in two months by simply becoming interested in other people than they can make in two years by trying to get people interested in them. Whether you're looking to develop better friendships or improve your relationship with your spouse, nothing builds a stronger relationship than focusing on the needs of your spouse before your own needs.

Additional Insight

Once you develop the habit of giving daily Warm Fuzzies to your spouse, you can take a more advanced approach by giving Warm Fuzzies in your spouse's unique "love language." In his wonderful book, *The Five Love Languages: How to Express Heartfelt Commitment to Your Mate,* Dr. Gary Chapman discusses how different people give and receive love differently:

"He sends you flowers when what you really want is time to talk. She gives you a hug when what you really need is a home-cooked meal. The problem isn't your love—it's your love language (which can be one of five: Quality Time, Words of Affirmation, Gifts, Acts of Service, Physical Touch).

"Your emotional love language and the language of your spouse may be as different as Chinese from English. No matter how hard you try to express love in English, if your spouse understands only Chinese, you will never understand how to love each other."

I recommend you obtain Dr. Chapman's book, learn your spouse's love language, and then begin giving daily Warm Fuzzies in his or her unique love language.

Date Night

As I have already discussed, while the years pass in our busy lives, it's all too easy for a husband and wife to become married singles—ships that pass in the night. To keep your love and communication alive and growing, I strongly recommend that you set aside one night every week when you and your spouse can be alone together. Select the night, say each Friday, and designate it **Date Night.**

A wife knows that on Date Night she is number one in her husband's life. Nothing interferes with this night. She does not cook or take care of the children. (Her husband makes the necessary arrangements.) This is her night to be courted. Taking her to a movie or a sporting event with friends doesn't count; you can do that afterward. Just be sure you take time for the two of you first. Don't double date on this night. You need to be alone to enjoy talking with each other. This is the time to show your spouse that he or she is the most important person in your life. Go somewhere where you can really be together such as a restaurant or a special, quiet spot. Sit across from each other so you can hold hands, look into each other's eyes, and simply talk.

During the conversation, ask your spouse the **Big Question:** *How can I be a better husband/wife, father/mother,, and person?* Then sit back and listen. Avoid reacting defensively when your spouse opens up. You may destroy confidence and pinch off his or her feelings if you do. Accept the advice openly. Write down what is said; the next morning, during your Daily Self-Care Routine, Feelings Journal about what was said. If it makes sense, carry the written suggestions with you and review them daily. And most important—begin taking ACTION!

You May Be Surprised by Your Spouse's Response

When asking the Big Question for the first time, some people (especially men) are surprised by their spouse's response. While they usually expect some suggestions, they are not prepared for the truckload they receive—"I thought I was doing a pretty good job as a husband and father, and then I asked my wife the Big Question and, boy, did I get an earful!"

Several years ago I did a survey of two hundred of my married clients. All two hundred of the husbands were successful businessmen, well respected in their communities, and all held some type of significant religious leadership position. Each husband was asked, "On a scale of 1–10, ten being wonderful and one being terrible, how would your wife rate your marriage?" Then each wife was asked to rate her marriage on the same scale. Out of the two hundred couples, how many would you estimate that the husband *and* the wife both agreed that their marriage was a seven or better? Out of the all the couples, there were only 9!

When most of my male clients are asked the above question, they respond with a seven or an eight. Most women, when asked the same question, rated a three or a four! There are several lessons to be learned by this survey:

1. In many marriages, one or both spouses can be out of tune with how the other perceives the success of the relationship.

2. It's easy to become so absorbed in a career and making money; so dedicated to giving service to one's church or community; or so caught up in a hobby or pastime, that the marriage relationship is neglected or ignored.

The wonderful thing about Date Night and the Big Question, along with other tools in this chapter, is that you take your marriage off of autopilot and bring it to the conscious level where you can discuss it openly and honestly and start taking steps to improve it.

Special Instructions Regarding the Big Question

Knowing that you might get more than you bargained for, prepare your mate for the Big Question by letting him or her know by saying, "I'm going to ask you the Big Question. You probably have five gallons of response, but I only have a thimble-sized container to receive your counsel, so please just give me a little. Let me work on that and then next week you can give me a little more to work on."

One individual who read about the Big Question neglected to pay attention to the **five-gallon bucket/thimble-sized container** counsel given above. There he was, sitting in his easy chair, his wife sitting at the far side of the living room, and with all the insensitivity and lack of timing of a baboon, he yelled out, "Hey babe, what can I do to be a better husband?" He was sure she would just go on and on about how great he was, but his wife responded, "What did you say?" When he repeated the question, his wife strolled over, sat down next to him, and proceeded to dump an entire truckload of response on him. Afterward, he declared, "That Big Question thing is a bunch of baloney. I'll never do that again!" If only he had read and applied the five-gallon bucket/thimble-sized container analogy.

A few years ago, while introducing the Big Question concept during an individual coaching session, I received an unexpected response. After I introduced the implementation steps for the Big Question, the man I was coaching responded, "My wife doesn't like me asking questions like that." I was incredulous! I had never known a wife who didn't love being asked that question. A few months later I ran into this man's wife at a meeting. In private, I asked her if she really didn't like her husband asking her the Big Question, and she confirmed the fact that she absolutely did not want him asking it. I was truly astonished! I asked if she wouldn't mind telling me why. She explained that earlier in their marriage he used to ask similar questions, and she would share her feelings with him. The problem was that he never changed anything; she could have been talking to the wall for all the good it did. It made her so mad that he would ask and then never follow through, that finally she told him to quit asking.

Imagine the mental models that were built and reinforced in the brain of this woman with each succeeding experience. What did her husband communicate when he never followed through on the feedback he requested from her?

The lesson is: If you're going to ask the Big Question, make sure you listen to the response and follow through. Otherwise, the Big Question will do more harm than good to your relationship.

Date Night along with the Big Question is key to making any marriage run smoothly. The feedback you receive from Date Night can provide valuable input for your Feelings Journaling and improve your marriage relationship in miraculous ways.

A Video and Pizza Aren't Enough

Recently, there was another interesting experience with one of my clients. He is thirty-one, married, with two children ages three and six. When it was suggested that he and his wife plan a date night, he honestly felt she wouldn't be in favor of it. He said, "She prefers a video and pizza at home rather than a date." He was strongly counseled that he needed to get her away from the phone, children, neighbors, and television, and go where just the two of them could talk. He explained how much they used to talk before their marriage. They would park and talk for hours, but now they talked very little.

NOTE: *This is quite typical. Many marriage partners feel other things are more important than talking. Little do people realize that lack of communication leads to more serious problems in a marriage.*

After some discussion he finally agreed to set up a date with his wife. He called her on the spot and she replied exactly as he'd predicted: "Honey, why don't you bring home some pizza and a video and we'll just stay here." With some encouragement, he held firm to his commitment to take her out on a date.

The night of the date arrived. He secured a babysitter and arrived home on time. She halfheartedly accompanied him to a local sandwich shop to pick up a sandwich and milk shake. Then they drove to a favorite area overlooking the valley.

For the first fifteen minutes their conversation centered on the weather and their children. After giving the five-gallon bucket/thimble-sized container statement, he asked, "What can I do to be a better husband and father?" At first she balked at the question, but when he didn't defend himself and tried to understand exactly what was being said, she felt free to continue. When the answer was exhausted, he asked a follow-up question: "Am I doing anything to cause you stress?" Then he listened some more. He was so natural with his questions and feelings that she didn't know he had been coached.

A late afternoon rain started falling gently on the roof of the car. The storm's pitter-patter along with the sharing mood prompted him to put his arm around his wife and hold her close. For the next two hours they talked and shared feelings, and then they left for home. On the way, the wife said little. But the following morning she was up early, singing, and fixing his favorite breakfast. As he came into the kitchen she said, "Honey, I really had fun last night." Later in the afternoon she called to tell him again how much she'd enjoyed the date.

The lifeblood of a successful marriage is communication *after the wedding*. Bringing a pizza and video home to set the stage for talking is not conducive to sharing feelings. Leave the house and go to some quiet, special place.

It is important that the husband takes the initiative and sets up the date. Kindle the romantic flame that you felt during your courtship days. Take the time to talk once again.

START ENJOYING THE BENEFITS NOW!

1. Select a night this week and follow the guidelines to prepare for and share a Date Night with your spouse.

2. In the proper setting, ask your spouse the Big Question. Listen without being defensive or interrupting. Write down your spouse's suggestions.

3. During your Daily Self-Care Routine, Feelings Journal about your spouse's suggestions. Carry the written suggestions with you and review them daily.

4. Schedule a Date Night every week (preferably the same night each week) from now on and repeat the same process.

5. After thirty days, assess the difference Date Night has made in your marriage relationship.

Couple's Statement of Promise

In addition to the Big Question on Date Night, I have developed an additional tool that is simple but highly effective in opening up communication and helping a couple to track how each is progressing in the relationship. The **Couple's Statement of Promise** is a contract or commitment between husband and wife. Designed as a review and accountability tool for couples, it contains brief statements of promise from one spouse to the other, and vice-versa.

Why is the Couple's Statement of Promise Important?

I see a high percentage of couples who have fallen into the married singles trap. Caught in its jaws and feeling the pain of rejection and apathy, many can't figure out how their marriage fell apart. Concerning this all-too-common scenario, one client commented:

"We were so in love when we first got married. We were determined to make sure our relationship stayed strong, not like so many other couples we knew—bored with each other, irritated, frustrated, friction, and discord. But then over the years the same things began creeping into our marriage. What happened to us?"

What happens is the phenomenon that befalls most couples after two or three years of marriage. The fabulous "in love" feeling fades away and couple's gradually fall out of love and marital entropy is in full force. The mating instinct runs its course, and only then does the opportunity for genuine love begin. Unfortunately, too many couples don't take advantage of this opportunity and instead elect to spend their lives pining for what they used to have when they first got married.

The Couple's Statement of Promise will recapture some of the feelings that filled your heart during those first years of marriage as well as the times of closeness, tenderness, and love since then. It will also provide you with a simple tool for recommitting to the nurturing of these feelings in the future.

NOTE: *It is most beneficial to create a Statement of Promise at the beginning of a marriage. It's a little easier in that part of life because you are committed to being the best spouse possible.*

Below are some exercises that will generate ideas to help determine the content of your Statement of Promise:

1. Strong Motive: Husband and wife must have a strong joint motive for creating the Couple's Statement of Promise. Why do the two of you wish to create this contract? What will it do for your relationship? Are both of you committed to the process? You should each Feelings Journal about your motives, then discuss this together and create a simple statement describing your motives. Place this motive statement at the beginning of the document. Without a powerful joint motive, your Couple's Statement of Promise will end up in a drawer.

2. Take Yourselves Back: Separately, take some private time to think back to when you were first married and the years that have passed. What made you fall in love in the first place? What were your hopes, dreams, and commitments to each other regarding your future marriage relationship? What are some of the most memorable bonding experiences you've had in your marriage? Journal your thoughts and feelings about these things, and then share your realizations and discoveries with each other.

3. Role Models: Talk with other couples you admire who seem to have wonderful, loving relationships. Ask them what they have done to keep their love affair going. Write down their suggestions and discuss these ideas as a couple.

4. Ask Each Other: Ask your spouse, "What can I do to ensure that you always know you're first in my life?" or "What can I do to always keep our friendship, romance, and love affair strong and growing?" This is a great opportunity to find out exactly what makes him or her feel the most loved, cared for, and cherished.

Create Your Statement of Promise

Your Statement of Promise is a very simple document. Take the information you have gathered and discussed from any of the four exercises above and create several brief "I promise you . . ." statements. Do this in two sections: one for the husband and one for the wife, with the husband stating what he promises his wife and the wife stating what she promises her husband. In order to get away from "we" statements and take full individual responsibility, I suggest you structure your statements like this: I, Jeff, promise you, Wendy, that I _____. I, Wendy, promise you, Jeff, that I _____.

The purpose of the following Statement of Promise is only as an example. Customize and organize your own Statement of Promise to fit your personalities, needs, and desires.

Jeff and Wendy Johnson Statement of Promise

We, Jeff and Wendy, each commit ourselves 100 percent to this Statement of Promise. It is with great love, tenderness, friendship, commitment, and tremendous optimism and positive expectation for our future that we do enter into this contract together. We desire with all our hearts to keep our love, romance, passion, and friendship always strong and growing. With this in mind, we do pledge to each other that we will review this Statement of Promise together on our Date Night the first Friday of every month. We commit ourselves to working together to keep every promise we make in this sacred contract. If or when we fall short, we promise to help each other, with love and forgiveness in our hearts, to continue moving forward, always forward.

I, Jeff, promise you, Wendy:

To ask and talk to you about your day, listening with my hands empty and making direct eye contact.

To do my best to help when asked and help before having to be asked.

To spend time every day with you one on one, being close, talking, and touching so you'll know that I cherish you.

To maintain my integrity and be honest in my profession and in our home.

To always avoid the temptations of pornography and sensuality.

To read out of a book with you every Wednesday night to strengthen our communication.

To invite at least one couple to come over and play games with us once a month.

To sit down with you to review our financial situation the first Monday of the month.

To keep a monthly budget.

To look for opportunities to feel the spirit together and strengthen our relationship with God.

To take you on a romantic and passionate honeymoon retreat every three months.

To eat healthy foods, exercise, and take good care of my body.

I, Wendy, promise you, Jeff:

To give you a kiss every night before going to bed.

To never go to bed angry at you.

To put your needs first in my life.

To compliment you daily (Warm Fuzzy).

To spend at least a half an hour each day talking and sharing with you to show you my love and to stay updated with the concerns of your life.

To always have "T" time with you (time to talk and touch).

To express my appreciation for you.

To go on our date night every week so I can discuss how to be a better wife, mother, and person.

To participate in running, mountain biking, walking, swimming, playing chess, hiking, or other activities with you at least once a week.

To initiate one act of service we can do together each month.

To never be alone with another man or participate in Internet chat rooms with men.

To take twenty-four hours to think before making a big financial decision.

Signed _____   Date _____

Signed _____   Date _____

Review your Statement of Promise Once Each Month

Once each month, preferably on your Date Night, go somewhere private to review and discuss your Statement of Promise. This is not meant to be a blame and bash session. This is a special opportunity for you to assess your relationship and lovingly and tenderly discuss how you can better love and serve each other by keeping the promises you have made. No one is perfect, no marriage is perfect, and Rome was not built in a day. Therefore, as you see and point out areas for improvement, lovingly discuss what steps you can take to help each other make these improvements. As time goes by and new insights are gained, you can edit and add items to your Statement of Promise.

Family Statement of Promise

If you are planning to have children, or your children are small, you can include with your Couple's Statement of Promise a **Family Statement of Promise** section. In this section, you as parents can make promises to your future or existing children. For example:

We, the Johnson family parents, promise you, our children:

To create a home environment of unconditional love, understanding, and refuge where you can grow and flourish.

To show you an example of love and tenderness through our relationship as your mom and dad.

To be positive, encouraging, and build you up in all our words and actions.

To help you discover your unique gifts, talents, and abilities, and provide you with opportunities to fully develop them.

As your children get older, they should be encouraged and invited to make some commitments to you, their parents, and to the family as a whole. This can be added to the Family Statement of Promise, which evolves into a statement containing the parents' promises to their children and the children's promises to their parents and family. Once a month, meet together as a family to briefly review your Family Statement of Promise and discuss how family members are doing. Imagine the powerful example children receive when they see and hear their parents being accountable, asking for help and suggestions, and making and keeping promises.

Once children are involved in the process, the Couple's Statement of Promise might well be separated from the Family Statement of Promise. Promises made between husband and wife should be discussed and reviewed privately as a couple. Of course, this doesn't mean that parents should hide from their children the fact they have made sacred promises to each other; parents should let their children know about this promise. It's a practice that provides children an important example and will help them succeed in their future marriage relationships.

Additional Insight

As with the LifeCreed, which I will present to you in chapter 9, the Couple's and Family Statements of Promise are not etched in stone. They should be added to, updated, modified, and expanded approximately as often as you revise your LifeCreed.

As mentioned, so many couples drift apart and forget why they even fell in love with their mate in the first place. These couples now carry mostly negative feelings about their spouse, the one who used be so special in their life. In as much as the mind cannot think of two dissimilar things at the same time, the commitments you make with your spouse in your Statement of Promise give you something tremendously positive to focus on. By creating and following a Couple's Statement of Promise, you are on the journey to becoming truly one as a couple.

START ENJOYING THE BENEFITS NOW!

1. Meet with your spouse and discuss the idea of the Couple's Statement of Promise. Before proceeding, make sure that you are both positive about participating. If one is not, implement the other Relationship Tools to improve the marriage relationship and then try again.

2. As outlined, begin journaling your feelings and gathering ideas for your Statement of Promise. Take time to compare notes and fully discuss your ideas together.

3. Create your Statement of Promise and make a copy for both spouses. Review is once each month on your Date Night.

4. Make revisions over time as you see fit.

5. If you have children, create a Family Statement of Promise. Review this as a family at Family Council once each month. (For details, see the "Family Council" section in chapter 8.)

Quarterly Honeymoon Retreat

With children, careers, and social and religious obligations, married couples often don't spend much, if any, extended quality time together. Date Night is an awesome tool, but it only lasts a few hours. Vacations are fine, but they're with the whole family. And by the time your head hits the pillow at night, you're usually too exhausted to spend any significant time rekindling the romantic flame.

For these reasons, it's good counsel to take time and get away as a couple once every three months or so, no matter what. The accommodations don't have to be expensive or elaborate. It can be an overnight at a local hotel or camping up the canyon. Once or twice each year the getaway can be more elaborate. The key is to be alone to nurture and fuel the romantic fire that can be easily extinguished in the grind of daily life.

At the beginning of every quarter, sit down together to schedule and plan your **Quarterly Honeymoon Retreat**. Make a list of all the arrangements that need to be made and divide them up between the two of you. Establish a budget and do whatever is necessary to allocate the funds.

While on your quarterly Honeymoon Retreat, leave the cares and concerns of the world behind. Approach this time together with the same enthusiasm and anticipation you had on your first honeymoon. Immerse yourselves anew in romance, tenderness, and friendship. Be fully present in the moment with each other while you're together. This is your time—just the two of you.

NOTE: *When first learning about this relationship tool, one LifeBalance client made the comment, "If we go away together every three months, we'll just be at each other's throats." The Quarterly Honeymoon Retreat is not a stand-alone tool. It is designed to be used in conjunction with the Feelings Journal, the Byte, and the relationship tools in this chapter. If you implement these tools as a total package, your marriage relationship will significantly improve. With a healthy marriage in place, the Quarterly Honeymoon Retreat becomes a wonderful reward you both look forward to.*

START ENJOYING THE BENEFITS NOW!

1. Schedule a time to sit down with your spouse within the next week to plan and schedule your first Quarterly Honeymoon retreat.

2. Prepare for and make this time together as special and productive as possible. Begin implementing the other relationship tools in this chapter at least thirty days prior to your first retreat.

3. Plan, schedule, and follow through with a Honeymoon Retreat every single quarter without fail. You will be amazed at how this tool fans the flames of romance in your marriage.

Important Ideas & Insights

_____

_____

_____

_____

_____

_____

_____

_____

_____

_____

_____

8

Enjoy a Close, Positive Relationship with Each of Your Children

You may be familiar with these thought-provoking lines:

A hundred years from now
It will not matter
What my bank account was,
The sort of house I lived in,
Or the kind of car I drove.
But the world may be different
Because I was important
In the life of a child.

With careers, commitments, community involvement, and a host of other balls in the air, many parents find they spend a very limited quantity of time—let alone quality time—with their children. The amazingly simple but powerful tools I have developed have been proven to significantly improve a child's self-esteem, attitude, sense of well-being, performance in school, and overall behavior and success in life.

Daily Family Connection

One of the simplest yet most important ways to encourage family unity is by gathering the family together each day at a set time to communicate and interact. This event often took place as families gathered around the dinner table at the end of each day. Unfortunately, in our fast-paced, fast-food, grab-a-snack, and see-you-later society, the art of gathering for the evening meal has been all but lost. Although it won't be easy, make this a priority in your home. Gather your family around the table. Pray together. Read a passage or two from scripture. Give children a chance to talk about their day, express concerns, and enjoy one another's company.

If the dinner gathering is not possible, then come together before everyone retires for the evening. Read a scripture together, allow family members to express concerns or share something important from their day, and end in prayer. It takes only fifteen minutes, but the rewards of helping family members feel close and connected will be more than worth it.

Making a Daily Family Connection

Take a moment to write down your feelings about how a **Daily Family Connection** would help your family become closer. Discuss this with your spouse and together determine what would work best for your family. Also very important, talk with your children about the idea and help them identify their own motives for doing it. If they have a strong *why* and feel like they have ownership in the decision, it will be much more successful. Hold your first one as soon as possible.

Kid's Day and Kid's Date

In my experience with executives, entrepreneurs, business owners, and others with jobs that demand significant amounts of time, energy, and focus, I find they spend very limited quantity and quality time with their children. In many cases the actual one-on-one time (TV and whole family activities don't count) amounts to little more than an hour or two in an entire month. While family activities are very important, children desperately need individual quality time with each parent. Done properly, this individual time has a more significant impact on the self-esteem, attitude, well-being, and the future success of a child or teen than virtually any other influence in their lives, including that of peers.

The most effective way to accomplish this one-on-one time is through what I call **Kid's Day.** You set aside one day a week for each of your children. If you have more than one child, select a different day for each one. If you have a large number of children, you can double up on one or more of the days. On their day, find a twenty-minute time slot (this is the minimum; it can be longer) when you can be alone with them one-on-one. With teenagers' chaotic lives, this time may have to be spent in bits and pieces throughout the day.

NOTE: *Please remember that the best time for you to be with your child may not be the best time for him or her. Trying to drag the child into your time slot when they aren't in the right mood or frame of mind will only prove counterproductive. Be alert and flexible, and you will know the right moment. It may be inconvenient for you, but waiting for the right time will pay big relationship dividends.*

Kid's Day time is not a time to criticize or come down on your child. Taking this approach will do more harm than good. Too often parents place their greatest emphasis on the negative, expressing displeasure, disappointment, reprimanding, and so forth. There is a tendency to practice negative reinforcement: "If you don't straighten up, you're not going to make it," "You'll never get into college with these lousy grades," "I thought you were capable of so much more," or "It's time to grow up and stop being a slacker."

These types of statements create powerful mental models and meaning for the child or teen. The problem is, it most often doesn't produce the positive outcome parents hope it will. Negative dialogue usually creates self-doubt, depression, anger, and rebellion. Negative reinforcement techniques practiced by parents typically affect a self-fulfilling prophecy in the child—a powerful expectation: "If my parents think I'm going to fail or that I'm a loser, they're probably right. I may as well give in to the inevitable."

Remember, striving for a positive reward or outcome usually generates far greater motivation to succeed than avoiding a negative consequence. The more powerfully positive the meaning, the more likely the attainment of the desired goal.

Kid's Day is your opportunity to let your child know how much you love and appreciate her. It's a time to shower her with positive affirmations about all the good things she's doing (this might be a challenge with some children, but hopefully you can find some positives). During this time, express your confidence in her abilities and potential, and tell her of her many unique gifts and talents.

After praising, affirming, and encouraging your child, if you have a suggestion for improvement, this is a good time to bring it up. Too often when you spend time with a child you want to get our frustrations and corrections out on the table immediately. If you do this, it poisons the remainder of your time together; your praise, affirmations, and encouragement do not have impact and may even be viewed as insincere or manipulative. Instead, wait until the end of your time together to bring up a suggestion for improvement, after trust and rapport have been established. Offer the suggestion gently and lovingly. Focus on only one area of improvement. Remember the five-gallon bucket/thimble sized container analogy from Date Night. Only give your child a little to work on at a time. The child receives this correction even more positively when it is followed by the **Big Question.**

The Big Question

Always conclude your twenty-minute time together by asking your child the question, "How can I be a better father/mother to you?" His response provides input for your Feelings Journaling. Imagine the powerfully positive effect on a child or teen's brain when he hears his mother or father ask, "How can I be a better mother/father to you?" We've received feedback from many kids who say, "I couldn't believe my dad was actually asking me how he could be a better father!" The humility, sincerity, and genuine love this communicates are unmatched. The full power of this process manifests itself after the father or mother Feelings Journals about the child's response and then actually starts living it. Imagine the impact on a child when he makes a suggestion for improvement and then sees his parent actually doing it!

Can Twenty Minutes Really Make a Difference?

How can twenty minutes a week make any real difference? Too often we believe it's only the major events that make a difference in our children's lives—trips to Disneyland, spending the whole day together, lavish gifts, and so forth. While these can be valuable relationship building events, they cannot compare to the consistent weekly praise, affirmations, and positive reinforcement Kid's Day offers. How often do we say to ourselves, "I really need to spend some time with my kids?" Then before we know it, months go by and we haven't taken the time. Guilt starts setting in. We think we can make up for it with a major event or extravagant gift.

With Kid's Day, after one year you will have completed up to fifty-two quality one-on-one sessions praising, affirming, and building trust and rapport with your child. Imagine the impact of doing this over five or ten years! Never underestimate the power of consistently doing the so-called little things.

NOTE: *Don't tell your child you have a specific day of the week set aside as his day. If you get tied up and can't get to it that day, you'll disappoint the child and make a major withdrawal in the relationship. In addition, your child (especially teenagers) may be busy on the day you've selected. Consider the selected day of the week as an extremely important commitment on your calendar, but be flexible when the unexpected happens. Stay alert for another time in the next day or two when you can get with your child. Remember, with teens especially, it may be ten minutes here and another five minutes there.*

Even though you don't tell your child that a specific day of the week is his day, you will find over time he intuitively begins looking forward to the day you've set aside for him, though he won't know exactly why.

Kid's Date

At least once a month, use Kid's Day as an opportunity to take a more extended period of time and participate with your child in an activity she chooses. Schedule this with the child and let her know this is a formal date. A father might tell his daughter that this is their daddy-daughter date or to his son that it's guys' night out. However you label it, the important thing is to allow your child to decide what the activity will be. This gives you a wonderful opportunity to learn about her interests and spend time doing what she enjoys. Find an appropriate time during the date to incorporate the informal dialogue you normally follow during the twenty-minute time slot on Kid's Day: praise, affirmations, the Big Question, and so forth.

Whenever we see or hear something, it is processed and produces a response according to the mental model we have for it. Imagine parents who consistently use negative reinforcement such as nagging, anger, ridicule, or criticism in their everyday interactions with their child. Imagine the resulting emotions and feelings stored in the mental models of that child. Each time the child sees one of the parent's faces or hears one of their voices, imagine the meaning that information has for the child as it is filtered through his mental models; imagine how he feels and responds—not just when the parent is negative, but at any time. This meaning creates enormous relationship barriers between parent and child.

Contrast this scenario with the parents who use positive reinforcement and rewards, who are kind, patient, encouraging, and loving. When the child sees the face or hears the voice of such a parent, what is the meaning and how does he feel and respond? As parents, the meaning that our eyes, face, voice, and presence communicate to our children is completely up to us.

It's never too late and our children are never too old for us as parents to implement this wonderful process. I have a seventy-year-old client whose children are now in their thirties and forties. I helped him start Feelings Journaling about each one of his children. With some prodding, he began extrapolating from these entries the content for little notes and letters expressing his feelings of love and appreciation to his children. A whole new world opened up for this fine man. He now has father-daughter date night and father-son guys' night out with his adult children. Of course he laments that he waited so long to do this, but for the next twenty to thirty years he'll be building fabulous relationships with his kids. He's even contemplating starting up grandfather-grandchild dates with his grandchildren. He told me recently that because of his efforts to connect emotionally with his wife and kids, these are the happiest days of his life.

Start enjoying the benefits now!

1. Follow the guidelines for this tool and schedule on your calendar a Kid's Day each week for each of your children. Once each month, turn the scheduled time into an extended Kid's Date.

2. Use this time to focus primarily on showering your children with praise and positive affirmations.

3. Ask them the Big Question, journal your feelings about this, and then add important points to your LifeCreed.

4. If you have suggestions for improvement, keep these down to one or two and save them for the end of the time with the child. State them in a loving and positive way.

Family Council

The days and weeks pass; our family members come and go. And too often when we do spend time together, it's in front of the TV. As parents, we need to set aside special time and call our families together for instruction, recreation, planning, counsel, conflict resolution, expressing appreciation, and building self-esteem. In today's busy world, we need to create an environment of refuge and unity in our homes. We know of no better way to promote this than through a weekly Family Council. Although this council can take several different forms, here are some suggestions based on what has worked for many families:

1. Set a specific day and time: Establish Family Council as a special family time and schedule it as a high priority on the family calendar. Parents and children should consider this an appointment to be kept. Everyone in the family is expected to adjust his or her schedule accordingly. I recommend Family Council be held once each week, perhaps just prior to or right after dinner. The duration can be as little as twenty or thirty minutes, depending on what needs to be discussed.

2. Key components: Key components of this family time might include:

- **Express gratitude and appreciation.** Take a minute to express appreciation for family members: the service each has given to others, the talents each shares, the accomplishments reached. (Take time to write down a list of these things in advance and then use it as a reference; it can make this activity much easier.) Also talk about the opportunities and blessings afforded you as members of a family and as free citizens.

- **Read from inspirational or educational materials.** Read together out of inspirational or educational books, periodicals, scriptures, and other uplifting materials. Give family members an opportunity to share their own experiences, thoughts, or insights, or to tell a good joke or story.

- **Showcase talents.** Family Council can be a time for family members to showcase their talents, whether it be a musical or dance number, an art project, a speech, or an athletic or academic achievement. Each family member can report on their proudest accomplishment for the previous week, and acknowledge the accomplishments they have seen in other family members.

- **Give everyone a turn.** Make sure everyone has a chance

to participate. Assign children to plan the Family Council, giving family members specific assignments such as leading a song, telling a story, planning a game, displaying a talent, or making a dessert.

- **Offer counsel and instruction.** Family Council is a prime opportunity for Mom or Dad to give instruction and counsel on specific topics such as integrity, selflessness, moral purity, faith, and kind words; educational topics might include safety in the home, finances, or chore responsibilities. Too many parents leave such instruction to the public schools and church classes. Yet the most potent and valuable instruction is delivered in the home.

- **Resolve concerns and conflicts.** Give each family member an opportunity to talk about the good things that happened this week and what went well. Then allow anyone who wishes to voice concerns and conflicts. Focus on positive resolutions, personal responsibility, and family unity and teamwork. This is a wonderful opportunity to teach members of the family how to resolve conflicts and remedy problems.

4. Set the tone: It is up to the parents to set the tone for Family Council, to create an atmosphere that is positive and uplifting. Patience, kindness, calmness, enthusiasm, and encouragement ought to prevail. Avoid conflict, preaching, and all other negative catalysts. Make this a time family members look forward to.

5. Recreation: You can set aside one Family Council each month for recreational activities, like going to a park, playing together, going out to eat, seeing a movie, visiting a museum, or attending some other cultural or social event.

START ENJOYING THE BENEFITS NOW!

Write down why you want to hold Family Council. Visualize having done it for several months and describe how your family is better for it. Refer back to this motive when you don't feel like having it or you've held one that hasn't gone well.

Review the details of this tool with your spouse (or your oldest child if you aren't married) and plan and hold your very first Family Council. As a family, select a set day and time to have Family Council every week. Put it on your calendars and consider it an extremely important appointment.

An Additional Insight: The Color Code

In seeking to better understand ourselves and to form close, loving relationships with others, we must understand that everyone's core motives are not the same. Something that motivates or is a priority for one person may be completely different for someone else. So many of us push ourselves to be just like everyone else in our dress, opinions, appearance, work, or relationships. At times, we attempt to manipulate others to be like us, or something else we believe they should be. In many cases, this results in tremendous stress, anger, illness, and failure. Every individual needs to discover their core personality and core motives, and embrace his or her innate gifts and talents, rather than trying to be like someone else.

I have spent many years adapting my good friend Dr. Taylor Hartman's *Color Code System* to many hundreds of my clients. Using this wonderful tool, you learn how various facets of personality, attitude, and behavior are grouped into four color categories: Red, Blue, White, and Yellow. While few people are completely one color or another, these categories represent a useful guide to personality types. Color Codes for personality are used because color is already an established metaphor for emotion and behavior: we see red when we're angry, we feel blue when we're sad, and so forth.

By using this color guide to personality, you can better see the core motives behind your own and other people's behaviors, helping you establish and maintain relationships with greater ease. And, most important, you can learn to incorporate within yourself the best of all the colors of life.

IMPORTANT Note: *The Color Code is not intended to pigeon-hole or stereotype anyone. It is a fun reference guide to identify your unique gifts and talents as well as your limitations. It will help you realize that you are unique and that you don't have to be like everybody else. The Color Code is simply a starting place that should lead you to incorporate the best qualities from all of the colors into your life. The Color Code can also open the communication lines with others in a light-hearted and non-offensive way.*

This section will provide you with a foundational understanding of the Color Code. To gain the full benefits of the Color Code and fully comprehend how to implement and utilize this powerful tool, you should obtain a copy of Dr. Hartman's amazing book, *The Color Code: A New Way to See Yourself, Your Relationships, and Life.* This book contains a forty-five question Color Code Inventory that allows each person to identify their own unique color code.

Color Code Overview

The Color Code Teaches Us the Core Motives behind Who We Are

Red—The Power Wielder

Strengths	Limitations
Pragmatic and Proactive	Abrasive
Active and Productive	Lacks Intimacy Connection
Competitive and Bold	Demanding and Critical
Assertive and Determined	Must Be Right
Relentless and Tenacious	Insensitive and Selfish
Resourceful and Self-Reliant	Emotionally Insecure
"King of the Jungle"	Disagreeable/Arrogant
Excellent Business Person	Knows Everything
Outstanding Leader/Delegator	Controller of People and Society
A Visionary—Plans Ahead	

Red Strengths

Healthy Reds are the lifeblood of humanity. They are the movers and shakers of society; they are known for their dominant nature; they are the powerful leaders and responsible delegators. Red personalities can be an asset to any organization. They enjoy competition and challenges, and they call easily on their inner core for self-motivation and direction.

Further, Reds focus precisely when setting goals and tenaciously assert their rights (and the rights of any organization, person, or cause they value). They value productivity and success, and willingly pay the price for both. Reds meet most aspects of life with self-confidence and tenacity. They are constant reminders of the power derived from rational thinking and assertive communication, and they model those leadership skills society seeks most to emulate. Their lights continue to burn brightly as a beacon of strength and productivity, warming and reassuring us with their resourceful and protective nature.

Red Limitations

Reds often see others through the eyes of power. They can be difficult to live and work with, unless they can get their way. Reds are taxing and demanding; they will argue at the drop of a hat. Their selfish nature is a constant reminder to other personalities that Reds will always consider themselves number one. They often are insensitive and arrogant, which creates distance and distrust. Intimacy is, perhaps, their least developed skill. They can suffer from loneliness due to their critical and disagreeable nature.

Reds argue from logic and are capable of manipulating with constant mind calculation. Highly verbal individuals, they often attack others and intimidate those who they perceive to be less-than-adequate human beings. They are particularly guilty of denial. They often are surprised to find out that others may see them in a negative light, but consider finding fault with others an essential part of their daily routine. Their tactless and stubborn behavior tends to expose a frustrated individual who blooms with positions of power and control, yet shrinks from social life when their leadership opportunities run dry.

Always processing another new thought in their mind, these often brilliant individuals must be constantly aware of their limitations in order to avoid sabotaging themselves from experiencing a quality life.

Blue—The Do-Gooder

Strengths	Limitations
Emotional and Admired	Perfectionist
Committed and Loyal	High Expectations/Demanding
Self-Disciplined and Stable	Unforgiving and Resentful
Self-Sacrificing and Nurturing	Worry- and Guilt-Prone
Appropriate and Sincere	Moody and Complex
Purposeful and Dedicated	Self-Righteous and Insecure

Blue Strengths

Like the earth that sustained and nurtured our early ancestors, Blues are also steady, ordered, and enduring. They grant us culture, beauty, and emotional sincerity. They love with a passion. For Blues, the finer things in life are intimate relationships and creative accomplishments, rather than material possessions (which many Reds particularly value). Blues bring culture and decency to home and society. They appreciate uplifting experiences and feel most comfortable in creative and productive environments. They seek a sense of purpose in life and willingly sacrifice luxuries in order to attain more meaningful accomplishments.

Blues are highly committed individuals. Loyalty to people and sincerity in relationships (at home and at work) are their trademarks. They believe in all causes that bring a higher quality to the human experience; they listen with endearing empathy and speak with emotional zeal; they truly value their connectedness to people and enjoy the accomplishments of others. And they don't require recognition.

With perfection as their guide, Blues stretch for the best within themselves and expect the same in their fellow beings. Obediently they accept the need for authority and put their energy into supporting law and order. Essentially, they are the glue that binds society together.

Blue Limitations

Blues probably find their greatest enemy to be themselves. Their self-righteous attitudes are often a guise for private insecurity. They can be too emotional and judgmental to enjoy intimacy. They continually depress themselves and others with unrealistic expectations or perfection. Lacking trust, Blues find themselves skeptical and suspicious of others. They can be bitter, resentful, and unforgiving of those who have crossed them in life. Overwhelming guilt and worry continue to drive them inward, seeking solace from the only one who truly understands them—themselves.

Blues are hard to please and tense about schedules. They are moody and find leadership a difficult dilemma. Blues aren't generally playful or spontaneous. In anger, they are the personality most likely to feel, "Life sucks and then you die." They often fail to see the humor in life. Blues become angry when others find them to be irrational and emotionally rigid in relationships. Typically, they exemplify the well-known phrase, "We have found the enemy, and it is us." Blues teach you to believe in yourself, but often they don't believe in themselves very easily.

White—The Peacemaker

Strengths	Weaknesses
Peaceful and Diplomatic	Insecure/Non-Assertive
Tolerant and Patient	Timid and Emotionally Insecure
Blendable and Kind	Withholds Feelings
Gentle	Unproductive Dreamer
Accepting and Objective	Silently Stubborn
Doesn't Have to Be Entertained	Unmotivated
Even Tempered	Indecisive

White Strengths

Whites are the satisfied ones. They are content and agreeable individuals who easily accommodate others through life. They complement every personality, regardless of their differences in style. Their gentle nature and diplomacy wins them many protective friends. Their agreeable and peaceful disposition makes them an asset to any family, friendship, or business that is fortunate enough to enjoy them. Whites typically are moderate people, without the extremes of other personalities. Like the water they represent, they flow over and around life's difficulties rather than demanding that obstacles in their path be moved.

Whites' leadership is solid and fair. They tolerate differences and encourage camaraderie with all team members. The chameleon is their trademark and reflects their ability to adapt and blend with everyone. Whites enjoy enviable strength and balance; they are receptive to every personality and willingly learn from all of them. They are most effective at putting life's crises in proper perspective. Satisfied and even-tempered, they ask little of life. Patient and tolerant, they have much to give. And give they do, with gentle approval for those fortunate enough to experience their accepting embrace.

White Limitations

Whites often seem bored and uninvolved. They are often unwilling to set goals. They frequently refuse to pay the price of involvement because they may fear the inevitable results of confrontation or rejection. Fear keeps them from experiencing intimacy; indecision limits their accomplishments.

In order to feel secure, Whites pay great attention to preserving the status quo and strive at all costs to please those they encounter in life. They express themselves reluctantly, preferring to let others believe as they will. Meanwhile, Whites go about their lives as they choose, avoiding conflict and confrontation and silently accepting whatever comes their way. What they don't value, in time they stubbornly discard. Often they do not bring to their lives those desirable experiences, which require the effort of risk, leadership, and honest expression.

Yellow—The Lover of Fun

Strengths	Weaknesses
Happy and Fun	Self-Centered and Uncommitted
Enthusiastic and Carefree	Irresponsible
Playful and Exciting	Superficial
Trusting	Naive
Charismatic and Popular	Impulsive and Undisciplined
Optimistic/Lands On His Feet	Disorganized and Incomplete
Genuinely Loves People	A Chatterbox/Flippant
	Lots of Alibis and Excuses

Yellow Strengths

Yellows are eager to experience all facets of life. They naively call for the spotlight to be placed on them as they play out their life as though it were on center stage. Yellows are our constant reminder that youth is in the eye of the beholder, as they are generally youthful in their attitudes towards new ideas, change, relationships, occupations, and the future. They carry a childlike quality of hope that inspires others to appreciate and value themselves as well as the wonderful world in which they live.

Yellows promote the good in others and willingly ignore their limitations. They are more inclined to like themselves just for what *they are* rather than what *they do*. They tend to be people-connectors, the social glue of any group.

Yellows express themselves candidly and genuinely. They give playful attention to living and inspire others to do the same. Freely, they offer their opinions as well as themselves, often spreading a contagious spirit of friendship wherever they go. Once a Yellow has intimately touched your life, you will appreciate more the incredible joy achievable by the human soul and the optimistic hope attainable within the human heart.

Yellow Limitations

Yellows have little regard for the property of others. They tend to be messy individuals, keeping themselves clean and polished in public even while their homes suffer from neglect. They want to give a particularly good impression to the world thus when social praise is a consideration, they are quick to comply with society's standards. Otherwise, they would rather not bother. Yellows often are disorganized in their environments and personal thoughts. Rather than focusing on real issues and important events, Yellows putter with minor concerns and the irrelevant much of their lives. They have a difficult time committing to anything that takes priority over playtime and, consequently, find themselves somewhat superficial and empty with regards to relationships.

Get Dr. Hartman's Book

In the limited space of this chapter, I can only provide you with a brief overview of the Color Code. To receive a complete understanding and to access the full benefits of this amazing system, you need to purchase Hartman's *The Color Code: A New Way to See Yourself, Your Relationships, and Life.*

Consider the following as just a sampling of some of the benefits and insights I and my clients have experienced as a direct result of Dr. Hartman's book.

1. The amazing forty-five question Color Code Inventory contained in the book will help you identify your own Color Code. After completing the inventory, many of my clients ask, "How can forty-five simple questions peg me so well?"

2. One of the greatest uses of the Color Code book is as a communication tool for couples. Here is an experience from my own life: My wife and I have spent hours discussing our own Color Codes. My dominant color is Red, so while reading aloud from the Red section of the book, I would comment whether or not I felt it accurately described me. Many times I would insist, "That's not me at all," and my wife would counter, "Oh, yes it really is!" Then she would offer—too willingly, in my opinion—examples of how I met the Red criteria head on. Because I answered the test questions, Dr. Hartman, rather than my wife, was making the points, I didn't feel like she was criticizing or accusing me. For us, the Color Code has been a wonderful communication and conversation device. It has

allowed us to talk about what might normally be sensitive or even negative issues in an open and healthy way. In fact, many times we joke about how Red or White one of us is acting.

3. Dr. Hartman discusses how different colors can interact and harmonize with each other in healthy ways; his is a primer on how to "celebrate differences." He points out potential areas of conflict between those of different colors and where the colors are more complimentary.

4. Again, from my own personal history: As adults, my own children have used the Color Code to identify their core personalities and motives, and this has helped me understand and communicate with them so much better. But how I wish the Color Code had been available to me as a father when my children were small! I'm certain that my Creator has a sense of humor, as evidenced by the fact that two of my beloved sons are full-fledged yellows—the polar opposite of my Red personality.

Pardon the personal note, but I am "Leo, son of Leo." My father was a fire chief, a true leader, a true Red personality. I always wanted to be just like him. So when my first son was born, I named him Leo, fully expecting he would follow in tradition and become a great leader like his grandfather. I was shocked when at age thirteen he came to me and bluntly said, "Dad, I don't want to be a leader."

Years later it all made sense when I discovered Leo Jr. is a hard-core Yellow. His core motives are very different from my own. A talented artist, he possesses gifts I never dreamed of. And since I began allowing him to be who he is rather than trying to force my Red motives upon him, our relationship has been so much closer. The Color Code is a priceless tool for parents to discover the unique, core motives of their children and then adjust their communication and approach accordingly.

5. Many of my clients purchase *The Color Code* and give it to their business associates, employees, parents, siblings, and grandchildren. The book opens up understanding and communication in a way that is nothing short of amazing. There are no bad colors; we all have strengths and limitations. The Color Code allows readers to use the knowledge of their own Color Code and that of others to better communicate, interact, and understand one another.

6. This wonderful guidebook will help answer the following critical questions:

- What are my core motives and dominant personality traits—what color am I?

- How can I capitalize on and accentuate my strengths to achieve a higher level of success in my life and relationships?

- How can I turn my weaknesses and limitations into strengths?

- How can I learn to recognize the Color Code of key people in my life and use this knowledge to significantly improve my relationships with them?

- Which colors tend to cooperate and harmonize and which ones more often are beset with challenges? How do I overcome these challenges?

- How can I use the Color Code to build successful relationships?

- How can I become my best color?

- How can I adopt the positive traits and core motives of other colors?

The answers to these and many other important questions can be found in Dr. Hartman's book. The ideas taught in *The Color Code* will help you cement a relationship with yourself, spouse, children, friends, colleagues, and employees. It is one more tool to help you in your journey toward your ideal relationships.

START ENJOYING THE BENEFITS NOW!

1. Purchase *The Color Code* and take the Color Code Inventory to discover your own core motives and personality colors. Then have your spouse and children take the inventory.

2. Initiate an open and fun dialogue about the colors and how they fit each family member's personality. This will stimulate healthy communication, understanding, and enhance family relationships in wonderful ways.

Important Ideas & Insights

_____

_____

_____

_____

_____

_____

_____

_____

_____

_____

_____

_____

_____

_____

_____

_____

_____

_____

_____

_____

_____

_____

_____

_____

_____

_____

_____

_____

_____

_____

_____

_____

The Ultimate LifeBalance Tool—
Your LifeCreed

9

Guarantee Yourself a Lifetime of Success through the Ultimate LifeBalance Tool—Your LifeCreed

Have you ever marveled at how time seems to fly by? We all have good intentions, goals we want to achieve, habits we wish to change, and relationships we hope to improve. But before we know it, another month, year, or decade has raced by and we're still stuck in our old ways.

In this book you have learned about simple but powerful tools that, when consistently implemented, are guaranteed to produce remarkable results in every aspect of your life. But how do you keep from simply putting this book on the shelf and falling right back into your old habits? Your greatest challenge now is figuring out a way to overcome your brain's dominant tendency to "keep things as they are." Working with thousand of people to overcome old habits and achieve desired goals, the easiest, simplest, and most effective tool I know of is called the **LifeCreed.**

An Easy Daily Method

We all live in the real world, a world filled with appointments, obligations, money, family responsibilities, pressures, and stress. It's easy to get distracted, to be busy, or to get stuck in the same old rut. It's impossible to constantly stop and consciously bring each important goal into our mind. But what if all you had to do to fully implement the process is put in a CD or cassette tape and listen? Once you create and record your own custom LifeCreed, it will be that simple.

Your LifeCreed is a written and recorded visualization of the ideal person you want to be and the ideal life you want to live in each of the **Six Key Relationships** or areas of your life: Spiritual, Emotional/ Intellectual, Physical, Family, Social and Financial (found in chapter 4). As you listen to your LifeCreed daily, you bring your goals into your mind where you can begin creating the new mental models and habits necessary to make those goals a reality.

Here are just a few ways your LifeCreed will lead to the life you've always dreamed of:

Self-Talk: Over your lifetime the voice you hear the most is your own. This is the voice that is most familiar to you. It is also the voice that you consider to be the most credible—you believe your own voice more than anyone else's. What you say to yourself is so critical! Studies show that self-talk dramatically increases mental force and the activation of specific mental models in your brain. Every day people reinforce and perpetuate negative mental models and habits through negative self-talk.

Through your LifeCreed, you will use positive self-talk to generate amazing results in your life. Record your LifeCreed when you are feeling especially good about yourself and positive about life. These emotions will be reflected in your voice. Then in the future, if you're having a down day, you can listen to your LifeCreed in your positive, optimistic voice and get an instant pick-me-up. This powerful self-talk in your LifeCreed generates tremendous mental force that can be used toward the formation of new mental models and habits.

Expectation: Your LifeCreed is recorded in your own voice; it states each expectation or goal in the present tense—as if it is already coming to fruition—and states your motive and how you feel having attained your goal. These elements combined communicate a powerful expectation to your brain. In the proper setting, and with powerful meaning, your brain cannot distinguish between what is real and what is hoped for.

Over time, you build mental models that become dominant and your brain begins responding as if what you desire is already a reality. As you listen to your LifeCreed on a daily basis, many of your goals and dreams will begin to unfold right before your eyes. You get what you expect. You attract what you think about most.

In addition, you also state every goal or ideal in the first-person. This directs you to take responsibility for your own future. You should never force or rely on others to make your dreams come true. You need to direct your own life and strive to lead and influence others to achieve greatness in their lives.

Accelerated-Learning Music: Have you ever noticed how much more powerful a movie is if the soundtrack is well done? It seems to be a more emotional experience, and everything else about the movie seems more powerful. Think of **Accelerated-Learning Music** as the soundtrack to your LifeCreed. Music has the ability to connect to the emotional areas of our mind, and our LifeCreed is carried along.

You need to record your LifeCreed with specific Accelerated-Learning Music playing in the background. As reported in Ostrander and Schrader's book *Super Learning*, scientists in the former Soviet Bloc made the startling discovery that a certain kind of music can put the brain into an accelerated-learning state. Since that time, extensive research has clearly shown that the larghetto or andante movements in Baroque concertos, a restful tempo of about sixty beats per minute, actually open up pathways and connections throughout the brain, accelerating the formation and expansion of mental models. Baroque composers typically scored this peaceful, soothing music for string instruments. Accelerated-Learning Music supercharges your Life-Creed and your results. You can visit my website at www.lifebal.net to get your own Accelerated-Learning Music performed by my gifted friend, Oneil Miner.

Visualization: As you listen to your LifeCreed, images of your ideal self and life will appear on the stage of your mind—as if it's already a reality. Because your LifeCreed is in your own voice, contains elements of powerful meaning, and is accompanied by Accelerated-Learning Music, you don't have to consciously force this visualization—it comes naturally into your mind. It's like seeing a movie of your ideal future, which triggers powerful feelings and emotions. These previews of your ideal future provide yet another source for building desired mental models and generating the mental force to activate those mental models to fulfill all that is stated in your LifeCreed.

While listening to your LifeCreed, ideas, impressions, new goals, and desires will come into your mind. Keep a small tape recorder or pen and pad near so you can make note of these things. Later, you can Feelings Journal about them, and at your discretion, add them to your LifeCreed.

New Mental Models: With all of the components of your LifeCreed combined, you will have one of the most powerful life-changing tools at the push of a button everyday. As you listen to your LifeCreed, you form new mental models with powerful meaning. After a short period of time, these will begin overriding and replacing old mental models. You will notice changes in your thinking, attitudes, emotions, and outlook on life—you will think differently and attract what you think about. Relationships will improve, stress will diminish, and your success will increase.

As you develop new mental models, your physiology will begin to change. In situations where you were normally stressed, you are calmer; where you have felt anger, you feel more peaceful; where there has been fear, you move forward with more confidence. You are teaching your brain to respond in positive, healthy, and productive ways.

Daily Practice and Repetition: Some weaknesses of virtually every self-improvement system lies in the fact that they are too tedious, complex, or ambiguous to create the consistent practice and repetition required over time. Most people give up and return to their old ways before new mental models and new habits can be formed. One of the reasons the LifeCreed produces such amazing results—when so many other programs fail—is that it's easy to implement on a daily basis. You simply turn on your tape player or insert your CD and start listening. These listening sessions, best done when you are doing something else like driving, exercising, or walking, comprise the consistent repetition that is so critical to creating new habits and lasting success. In your LifeCreed, you have a dynamically evolving lifetime vehicle to which you can attach any new insights, ideas, or goals and make them a permanent part of your life. I have listened to or read my LifeCreed an average of five times a week for almost forty years. Every year I update and record it again.

Key Concept ⬦⊸ ───────────────────

Just as advertisers design commercials to activate powerful mental models and emotions in your brain, causing you to respond in a specific way, your LifeCreed will likewise be your own custom "advertisement" in moving you toward the future you desire.

───────────

Creating Your First LifeCreed

The idea for the LifeCreed was an extension of conversations I had with Napoleon Hill. In his interviews with over five hundred of Carnegie's friends, he found they all had seventeen areas of focus they used in varying degrees. But the number one tool they all had was a Definite Major Purpose (DMP). This DMP identified what they were trying to accomplish with their life committed to paper. They had written it down. As I learned more about how people respond to emotional motives, I developed this into the LifeCreed.

The LifeCreed is the most exciting personal growth tool ever developed. Beginning with just a few specific goals, your LifeCreed will grow to encompass all of your Six Key Relationships. Feelings Journaling will help identify your goals or the specific details of your ideal self and life. Turning your goals and ideals into **LifeCreed Statements** is the first step in turning the picture of who you want to become into the reality of who you are.

Don't get bogged down trying to make your LifeCreed perfect the first time. Keep in mind two very important points as you begin the creation process for your initial LifeCreed:

1. This is only the beginning. The purpose of your LifeCreed is to act as a catalyst and a source of inspiration. As you listen to your Life-Creed daily and write in your Feelings Journal, a flood of ideas, realizations, and desired goals will come into your mind. After two or three weeks, you will be ready to revise your initial LifeCreed by adding some of this new information. Remember, your LifeCreed is not static; you don't create it once and that's it. Your LifeCreed is an ever-evolving document. As you discover more about who you truly are and the life you really want, you will continue adding these discoveries to your LifeCreed for a lifetime of increasing success, happiness, and fulfillment. Your initial LifeCreed is only the beginning of a lifelong refining process.

2. Get the discovery process moving. Remember the old steam locomotives you've seen in western movies? From a dead stop, the locomotive strains and groans; the first few chugs turn the wheels, but they slip on the hard steel tracks. With the next few chugs the wheels gain some traction, and the train slowly creeps forward, gradually picking up speed until it's sailing smoothly down the tracks.

The key to discovering and attaining your ideal self and life is to start the journey—get the train moving. Create your initial LifeCreed as quickly as possible and start using it to generate amazing results in your brain and your life. Don't worry that it isn't good enough; you'll have lots of opportunities to improve it in the future. Just get the train moving!

STEP 1: ANSWERING THE LIFECREED QUESTIONS

The first step in creating your LifeCreed is to begin the process of discovery, of uncovering the hopes, dreams, gifts, and talents that are the real you—the picture that you carry in your heart. You already have begun this process by writing daily in your Feelings Journal. Answering the **LifeCreed Questions** will greatly help you expand this process.

Keep in mind that because of expectations or limitations placed on you by others, or simply as a by-product of your own doubts, fears, or negative thoughts, some aspects of your true identity may have lain dormant or been repressed for many years. Some of my clients have expressed a feeling of frustration in their first attempt at answering the questions: "I feel like two people: one part of me wants to open up while the other is preventing it." This is a case of the *true identity* fighting to be recognized while the *false identity* wants to remain as is, in its safe little comfort zone. After years of listening to their own self-talk or the comments of others, many clients have trouble getting in touch with their true self and potential, to think and dream big, and to think in terms of their ideal. It's time for you to begin the process of discovering and freeing your true identity and get in touch with your ideal self and life by creating new positive mental models to guide your life. A client recently wrote me:

I began Feelings Journaling several months ago, and had some difficulty moving on to the LifeCreed. As I began the process, I kept stumbling with the concept of my "ideal self." I didn't think I had one. So many years of living my life to please others, and feeling insecure and doubtful about my own abilities, made it hard for me to imagine anything for myself. You asked me what was exciting to me, and so I began to take some time in Journaling to write about it. I couldn't believe what came out. I have dreams and hopes for myself and my family that are still exciting when I read them today. These became the focal point of my first LifeCreed. It was only a few statements, but they mattered very much to me. Every time I listen to my LifeCreed I hear them again, and the same excitement is there.

LifeCreed Questions

In the next few pages are lists of questions that have proven very effective in helping people tap into their true identity and, in this mind set, discover their vision of their ideal self and life. In the process you may feel inward pressure to answer the questions in a certain way— how you should feel or ought to feel, which is derived over the years from parents, spouses, bosses, society, or self-talk. Temporarily place these feelings and responses in the "false identity category" and allow yourself the complete freedom to express your true identity.

NOTE: *The LifeCreed questions are separated into seven sections to provide simplicity and structure in exploring the various elements of your relationships, ideal self, and ideal life. As you begin to put together your initial Life-Creed, please understand it is not intended to be created in sections. Your LifeCreed content may be stated in whatever order or placement that makes sense to you.*

You don't have to answer every question. They are presented only as a catalyst to help you unlock your true identity, goals, dreams, and talents. As you review the questions, answer only those that provoke a thought you would like to explore or that trigger powerful feelings. If other ideas and feelings come to you in the process, write them down as well. Use a separate piece of paper for each section. As you answer the questions, write whatever comes into your mind. Be completely truthful and honest, and even negative if necessary. Just get everything you're thinking and feeling down on paper. In essence, this is a Feelings Journaling exercise. If something doesn't come to you in an area, skip it. Don't let it hold you up. You don't have to address each area immediately. You may find that these areas provide a starting point for Feelings Journaling in the future. But don't let them bog you down now. It's important to get the most immediate areas down now and begin the process.

Some questions pertain to your future goals. Answer these questions according to the *ideal* you would like, not what you perceive as realistic or where you are today. Remember, the purpose of the Life-Creed questions is to begin the process of discovering your true identity and your vision of your ideal self and life. Write as freely and openly as you can. Don't worry about structure, grammar, or spelling. When you are finished, you will go back and convert your entries into LifeCreed Statements. At this point, your only aim is to get your thoughts and feelings on paper or on your computer screen. Using the Six Key Relationships as general categories will get you started.

Spiritual: My relationship with my Creator
- Is there anything I can do to make my life more spiritual? If so, why do I want to be more spiritual?
- Do I honestly want to become more religious? In what way(s)? Why?
- Should I spend more time reading or listening to religious or spiritual literature? Like what? What would this do for me?
- Am I tolerant of others' beliefs? What concerns do I have about my attitude in this area?
- What blessings in life am I most grateful for? Why?
- What kinds of people or events make my inner spirit come alive? Why?

Emotional/Intellectual: My relationship with myself
- What mental strengths would I like to foster in myself? Why?
- What intellectual strengths would I like to nourish? Why?
- What can I do to cultivate a better self-image?
- What behaviors or thoughts would I like to change? If these were changed, how would my life be different?
- What books would I like to read? Why?
- What special knowledge or educational degrees would I like to obtain? Why?
- What are some other personal qualities I would like to promote in myself? Why do I believe these are important?

Health/Fitness: My relationship with my body
- How do I feel about the way I look? Why do I feel this way?
- Looking at my physical appearance, the aspects I like most or am most proud of include _____. Why?
- The aspects I like least or am least proud of include _____. Why?
- What are my ideal weight and measurements? Why do I believe these are ideal?
- What elements of an exercise program would I like to include in my daily/weekly routine? (Give details.)
- What part of my diet would I like to change? Why?

Family: My relationship with my spouse and children

- What can I do to be a better spouse? How would this improve my marriage?
- I can show my spouse I love him/her by _____. I can do this daily by _____.
- I can show my spouse I want to improve our marriage by _____.
- What positive qualities in my spouse do I want to reinforce?
- How would having a date night with my spouse each week improve my marriage?
- How can I show my spouse how I truly feel?
- I show my spouse I put him or her first, by _____.
- I express approval to my spouse by _____.
- What things about my family am I proud of? Why do these things make me proud?
- What in my family life would I like to change? If this were changed, how would my family life be different?
- How can I encourage more love in my family?
- How much quality time do I spend with my family? How much time, quality and quantity, would I like to spend? What would I do with this time?
- How can I spend twenty minutes a week with each one of my kids?
- I show affection and attention to each family member by _____.
- I can openly and honestly communicate with each family member without being defensive by _____.
- My loved ones can tell me how they feel without fear because I _____.
- I sometimes make my family feel like I put my work first when I _____.
- I can show my family they are more important to me than work by _____.

Social: My relationship with others
- How do I feel when I'm around other people? Why?
- How would I like others to treat me differently? Why?
- What can I do to be more open and free with others?
- What dreams of leadership do I have? Why?
- What can I do to be a better listener? How would this improve my social life?
- Whom do I offend, and why?

- What can I do to find the courage to open up and ask trusted friends for advice on how I can be better?

Financial: My relationship with money and my career
- If I could have the ideal job, what would it be? Why would this be ideal?
- What excites me the most about my present job? Why is this exciting?
- What things about my work would I like to change? Why?
- Do I work too many hours? Why do I do this?
- What one thing could I do to increase my effectiveness at work? How, specifically, would this increase my effectiveness?
- How much money would I like to earn each year? What would I do with the extra money? Why am I not making this much now?

General: My relationship to my overall life
- Who am I? (This question can stimulate a flood of thoughts.)
- My role in life is to _____. Why do I feel this is my role?
- I would like to be recognized for _____. Why?
- What are my greatest talents, skills, or gifts?
- My greatest frustrations about me are _____. Why are these things frustrating?
- The habits I would most like to get rid of include _____. How would my life be better if these habits were eliminated?
- The habits I would most like to acquire include _____. How would my life be better if I fostered these habits?
- If I had just won the lottery and money was no longer a concern, what would I do with my time? Why would I spend my time this way?
- The one thing I have always wanted to do is _____. Why?
- Where would I like to travel? What would I do once I got there?
- Ultimately, who do I want to be? Why?

STEP 2: CREATE YOUR LIFECREED CONTENT

The next step is to create the initial content for your LifeCreed by converting your answers to the questions in step 1 to **LifeCreed Statements**.

You can easily construct a LifeCreed Statement utilizing Five Building Steps:

First: Identify Your Goal

Review your answers to the LifeCreed questions. Underline any sentences or phrases that contain a goal you want to achieve.

For example, one of the questions under the Family section states: I can show my spouse I want to improve our marriage by _____.

Let's assume that you answered the question as follows: *I can show my spouse I want to improve our marriage by spending more time with her.*

You underline your goal: *I can show my spouse I want to improve our marriage by* spending more time with her.

Second: State Your Goal Clearly

Is your goal clear and defined? If a complete stranger were reading your goal, would they know exactly what you mean?

Your brain will not lock onto a goal that is too general in nature. You need to be as clear and specific as possible. As you review the goal you have underlined, ask yourself, "What do I mean by that?" Keep asking this question and expanding your goal until you can go no further. Using the previous example of *I can show my spouse I want to improve our marriage by spending more time with her,* your goals could be more specific and clearly defined as follows:

I show my spouse I am committed to improve our marriage by taking her on a date night every Friday night and asking her the Big Question.

Third: Write in the First Person

Always state your LifeCreed goals in terms of what *you* can do.

Your LifeCreed is your own personal map to the ideal self and ideal life you desire. It is for your eyes and ears only, so there is no reason for it to contain instructions for anyone else. In addition, you cannot control the actions of others or rely on them to make your goals and ideals a reality. Search through your LifeCreed Statements where you attempt to control or direct the actions of others. Change these to the first-person and adjust the wording so that it indicates what "I can do."

For example, "If only she would . . ." could be changed to "I create the environment where she can . . ." "My boss needs to . . ." can be amended to read, "I create the environment where my boss can . . ."

Fourth: Write in the Present Tense

State your goal as if you have already attained it.

In chapter 2, you learned about the power of the Byte and the brain-science principle that states: When the emotion or meaning of a mental model is powerful, your brain does not distinguish between what is real and what is imagined—it simply takes action!

One of the most effective ways to create powerful meaning in your brain is to express an expectation—to state something as if it is already a reality. As your brain forms new mental models based on your expectations, you will find your expectations become *self-fulfilling prophecies*.

In your LifeCreed Statements, express all of your goals in the *present tense*. Instead of "I hope," "I wish," "I will," or "I want," use phrases like, "I am," "I do," "I deserve," and "I am becoming." For more examples of present-tense statements, please see Appendix A.

Fifth: Check for Negative Statements

Change any negative statements to the positive.

Many traditional self-improvement and therapy programs teach individuals to break negative habits by focusing on avoiding the negative consequences. That is, when you get the urge to act out a particular behavior, you simply remind yourself of all the pain it will cause you, and this motivates you to avoid it. While this works for some people, it is ineffective for many. Think of the millions who smoke, all the while knowing it's killing them. Brain science clearly shows that we are far more motivated by a positive reward or outcome than avoiding a negative one.

As you create your LifeCreed Statements, be aware of any phrases that are the least bit negative, such as: "I never want to," "I don't," or "I shouldn't." Replace them with a positive: "I always," "I do," or "I am committed to." Follow the positive phrase with a statement of what you are doing to create a positive outcome—be proactive! Remember, as you listen to your recorded LifeCreed, your brain will begin responding and your positives will become a reality.

Use the Five Building Steps to create and then continually add to and revise your dynamic, ever-evolving LifeCreed. This simple yet powerful tool will become the vehicle to which you can attach and achieve any goal you set for yourself.

Add a Motive and a Hook

Once you have finished converting all of your LifeCreed questions responses to LifeCreed Statements, review the document and select the *top three goals* you really want to focus on and give special attention to. In order to supercharge these goals and speed you on your way to their realization, you should attach a **motive** and a **hook** to each one.

Motive: As I stated in chapter 1, "The single most important factor in changing mental models is your motive." The only way to override your brain's resistance to change and tear down the twenty-foot security fence around your existing habits is to clearly identify, put in writing, and continually review your why.

Brain science is proving what we have sensed all along—the catalyst, the fuel, the key to change is not in your head, it is in your heart. Brain scans clearly show that when you focus on a powerful motive (connect to the feelings and emotions of your heart), a mental force is generated that literally changes the physical structure of your brain. If you want to change your dominant mental models, you must learn how to tap the power of your heart, the power of motive.

Take each of the three goals you have selected for major focus and add a written motive. How?

> **1. Clearly and simply state** in writing why you want to achieve it—what is your motive?

> **2. Clearly visualize yourself** in the future already in possession of the goal and briefly describe how you feel having attained it. How is your life better? Describe how proud specific people are of you and how they respond to you. Be descriptive, precise, and detailed. Create as much positive and powerful emotion as possible. Be careful not to state "I will feel . . ." or "When I have it I feel . . ." See yourself already having achieved it and state how you feel as a result. Only by stating the feeling in the present tense can you produce the full power of meaning.

Hook: As you review the goal you have selected, ask yourself, "How can I add more detail regarding the steps and process I will follow to achieve this goal?" and "How can I be more precise with dates, days, or times relating to these action steps?"

A **hook** is the *how, where,* and *when* of a specific goal. If you have a powerful motive to go from Los Angeles to New York City, but your goal simply states, "I get on the freeway and head east," it doesn't matter how strong your desire is, you won't get there. So while the goal and your motive are incredibly important, the hook—the how, where, and when you will do the things you've identified—is essential. So a goal to get from Los Angeles to New York could have the hook: "To get to New York, I take US 101 North; I leave today at 4:00 p.m. in my car."

BEFORE AND AFTER

Here are some examples of LifeCreed Statements before and after a Motive and Hook have been added:

Goal with *No* Motive and Hook: I tell my wife I love her.

Goal with Motive and Hook added: Because I have a strong desire to be closer with Susan and improve my marriage, each weekday at 5:30, when I arrive home from work, the first thing I do is find Susan, take her in my arms (hook), look into her eyes (hook) and say, "I love you" (hook). The way her face lights up and the warm feeling I get are wonderful (motive). This simple daily act is bringing us closer together (motive) as husband and wife. I am highly motivated to keep doing it from now on!

Goal with *No* Motive and Hook: I am committed to losing weight.

Goal with Motive and Hook added: I am determined to be lean and have a body I am proud of (motive). By June 1, I have lost thirty pounds (hook). I have achieved this amazing goal by exercising from 7:00–8:00 a.m. Monday through Friday (hook); drinking at least eight glasses of water every day (hook); and not eating after 7:00 p.m. at night (hook). Having lost thirty pounds I feel incredible (motive)! I feel lean and light on my feet (motive). My new clothes look incredible on me (motive)! When I look in the mirror I think to myself 'You look fabulous!' (motive). My friends and family keep commenting on how great I look and asking "How did you do it?" (motive). This is the new me and will be for the rest of my life (goal)—I love it!

Attach a motive and hook to your top three goals and watch their realization unfold before your eyes! As you achieve each goal, choose the next most important one in your LifeCreed and add a motive and hook to it. You should keep the number of goals in your LifeCreed with motive and hooks to three or four.

Additional Resource: In Appendix B are some examples of LifeCreed Statements with Motive and Hook added to the goal. Feel free to use these to help you get started in the process.

Additional Insight

As you have learned repeatedly throughout this book, motive is essential to changing your mental models and achieving your desire goals and dreams. While I have recommended that you begin by attaching a motive to your top three goals, this is only a starting place. With practice you will become more skilled at discovering and expressing your motives in writing. In future versions of your LifeCreed, you can add motives to many of your goals. As listen to your LifeCreed daily, these motives will only increase the rate at which you achieve your goals.

While adding motive to many of your goals, I do recommend that you limit hooks to only three or four goals at a time. Too many hooks in your calendar can become overwhelming—your brain can glaze over and ignore all of the to-dos in your schedule. Keeping the tasks to a manageable few at a time will greatly increase your success. Once achieved, you can add new hooks to replace the old ones—in this way *success breeds success* as you build one achievement upon another. While having a few hooks in your daily schedule may not appear as impressive, this approach is far superior to having a long list of commitments that you never get to.

As I have worked with my clients, there were eight areas that most of my clients had a desire to focus on. The following are the goal, motive, and hook for each of these areas. Feel free to use a few of them that cover areas you are interested in.

1. Being a Better Listener: I am a genuinely interested, active listener. I look people in the eye with my hands empty and with only what they are saying on my mind. I ask thoughtful questions that help others share the feelings they want to express. I always listen one minute before speaking, so they can know that I care.

2. Remembering People's Names: I have a great memory of names. When I first meet someone I use their name three times in our conversation. When I want to recall a name I say,

"What is that person's name?" It will come to me in a moment. I give people a reason to be in awe of this ability.

3. Praying: I love discussing my life with God and dedicate five or ten minutes every morning and evening for this, always with the goal of spending more time to develop our relationship to a deeper, more spiritual level. I am always seeking for what God would have me know and do to serve him better.

4. Reading Inspirational Material: I am always eager to study scriptures and other thought-provoking material, which prepares me to connect with my infinite intelligence. Every day at 7:00 a.m., for fifteen minutes, I read and seek to develop those habits that will help me identify and fulfill my purpose.

5. Controlling Temper: I am in total control of my voice and temper, always thinking before I speak, so that my spouse, children, neighbors, and co-workers can respect me for the self-control I demonstrate.

6. Stop Worrying: I expend energy on that which I can do something about, and let go or that which is not within my control.

7. Letting Others Get to Me: I allow all people their weaknesses. I look for a good point in everyone I meet and mention it each time it is appropriate.

8. Reading Books Regularly: I have prioritized the top five (or ten) books on my reading list. I read the top book on my list every Thursday and Saturday evenings from 8:00–10:00 p.m. I do this because it makes me feel _____.

Additional LifeCreed Content

In addition to your LifeCreed question responses, there are some optional things you can add to your LifeCreed. Consider the following:

1. LifeBalance Tools: Simple LifeBalance Tools have been tested and proven to bring success and fulfillment in every area of life. These tools include Feelings Journaling, the Byte, the Daily Self-Care Routine, Date Night, Kid's Day, and many others. In the busyness of your daily schedule, obligations, and distractions, one of the greatest challenges you will face is remembering and being motivated to consistently implement these tools in your daily life. An easy and highly effective way to do this is through your LifeCreed. Apply the Five Building Steps to create goals to daily use the LifeBalance Tools mentioned above and then record these as part of your LifeCreed. If any of these are one of the three or four goals you wish to give special focus on, be sure to attach a motive and a hook.

2. Be Grateful for Unique Gifts and Talents: Too often in our hectic lives we don't stop to reflect on the things we're really good at—our own unique gifts and talents. You may have had a much better connection with these gifts and talents when you were a child. Then as a result of career counseling, college majors, the pressures and expectations of others, or just getting into daily routine and the grind of life, you likely lost track of these things or buried them completely.

What are you great at? What unique gifts and talents has your Creator endowed you with? What are some blessings in your life that you are grateful for? You may have difficulty identifying some of these things yourself. Perhaps you should ask your mother, your spouse, or a close friend to help you. Adding a brief description of a few of your greatest gifts and talents to your LifeCreed, then listening to your own voice reminding you of them will generate a powerful response in your brain and in your life. If you don't feel comfortable asking anyone else, just imagine what positive things they would say about you if you did ask them. If you're religious, think about the positive things your Creator would have to say about you.

State each gift or talent briefly, simply, and in first-person present tense. Place these in your LifeCreed wherever you feel appropriate. Some examples are:
- I am a great listener.
- I have a unique ability to lift the spirit of everyone I meet.
- I am extremely creative and artistic.
- I have the gift of great faith.
- I have tremendous empathy for others.
- I'm really good with my hands and fixing things.
- I'm really smart with electronics.

3. Slogans, Quotes, and Lyrics: Many of my clients have inserted slogans, quotes, song lyrics, and so forth that they personally find inspirational or motivational. These can come from a variety of sources:

scripture, famous people, novels, self-help titles, songs, or movies. One client is a big fan of *The Lord of the Ring* movies. In one scene, Gandalf the wizard is perched on a narrow rock bridge spanning a deep chasm. Facing off with a huge fiery beast, he slams his staff into the rock and boldly shouts, "You shall not pass!" My client has inserted this into a section of his LifeCreed where he talks about achieving a significant goal in the face of staggering obstacles. Imagine the mental models this activates and the meaning it has as he recalls that movie scene and imagines himself as Gandalf the fearless wizard!

Consider all the time and expense that goes into creating a powerful scene like this in a movie. Then think about how it makes you feel. Think about hearing an old song you heard first in high school or on your first date with your sweetheart. Those emotions and feelings are available for you; you just need to connect them to the areas of your LifeCreed that need that extra emotional punch. While the mental model you create for a new goal may seem small to begin with, connecting it to a powerfully emotional mental model that already exists for you is the ultimate shortcut!

Add your favorites to your LifeCreed and keep adding as you find more—especially those that elicit deep feelings, emotions, or meaning within you. My parents used an axiom that became one of my favorites: Any job worth doing is worth doing well. Another favorite was quoted to me by Napoleon Hill: Every adversity and every defeat carries with it the seed of an equivalent or greater benefit, if you look for it.

4. Special Moments: Take time to remember those experiences in your life when you were deeply moved or greatly inspired, when your perspective was incredibly clear, when you perceived truth, when you felt the presence of God, and when you were incredibly motivated, positive, and optimistic. These experiences can come to you while watching a movie, reading a book, listening to music, or attending a speech or seminar. They can come during a special moment with spouse, children, or friends, or while meditating, praying, or attending a religious service. These powerful moments can bring you to tears, raise your spirits to soaring heights, and fill you with resolve and a commitment to improve or take action.

Unfortunately, these moments are brief and intermittent. Before you know it, the reality and immediacy of life crowds back in and the moment passes. But what if you could forever capture the magic and power of those moments? What if you could experience them over and over again? What if you could call on them to lift and strengthen you in times of trial and despair? You can.

Carry a small notebook or mini-digital recorder with you in your pocket at all times. This will become your **LifeCreed Ideas Notebook**. When you experience one of these inspiring, life-changing events, describe in detail what you saw, read, or heard. Describe your insights, feelings, and why it touched you so powerfully. Record how you can use the information and what goals, commitments, and resolutions it inspires you to make. Brief details can be recorded in your notebook, or recorder, and then expanded in your Feelings Journal. Then, take this information and integrate it into your LifeCreed.

Every time you listen to your LifeCreed, you can relive these powerful experiences and be uplifted anew. Never allow the power of these sacred moments to be lost again. When they break through the surface into your conscious mind, capture them in your notebook or pocket recorder, and then forever in your Feelings Journal and LifeCreed. It is easy to be satisfied to have these experiences just be fleeting moments. But with the LifeBalance Tools they will be lasting and treasured experiences.

Review Sample LifeCreeds

In building your first LifeCreed, it can be very helpful to review the LifeCreeds of others for ideas and formatting guidance.

While reviewing the LifeCreeds of others can be insightful, there is no point in simply copying them verbatim. Your LifeCreed is unique to you. This is precisely why you *should not* review the Sample Life-Creeds section until after you have answered the LifeCreed questions and done your best to build your own LifeCreed. Use the sample Life-Creeds as a tool to help you expand and refine your own LifeCreed.

NOTE: *These sample LifeCreeds were never written for anyone else to see or hear let alone be published. (I did get my clients' permission, of course.) The samples are my clients' innermost thoughts. Look for sentences you agree with and ignore those that are not the way you think or speak.*

Important: Do not get bogged down in your review of the sample LifeCreeds. Avoid the temptation to compare your LifeCreed to others. Creating a LifeCreed is not a writing contest to see who can produce the most flowery, eloquent statements or the most elaborate or complete

LifeCreed. Your LifeCreed is for you and you alone. No one else should ever be allowed to read it. It is the unique expression of your deepest feelings, dreams, and ideals.

As you review the sample LifeCreeds, don't allow yourself to be sidetracked by feeling "mine isn't good enough—I need to work on it before I can record it." Many clients have spent months or even years working on their initial LifeCreed, trying to make it better or perfect before they record it. This violates the very purpose of the LifeCreed. Your LifeCreed is a tool of discovery. As you listen to it each day, you will uncover new insights, ideas, feelings, dreams, gifts, talents, and aspirations. Add these to your ever-evolving LifeCreed. Consider the following experience of one of my clients:

After weeks of creating, revising, starting over, and over again, I still didn't have a LifeCreed I liked. My wife had picked up some of the materials I received from you and got very excited. She started Journaling and working on her LifeCreed. Within a week she had recorded hers! This motivated me to get with it. I sat down and gave it my best shot. I recorded it the next day. I've been listening to it for several weeks and can already see the areas I want to improve. I have to thank you and my wife for the motivation to get something recorded and not wait for it to be perfect.

After awhile, some parts of your initial LifeCreed might give you **Creed Nausea**—"If I have to listen to that one more time I think I'll throw up!" When this happens, don't stop listening to your LifeCreed. Simply make a note to change it when you next make revisions. It takes time to filter all the boring parts out of your LifeCreed that sounded so good when you included them. Remember, this process is allowing you to move to higher levels of thought, attitude, and action. So be patient; keep listening and keep Feelings Journaling. When in fact you do get to the point that you stop listening, then it's time to rewrite.

Trying to create the perfect LifeCreed is an illusion. You will never do it—it will simply continue to expand and evolve as you do. It is a work in progress, a continuing journey of discovery and achievement that hopefully will never end.

Glean a few ideas from the sample LifeCreeds, make some modifications to your own accordingly, then move on as quickly as possible to the recording of your LifeCreed. The sooner you are listening to your LifeCreed every day, the sooner you will begin seeing the realization of your ideal self and your ideal life.

Put Together Your First LifeCreed

You now have everything you need to assemble the content for your first complete LifeCreed. Do the following:

1. Answer the LifeCreed Questions as instructed in this chapter.

2. Use the Five Building Steps to create your initial LifeCreed Statements.

3. Attach a Motive and Hook to three or four goals you want to focus on.

4. Review the categories of Additional LifeCreed Content and add to your LifeCreed as you deem appropriate.

5. Review the Sample LifeCreeds section in Appendix B to obtain ideas for content for your LifeCreed.

6. Put all of the above in writing before proceeding to the next section.

Remember, initially your LifeCreed is just a compilation of the various thoughts and ideas you have. It will grow and become more detailed and specific as you listen to it over time.

Please go to Appendix B and review the Sample LifeCreeds section.

STEP 3: RECORD YOUR LIFECREED

You are now ready to complete and record your LifeCreed!

Studies show that your self-talk dramatically increases the meaning and credibility of any information as it enters your brain. You will use the powerful brain science of self-talk to your advantage by recording your LifeCreed in your own voice.

Many find the first recording of their LifeCreed a somewhat awkward experience. The following suggestions come from years of experience with my clients. These ten tips will help you through your first experience.

1. Use your LifeCreed question responses. Your recording will come directly from the responses to LifeCreed questions, additional ideas, or client samples you have converted into your own LifeCreed Statements. Remember, don't worry about the order. Simply put all of your LifeCreed Statements and content together in whatever way feels right to you.

2. Choose the right setting. It can be quite a challenge to find a quiet, private place to record your LifeCreed—phones ring, family members interrupt, and you fear someone might overhear you. Ideally, you want to avoid all distractions. One secluded place to record your LifeCreed is in your car. It's quiet, private, and usually has a built-in stereo system to play the accelerated-learning background music. Avoid places where passing cars will be disruptive. Your garage or a secluded parking spot can work really well. If recording in your home or office, you may want to put up a "Do Not Disturb" sign on the door.

Whatever you do, choose the location that would make it easiest for you to make the recording without interruption. Be sure to tell your spouse what you're going to do. (I had one client who went out to the garage, closed the garage door, and got in his car. His wife thought for a moment he was trying to do himself in!)

3. Gather equipment and materials. Make certain you have everything assembled that you need to record your LifeCreed. Study out the operation of the equipment, check for fresh batteries, and make sure your cassette tape is blank.

Option 1: Recording in the car
    Tape recorder, battery operated
    CD player in car
    Blank audiocassette tape
    CD with Accelerated-Learning Music
    LifeCreed Statements and content

Option 2: Recording in the home or office
    Tape recorder
    CD player
    Blank audiocassette tape
    CD with Accelerated-Learning Music
    LifeCreed Statements and content
    "Do Not Disturb" sign

4. Make sure you're upbeat and positive. When you record your Life-Creed, make certain you're in a state of mind where you're feeling positive and enthusiastic. This attitude will be reflected in your voice and communicated to every cell in your body each time you listen to your LifeCreed. If you're having difficulty getting into this frame of mind, select a LifeCreed Statement and read it. Visualize how it will feel to be that person, accomplish that goal, or to be in that situation. Take whatever time you need to feel the excitement again. Then you'll be ready.

In the future, if you are feeling negative or depressed, play your LifeCreed. Hearing your positive voice will give you a lift. Never underestimate the power of self-talk—positive or negative self-talk. When you find your self-talk is down and negative, turn on your LifeCreed recording and let your positive self-talk dispel the negative.

5. Rehearse beforehand. Before you start recording, take a minute or two to rehearse. Read aloud from your LifeCreed Statement pages with the music playing in the background. Become familiar with what is there and comfortable with hearing yourself read it out loud.

6. Choose your music. As we have already discussed, certain kinds of music can put the brain into an accelerated-learning state. Larghetto or andante movements in Baroque concertos open up pathways and connections throughout the brain, intensifying the formation and expansion of mental models. Baroque composers typically scored this peaceful, soothing music for string instruments. The LifeBalance Institute website contains a list of additional composers and specific arrangements that are appropriate.

NOTE: *People invariably ask, "Can I substitute the classical CDs or tapes with some of my favorite tunes?" The answer is no. The choice of music has nothing to do with personal taste or entertainment value. Accelerated-Learning Music is used to evoke a specific psycho-physical state of relaxed concentration in the brain, allowing for the unrestricted absorption of information.*

7. Adjust the volume. You'll need to experiment a little to find the proper balance between the volume of the music and your voice. After a minute or two of recording, you will notice on playback that, compared to the volume of your voice, the background music from your stereo is generally softer than you thought. To balance it out, turn the volume of the music up so it is just a bit louder than that of your own voice. At first, speaking over the volume of the music will be a bit awkward. Experiment with different volumes until you get it right. When the proper recording balance is achieved, you should hear your own voice just above the background music.

8. Get accustomed to the sound of your voice. On first hearing the recording of their LifeCreed in their own voice, many people complain,

"Does my voice really sound like that?" or "It sounds like I'm giving a funeral sermon." Don't worry about how the initial recording sounds. Remember, your LifeCreed is always evolving. Hopefully, you will modify and re-record your LifeCreed many times. As the months and years go by, you will come to appreciate and even enjoy hearing your own voice. You will become more comfortable and polished each time you make a new recording. Remember, your LifeCreed is for your ears only, so you needn't be self-conscious or worry what others will think when you record it. Remember, when Creed Nausea hits, you need to rework and re-record, or else end up not finding the time to listen to it because it's boring or irritating.

NOTE: *You may have the inclination to keep re-recording until you get every-thing perfect—DON'T! Practice a few times, then make the recording, complete with stutters, mispronounced words, and so forth. Just get it done so you can start listening to it and begin the process. Your LifeCreed is not for motivational hype—it is intended to open your mind and continually feed it specific informa-tion and positive instructions.*

9. Leave a four- to five-second gap. Your LifeCreed most often is divided into sections—a specific goal—also known as a LifeCreed Statement. After each complete LifeCreed Statement, leave a four- to five-second gap of silence before you proceed to the next section. This gap allows your brain to absorb the information before going on. As you listen daily to your LifeCreed, you will find during these periods of silence that you begin to visualize or see in your mind's eye the realiza-tion of your goal or ideal. During these moments, ideas and feelings will likely flood your mind. Make sure you have a tape recorder or pen and pad handy to jot down these impressions as they come.

10. Listen to your LifeCreed daily. Listen to your LifeCreed twice daily for three weeks. You don't need to listen to your entire LifeCreed at one time. Just start the tape up where you left off. Soon you will begin to develop Creed Nausea (If I listen to my Creed one more time, I'll throw up!). At this point you will be ready to make your first Life-Creed revision.

Important: Your LifeCreed Is for Your Eyes and Ears Only!
Your LifeCreed is all about you and the realization of your ideal self and life. If others were to read or listen to it, they might not understand.

With everything stated in first-person present tense, they could interpret your LifeCreed as arrogant or silly. Suppose, for example, you are working at controlling your temper, so you create language in your LifeCreed to that effect. You state, "I'm in complete control of my voice and temper. My wife and children are in awe at how cool and calm I am under pressure. I feel great knowing I'm in control."

Now imagine your spouse gets hold of your LifeCreed and reads this or hears you saying it on your LifeCreed recording. Later that day you lose your temper with one of your children, and your spouse eyes you with a look of smug reproach. It's like somebody just dropped some chewed gum in your soup—it ruins the whole thing! Your LifeCreed is for your eyes and ears only.

How Do I Coordinate My LifeCreed with My Calendar?

You may be wondering how dates and times in your LifeCreed are coordinated with your daily calendar. Once you complete your LifeCreed, review it for any dates and times that should be entered in your daily schedule. Put these in your day-planning system—PDA, day-planner, or computer.

Limit the number of date and time hooks in your LifeCreed—you don't want to overload your daily schedule with a multitude of entries. If there are too many it becomes overwhelming and your brain becomes desensitized to it.

For instance, one client scheduled out in minute detail many of the goals in his LifeCreed and entered them in his PDA with alarms attached. Multiple times each day his PDA alarm sounded off. After awhile he just started hitting the "cancel" button and pushing the scheduled activity back, putting it off until later. Too often he ended up forgetting about it all together.

So rather than trying to schedule everything, only schedule on your calendar appointments and reminders for the most important goals in your LifeCreed; no more than a few each day. This way you can focus on a few at a time and not be overwhelmed. Over time, as these activities become a habit, or you accomplish the goal, you can replace them with a few more important items on your daily calendar.

Keep in mind that although many of your goals and ideals may not be physically entered on your daily calendar, just Feelings Journaling and listening to your LifeCreed on a daily basis will cause your brain to naturally focus on your goals and bring them to fruition. Many of my clients are amazed when they realized they have achieved many of the goals in their LifeCreed without being aware they were being accomplished. Such is the power of the daily LifeCreed in the habit formation and goal achievement processes.

Your LifeCreed is an amazing document. It defines the picture of yourself that you will carry in your heart each day and is a constant reaffirmation of who you really are. It's the definition of yourself that everyone else will begin to see. As you begin the process of using your LifeCreed each day, hold on. You will be amazed at how your perspective of yourself and those around you begins to change. It's like getting new glasses. People will ask, "What's different about you?" Just smile and say, "Everything and nothing!"

Record Your LifeCreed NOW!

Following the instructions in this chapter, record your first Life-Creed and begin listening to it twice daily for the next three weeks.

NOTE: *Do not procrastinate the recording of your LifeCreed because you want it to be perfect. Just get the first recording done as quickly as possible so you can begin listening to it and receiving the amazing benefits. After three weeks you can make all of the corrections you desire and then re-record your LifeCreed.*

Your Ever-Evolving LifeCreed

Is it true that you can't teach old dogs new tricks? Many old dogs have tried the LifeBalance System—many who really doubted their ability to make a significant and lasting change in their lives. Many had tried a multitude of self-improvement programs, with minimal success and much frustration. But with the LifeBalance System they achieved remarkable results.

The reason most people don't succeed in making the changes they desire is they lack a clear, strong motive and the understanding of a simple, practical daily system with the necessary tools to make needed changes in their lives. The LifeCreed is a simple yet powerful tool you can use every day for the rest of your life. Each time you want to change a specific habit, achieve a certain goal, or progress to a new level, integrate this desire into your Feelings Journal and LifeCreed, and it will become a reality.

Can a person really, truly, permanently change? Yes—in wonderful and amazing ways! With your LifeCreed, your upward spiraling evolution will never end. You can begin this evolutionary process with the first revision of your LifeCreed.

Revising Your LifeCreed

After approximately three weeks of listening to your initial Life-Creed recording, Creed Nausea will start to set in with certain parts of your LifeCreed, and you will be ready to revise it. Follow these guidelines:

1. Read and Listen: Sit down with a written copy of your LifeCreed and follow along as you listen to your LifeCreed recording. It's very important that you listen and read at the same time. Do not review your written LifeCreed without simultaneously listening to the recording. This will give you the best feedback regarding which parts you want to change.

2. Edit as You Go: Draw lines through the parts that have become irritating, boring, or that you want to eliminate. Circle those you want to revise or expand. Make notes in the margins, indicating what revisions or additions you have in mind.

3. Listen for Voice Revisions: Make note of places where your voice sounds monotone or tedious, where you could add more inflection, enthusiasm, speed up, or pause.

4. Review Your LifeCreed Ideas Notebook: This is the notebook you've been keeping with ideas for your LifeCreed revisions. Daily, as you listen to your LifeCreed and keep your Feelings Journal, ideas for additions to your LifeCreed will come to you. In addition, you will have a Special Moment; use your LifeCreed Ideas Notebook for recording these ideas. Add these ideas to the appropriate places on the written copy of your LifeCreed. Remember—don't worry about dividing your new ideas and revisions into sections like family, financial, physical, and so forth. Place new additions in various locations throughout your LifeCreed, depending on what makes the most sense and feels good to you, and what will create the most powerful meaning and motive. For example, statements about God, your spouse, or your children may be placed in various sections of your Creed because they are an integral part of many areas of your life.

5. Jot Down Self-Improvement Ideas: Over the years you've probably read a number of self-improvement books or attended seminars and gleaned some great ideas. At the time you probably thought, "I'd really like to implement that in my life." The same thing may happen to you when you listen to religious ministers or leaders, listen to good programs on the radio, or watch uplifting TV programs. The moment you come across these ideas, write them down in your LifeCreed Ideas Notebook, and why they are important to you so you can include them in the next revision of your LifeCreed. Once in your LifeCreed, you will start living them—guaranteed!

6. Borrow Ideas from Others: Review the sample LifeCreeds of my clients in Appendix B to get additional ideas and insights for refining your LifeCreed. Feel free to borrow from other sources as much as you like. Eventually, you will take others' ideas, extrapolate them, revise them, and finally put them into your own words and make them a part of your LifeCreed.

7. Draft Your Updated Version: Using the edited copy of your original LifeCreed (with all the scribbled notes, corrections, and additions you have made), write or type your new, updated LifeCreed.

8. Record Your Revised LifeCreed: Record your revised LifeCreed following the same steps used to record your initial LifeCreed. However, this time, as per your notes, see if you can add enthusiasm to parts that seemed boring in your first recording, read it with more emphasis, or add inflection.

9. Maintain a Positive Frame of Mind: As before, record your revised LifeCreed when you are feeling positive, optimistic, and enthusiastic. This attitude will be reflected in your voice and communicated to your brain every time you listen to it.

Future revisions of your LifeCreed

Every three to four months (or as needed) during the first year, repeat the entire process outlined in this chapter to further refine your LifeCreed. In the second year, repeat the LifeCreed revision process only every six to eight months, or as needed. From the third year on, you'll probably revise your LifeCreed about once a year. However, any time you feel the need to change or add to your LifeCreed, don't hesitate to do so. As you accomplish goals and see ideals realized, add new ones.

As you continue to use all of the tools and resources in the Life-Balance System, you will discover even more additions for your future LifeCreed revisions. Your LifeCreed will become part of an upward spiraling pattern of success and happiness that will last a lifetime.

NOTE: *Always remember that your LifeCreed is a vehicle to which you can attach any goal, ideal, principle, practice, or desire you want to achieve and make a permanent part of your life. Anytime in the future, when a new idea or desire hits you, or when you discover a new principle, seek a new direction or for any reason find yourself thinking about a change or improvement you'd like to make, write in your Feelings Journal about it, add it to your LifeCreed, then watch it become a reality!*

Be sure to save the written versions of your old LifeCreeds. It is so enlightening and motivating to see how your thoughts and habits evolve over the years. Mine are kept in my journal or life story, which I call *Leo's Life*. It's over three thousand pages now. It is one of my favorite books to read because there are so many neat things that have happened in my life that I would have forgotten.

Within the next three to four weeks, when Creed Nausea begins to set in, schedule several hours to revise your LifeCreed. Be sure to calendar this time as a must-do appointment, or you will likely pro-crastinate. This becomes a problem when people grow nauseated with their initial LifeCreed and stop listening to it with the full intention of doing the revision. Before they know it, months have passed and they don't have a revised LifeCreed, nor have they been listening to their old LifeCreed. This is how people could fall out of the LifeBalance System and back into old habits and ruts.

Remember, the LifeCreed is a tool that will develop new mental models, which are the muscles that will lift your life to new heights. Like other exercise programs, you must commit to continuing this effort for the rest of your life. Listening to your LifeCreed is the tool to keep you in shape.

Important Ideas & Insights

_____

_____

_____

_____

10

Marvel at Your Progress with Your Scoreboard For Life

Too often people live their lives like they're playing in a basketball game with no scoreboard. They hit some great shots, get some rebounds, make some good plays, but they have no idea where they are in the game—whether or not they're really progressing or accomplishing anything. We live in a society that likes to keep score. While keeping score determines the winner in an athletic event, it also can be a powerful motivational tool when used to track and monitor personal progress.

It's easier to measure progress when you can review where you've been. With the **Scoreboard For Life**, you can see exactly how far you've progressed with the goals in your LifeCreed, and how much you have improved your most important relationships. It's a wonderful tool for continual discovery and voluntary accountability. Each time you review your Scoreboard For Life, you'll be amazed at how many things stated in your LifeCreed have been realized and how much progress you have made in the six key relationship areas of your life. The Scoreboard For Life also reveals areas in your LifeCreed and relationships where you need to put more focus in the future. Often we are unaware or unconscious of how much progress we make in our lives, or where we need improvement. The Scoreboard For Life brings the goals in your LifeCreed to the surface where you can see where you've been and be better able to chart your course forward.

I am grateful to Glade Jones, who gave me the original idea for the Scoreboard For Life.

Creating Your Initial Scoreboard For Life

In the last chapter you learned you should periodically revise your LifeCreed. The first revision comes after listening to your initial Life-Creed recording for approximately three weeks. During the first year, revisions are made every three to four months. In the second year, the LifeCreed revision process is completed every six to eight months. From the third year on, you'll probably revise your LifeCreed about once a year. However, any time you feel the need to change or add to your LifeCreed, don't hesitate to do so.

The first time you revise your LifeCreed, you should put together your Scoreboard For Life. Then with each LifeCreed revision in the future, you can simply edit your existing Scoreboard For Life. To create your first Scoreboard For Life, please proceed as follows:

1. Review your LifeCreed and on a separate page make a list of each specific goal you want to work on, now or in the future. (If your LifeCreed was created using a computer, you can copy and paste it.)

2. Number the list. All LifeCreeds are different. Some may contain a few dozen goals, while others can have seventy or more specific goals or items that can be placed on the Score-board For Life list.

3. To the left of each goal, make a line. On this line you will indicate a score of how well you're doing.

4. Place a title and date at the top of the list.

Below is a sampling of a few of the goals taken from a LifeBalance client's LifeCreed and put into the Scoreboard For Life format. (The client's actual list was much longer.)

My Scoreboard For Life
March 1

Score
1–10

_____ 1. I look for the good in people.

_____ 2. I compliment people on at least one point during every conversation.

_____ 3. I am a great communicator.

_____ 4. I am positive about others and I hate gossip.

_____ 5. I write thoughtful notes to those I appreciate.

_____ 6. I am a great listener.

_____ 7. I have a great memory for names.

_____ 8. I am a mover and a shaker, a creator of innovations.

_____ 9. I have an uncanny ability to change my thoughts appropriate to the situation.

_____ 10. I am in control of my emotions and I remain calm.

_____ 11. I am alive spiritually.

_____ 12. I read inspirational material for half an hour every morning.

_____ 13. I pray and meditate sincerely each morning and evening.

_____ 14. I write religiously in my Feelings Journal five days a week at 6:30 p.m.

_____ 15. I am a moral and honest person.

_____ 16. I give Susan at least three warm fuzzies in her love language every day.

_____ 17. I have kid's day with Michael every Tuesday.

_____ 18. I have kid's day with Megan every Wednesday.

_____ 19. I have kid's day with Shawn every Thursday.

_____ 20. I am healthy and I work out for half an hour five days a week at 7:00 a.m.

_____ 21. I earn $150,000 a year.

NOTE: *As you review your LifeCreed for specific goals, as I've said be sure to break any general references into separate goals. For example, if your goal states, "I show unconditional love to each of my children by . . ." and you have three children, make separate entries for each child: "I show unconditional love to Michael by . . ."*

Using Your Scoreboard For Life

Once you have created your Scoreboard For Life with a complete listing of all the goals from your LifeCreed, before scoring yourself, make some copies. Use your Scoreboard For Life sheets as follows:

1. Score yourself: Use one copy to score yourself. On a scale from 1 to 10, score yourself for each listed goal or ideal. A one means you never do it or are just starting to work toward it, while a ten means you do it consistently or have already achieved it. The scoring is totally subjective. Just be as honest as you can be.

2. Identify goals that need more focus: After you finish scoring yourself, review your Scoreboard For Life. You will notice that you have made progress, or even achieved some of your goals, without really thinking about it. Feelings Journaling and listening to your LifeCreed each day have harnessed and directed your natural built-in ability to create surprising progress. As you review your scores, you will find other goals that have become a reality because you have consciously focused on them and worked hard to bring them to fruition. However, you will also notice that there are some goals where you have made little or no progress. Place an asterisk (*) next to each of these. Review all of the goals with an asterisk and choose the top five goals you want to focus on from now until your next LifeCreed revision (every three months for the first year).

Go to your LifeCreed and find the five goals you have selected. Clearly mark where these five goals are.

3. Motive-Hook expansion: In chapter 9 you learned how to attach a motive and a hook to a few of the goals in your LifeCreed. A motive and hook are essential to harnessing your brain's natural abilities to achieve your goals. Some goals require a more extensive or expanded motive and hook, and a more concentrated focus before they become a reality. In your LifeCreed, expand the motive and hook for the five goals you have selected:

> **Motive and Meaning:** As you review what you have written about each goal in your LifeCreed, ask yourself, "How can I add more powerful motive and meaning?" See yourself in the future already in possession of your goal and really elaborate on how you *feel* now that you are in possession of it. How is your life better? Describe how specific people are proud of you, and how they respond to you. Be descriptive, precise, and detailed. Create as much positive and powerful emotion as possible. Add these additional details to each of the five goals you have selected in your LifeCreed. Make certain to use first-person and present tense in your statements. If you feel it would help to develop more detail, you can use the 5-Step Discovery Process on some specific goals as described in chapter 3 on page 37.

Hook: As you review each of the five goals, ask yourself, "How can I add more detail regarding the precise action steps and process I will follow to achieve the goal?" and "How can I be more precise with dates, days, or times relating to these action steps?" Add these details to each of the five selected goals in your LifeCreed. Be sure to use first person and present tense in your statements.

4. File your score sheets: Put the Scoreboard For Life sheet you have just scored, along with the unscored copies, in your file. Do not look at your scores again until the next time you revise your LifeCreed. At that time, take an unscored copy of your Scoreboard For Life out of your file and score yourself. Compare it to the previously scored Scoreboard For Life sheet in your file. Note the differences. Some goals will have significant progress, others may remain about the same, and there may be a few goals that have slipped. And there likely will be several goals that have progressed or have been realized without any conscious effort on your part.

A Perfect Opportunity for Self-Assessment

As outlined in step 4 above, at the next revision of your LifeCreed, open your Scoreboard For Life file. Do not look at your previous scores until after you score yourself on the unscored copy. Once you have scored yourself on a fresh Scoreboard For Life sheet, compare your scores with those from before. When comparing her scores, one Life-Balance client commented: "After three months of Feelings Journaling and listening to my LifeCreed, I took the Scoreboard For Life sheet and scored myself again. When I compared that score with the one from 3 months before I was amazed at the progress I had made! There were some areas I had greatly improved in and I wasn't even consciously working on them. The LifeCreed is a powerful tool!"

Your Scoreboard For Life will provide you with the following benefits:

1. Success breeds success. Comparing your current Scoreboard For Life with the previous one allows you to clearly see your progress and give yourself a well-deserved pat on the back. This is tremendously motivating and spurs you on to attain ever-greater heights. In essence, success truly does breed success.

2. Areas for improvement and LifeCreed revision. Keeping score of your progress lets you identify areas for improvement and goals where you aren't making much or any progress. You can Feelings Journal about these areas and ask, "Why am I not making progress?" This may be due to one or more of several reasons:

- Your motive and meaning may not have sufficient clarity or power: Remember, if your *why* is strong enough, your brain will make it happen. If you determine this is lacking, expand your motive and add this particular goal in your LifeCreed.

- Your hooks (how and when) are not specific and clearly stated. If this is the case, expand the hooks for each goal you are having trouble achieving and put these hooks in your LifeCreed. You can also put these hooks in your calendar.

- You don't really want the goal or ideal that much after all. After thinking and Feelings Journaling about a specific goal, you may come to realize that it's not that important to you. If so, eliminate it from your LifeCreed and replace it with something you are passionate about—something that carries a powerful motive and meaning.

3. Personal assessment and accountability: Although your Scoreboard For Life is completely subjective, it can be a wonderful personal assessment and accountability tool. Some of us can go for years and never really know if we're making progress or where we need improvement—we have no simple, practical way of keeping score. With your Scoreboard For Life, you will always know exactly how far you have progressed and where you need to improve. You will hold yourself accountable to the ideal person you want to become and the ideal life you want to live.

START ENJOYING THE BENEFITS NOW!

Take your LifeCreed and follow the process outlined in this chapter to create your first Scoreboard For Life. Score yourself for every goal in your LifeCreed. File this scored sheet with an unscored copy. Next time you revise your LifeCreed, score yourself on the unscored Scoreboard For Life copy in your file. Compare it with your last Scoreboard For Life. Use the results to fine-tune specific parts of your LifeCreed.

Important Ideas & Insights

_____
_____
_____
_____
_____
_____
_____
_____
_____
_____
_____
_____
_____
_____
_____
_____
_____
_____
_____
_____
_____
_____
_____
_____
_____

Helping Others Gain
The Slight Edge

11

Achieve the Highest Level of the Slight Edge by Mentoring Others

Some of the greatest satisfaction and fulfillment you will ever experience will come as a result of mentoring others in the LifeBalance System. Once you have experienced the wonderful blessings of these tools, I encourage you to share them with others. Teach your family, friends, and colleagues how to implement Feelings Journaling, the Byte, and other LifeBalance tools into their lives.

One of the most effective ways I know to utilize the LifeBalance System is through another of my tools known as the **Personal Performance Review or PPR**.

The PPR

In the hectic business world where getting things done is so prevalent, it's easy to lose sight of the importance of serving and nurturing positive relationships with the people around us. With all of our deadlines, details, and unexpected detours, it's easy to go on autopilot when it comes to interacting with others. It's difficult to stop and focus on doing the little things that mean so much to our co-workers. To help with this challenge, I have developed a simple tool called the PPR.

The PPR is a tool you can use in your career or in any other environment where you are responsible for monitoring the performance of others. Based on past experience, many perceive performance reviews in the workplace and other similar environments as negative; the focus, it seems, is always on what they're doing wrong. When called in for a performance review, most employees react, "Oh great, another venting session to tell me all the things I'm doing wrong!" Imagine the meaning this has and the disastrous impact it can have on morale and intra-office relationships. No wonder most people dread performance reviews.

The PPR takes an entirely different approach. Truly effective leadership and accountability is not constructive criticism—I don't believe there is any such thing as *constructive* criticism. Effective accountability involves sharing with another your appreciation for all the things he or she is doing well and right. The PPR is all about reinforcing positive behaviors, building meaningful relationships, and creating an environment and mind-set where individuals want to improve their performance. In contrast to typical performance reviews, PPRs focus on rewarding positive behaviors. In this setting, suggestions for improvement are welcomed and viewed as helpful rather than critical or hostile. Leaders and managers also use PPRs to ask a form of the Big Question: "How can I be a better employer/manager/leader?"

The PPR demonstrates that a leader truly cares about those in his or her organization. Contrast this with the customary employee or subordinate review practices that focus primarily on criticism or are called only when there's a problem.

Simple Steps for the PPR

The PPR is simple to implement when you follow these guidelines:

1. Create a written understanding. Too often in business environments there is no clear job description. Have each person under your supervision create a written understanding of their responsibilities. Have them be completely clear and detailed about their responsibilities. Then you review it and add to or delete statements from the list. This gives you an opportunity to discuss it with the individual and revise it as needed.

2. Have the PPR weekly, if possible. The PPR normally lasts no more than ten or fifteen minutes. It is best held weekly, if possible, at the same hour and the same day of the week, but no less often than every two weeks.

3. Limit the number of PPRs. An employer, manager, or supervisor normally should be responsible to hold PPRs with three individuals (ideal), five being the maximum. Any individuals above these levels should be delegated to others along lines of authority.

4. Know the overriding purpose for the PPR. As a part of the PPR there is a review of the employee's responsibilities and your expectations. Keep in mind, however, that the purpose of the review is not to point out all the employee's weaknesses and failures. Rather, the primary purpose of the PPR is to offer praise, recognition, and appreciation for all the good things the individual is doing.

5. Give suggestions for improvement. Once you've given plenty of praise and recognition, you can then offer one or two suggestions for improvement. Rather than overloading your employee, give the individual an opportunity to improve in one or two areas. At the next PPR, praise the employee for her improvement and then offer additional suggestions. This creates an environment where she can succeed one step at a time.

Remember, to the brain, meaning is everything. When suggestions for improvement are preceded by praise, recognition, and appreciation, these suggestions are more likely to be associated by the brain as positive. This individualized, positive process is further reinforced when at the next PPR she is praised for additional improvements made. In this environment, many employees actually look forward to receiving suggestions for improvement, so that they can make progress and receive accolades at the next PPR. In addition, the leader is perceived as caring and fair, the kind of leader others want to follow.

6. Ask the Big Question. Close to the end of the PPR ask, "How can I be a better manager/employer to you? How can I better help you succeed?" Then sit back and listen to some incredibly valuable feedback. Imagine how the individual feels (the meaning) when you ask him or her to tell you how to improve! Write these suggestions down, Feelings Journal about them, and as you deem appropriate, create and implement a plan to make them a reality. A manager who asks for and then acts on suggestions for improvement from employees enjoys loyalty and support at an astounding level.

7. Prepare for the PPR by Feelings Journaling. Prior to the

PPR, write some comments of your own about the individual—what he's doing well, some areas for improvement, why you value and appreciate him, and so forth. Doing this will allow you to crystallize your thoughts, get rid of the emotions connected to negative feelings, and receive much-needed inspiration. Writing in your Feelings Journal is an excellent way to prepare for your PPRs.

A PPR Testimonial

Recently I received a letter from Virginia, a client. She is the executive assistant to another of my clients, Jim, who is a successful executive. Virginia is so excited about her weekly PPRs with Jim that she wrote to tell me about it. Her words serve as both a testimonial and an overview for anyone considering implementing the PPR:

Jim and I have worked together for nearly ten years, and we've been a very good team. But now Leo has introduced us to a new tool that will, I am confident, take us to a higher level of performance and communication. Therefore, I would like to share my candidly bullish comments about the recently implemented weekly Personal Performance Review that we have begun:

First and foremost, in my opinion, this is a natural extension of the LifeCreed that Leo helped me write that I listen to daily. And, just as listening to my Creed, recorded in my voice, reinforces my self-image of who I am and hope to become, the weekly PPR with Jim reinforces what I do and hope to do professionally. Every week I hear, in my boss's voice, what I am doing right and a few suggestions to achieve higher levels. This is a very powerful adjunct to my LifeCreed.

How wonderful to hear his comments about what I'm doing well! It is dramatically reinforcing to know that my boss is noticing these things. We all know that in most offices, what you do right always goes unsung and is taken for granted. Instead, it's what you do wrong that is mentioned. But not here. Now I hear weekly that Jim is noticing what I'm doing RIGHT!

In most office structures a supervisor is so busy with their own responsibilities, they hardly know what their subordinates are doing, let alone how to measure the effectiveness. With a weekly PPR and modifications, there is no mistake.

As a professional, I want to be a truly world-class assistant to Jim. Because I know that as I get better I enable him to be more effective. And as he becomes more effective it empowers him to increase the number of clients. And voila—my salary and value increase! I believe a person's pay should be tagged to their performance. The PPR is a great barometer.

By reviewing my job description weekly, we examine and discuss the points so there can be no misunderstanding of what's really expected. And in the discussion, we communicate what Jim would like—exactly. Believe me: there is nothing so reassuring for an employee as to know exactly what is expected.

As Jim reviews my performance and shares his vision of what would be "most perfect," he actually asks me how he can improve! Imagine a boss asking an employee that question! I can give him my feedback in return and help him tweak his performance so we can both participate in our goal of perfect execution.

And how wonderful it is to know my boss is happy with me and appreciates all I do. It makes all the hard work worthwhile.

In my opinion, with effective implementation of this powerful tool, businesses throughout the country could be transformed. At a time when companies are looking for more output from their workers, this is a brilliant tool. I hope you'll give it a try.

Applications for the PPR

The PPR works in any organization or environment where there is a leader and subordinates. These would include small businesses, corporations of all sizes, charitable foundations, religious institutions, educational groups, and family organizations.

Schedule Your First PPR Now!

Following the guidelines in this chapter, schedule your first PPR with someone you have responsibility over. This could be at work, in a volunteer capacity, at school, at home, and so forth.

Important Ideas & Insights

_____

_____

_____

_____

Author's Final Words: YOU CAN DO IT!

I am so grateful to provide this book for you. In some small way, I hope I have honored Napoleon Hill's challenge to me forty years ago. It has been an exciting journey, both in discovering these tools and principles, and in writing this book.

It is an amazing experience to see people catch the spirit of Life-Balance, to hear the excitement in their voices, and to receive letters, sometime years later, thanking me for the help I provided. This has been my greatest reward. I am grateful for the opportunity to share so many heartfelt emotional experiences with them. Now I look forward to hearing from you with your own success story.

This work could never have been done without the help of my sweetheart Shirley. So much of the relationship material I teach comes from her. I'm also grateful for the devotion and help of Mark Kastleman and Bob Wright, my two unbelievable partners in this LifeBalance work.

Please let me know how you are doing, any personal insights you have about this work, and any questions you have via my website at www.lifebal.net.

I hope my efforts, and this book, will benefit your life and help you have the relationships you so much deserve.

Leo Weidner
2008

Appendix A:
First Person, Present-Tense Phrases

I am pure energy and I . . .

I am strong when I . . .

I am strong and able to . . .

I am strong and self-reliant in . . .

I am successful at . . .

I am unique because I . . .

I am wealthy and . . .

I attract money from . . .

I attract success because I . . .

I begin again to . . .

I believe in myself and my
ability to . . .

I breathe deeply when . . .

I buy only healthy foods

I can do it because . . .

I control what I eat because . . .

I deserve good things

I deserve money

I deserve success

I deserve the good life

I do it

I do it easily

I do it for me

I do it now

I do it today

I do one thing at a time

I eat right

I enjoy success

I enjoy exercise

I exercise everyday

I feel fantastic when I . . .

I love . . .

I realize . . .

I go . . .

I treasure . . .

I work toward . . .

I search for . . .

I am . . .

My mind is open

My strength is multiplied
when I . . .

My will moves mountains

I hold my head high and I . . .

I am satisfied with smaller
portions

I am successful

I like myself

I love myself

I move lightly when I . . .

I practice . . .

I read food labels because . . .

I relax when . . .

I relax and enjoy eating less

I remember _____ easily

I remember _____ vividly

I rise above all obstacles

I smile when . . .

I speak up when . . .

I stick to it easily, naturally

I succeed because . . .

I succeed again and again at . . .

I take action now

I feel at peace

I only eat fresh, natural foods

I follow my instincts

I follow success

I have concentrated my will on . . .

I have energy and enthusiasm

I keep an open mind

I let go of . . .

I have . . .

I commit myself to . . .

I focus on . . .

I lead others to . . .

I hold . . .

I seek . . .

Appendix B:
Sample LifeCreeds

ATTENTION: *Do not review these sample LifeCreeds until after you have answered the LifeCreed questions in chapter 9.*

LIFECREED EXCERPTS

These are excerpts from the actual LifeCreeds of some of my clients. Having completed your initial LifeCreed statements, you know what it takes to create a LifeCreed: the effort, the soul-searching, the expression of your deepest feelings, dreams, and ideals. I'm grateful to my clients for their willingness to share excerpts from their private LifeCreeds with you.

Remember: These excerpts reflect the ideal self and life my clients were striving for. Many of these ideals were not yet realized when the Creeds were written.

My Relationship with My Creator

Sample Creed Excerpt 1: Spiritual

(This excerpt is written like a prayer to God.)

Heavenly Father, I am a true disciple of Christ and strive to emulate his example. I want to be like him and serve people as he did. I start every day at 6:00 a.m. by talking with you, and I always ask for your help in overcoming my faults and in being more Christlike. I strive to communicate with you all day long and listen carefully for your counsel. Since I desire to become more Christlike, I study his example from the scriptures every day in my office from 7:30 to 8:00 a.m. As I am doing this I feel your spirit and I learn how to think and act more like my savior. This time brings me feelings of great peace, perspective, and joy.

I know you love me, and I love you, and when I talk to you I feel that we are talking face to face. Because I love you, I obey your commandments.

I seek each day to understand the commandments and why you have given them. I strive to see the direction that obeying the commandments points me in, and I work harder to obey my understanding of "the higher law."

I magnify my Church participation by working with all my heart and soul when asked to help. I am not content to do what others have done, but I study the assignment and apply my special talents of empathy and leadership to do more than is expected. I am worthy at all times to be guided by the Holy Spirit, and I seek diligently to listen and obey all promptings. This helps me be a much better father, husband, and servant to everyone around me.

I strive to treat all people equally. I seek those who have spiritual and physical needs. I help them because I see the face of the Savior in every individual. My greatest joy comes from serving others and I love it.

I lead my family by example. I am prepared for every Sunday. I assist all members of the family in their preparation and keep Sunday a relaxed, pleasant day. I spend all of Sunday seeking to serve my family and draw closer to them. My efforts on Sunday have a positive impact on my relationships with my family all week long.

I meet with my Sweetheart from 6:30 to 7:00 p.m. on Sundays to plan our week and to make certain that I am aware of any special events or needs in the family during the coming week.

Sample Creed Excerpt 2: Spiritual

I love searching the scriptures and other spiritual materials every morning at 7:30 for twenty minutes, seeking for what the Lord wants me to know and do to serve him better. I have committed to him that I will read the scriptures every day without fail. I honor this commitment, and doing so makes me feel good and brings me a rich outpouring of his spirit. I always spend one hour at 10:00 Saturday evenings reading and pondering Sunday School lessons so I can fully participate and contribute in church. It's very fulfilling and satisfying to join in the Sunday School discussions with my brothers and sisters.

I am a dynamic spiritual leader in my home. I lead by providing a positive example for my family by studying the scriptures, saying my personal prayers, and calling the family together for our family prayer every morning at 8:00 a.m. Through my example I invite the spirit into our home, and this makes a positive difference in the peace and harmony that is there.

I love discussing my life every morning with God. I thank him for all the blessings he has given me, and I constantly strive to spend more time praying to improve our relationship to a deeper, more personal level. My relationship with him is so vital that I love taking time to communicate my innermost feelings to him all during the day and evening. Doing this makes me more successful in every other part of my life.

I have mastered the habit of going to bed by 10:30 p.m., and I realize that this is the solution to the accomplishment of many of my spiritual goals.

I am the head of my family and I take the lead in our weekly Family Councils on Monday nights. I know the Lord smiles as he watches the way I lead out in my family

I am young, healthy, and happy. I am complete. I am proud of my body and my face. I am gifted in body and mind. I overcome any obstacle. I am alive and aware. I am in control. Life is wonderful!

I am a caring person. I am sensitive and responsive to people's needs. I am expressive and loving. I create great friendships and loyalties because I give great love and loyalty.

I am intelligent and sensitive and love a good time. I have the ability to see humor and use my wit to soften life's stressful times. I am resilient and strong.

I love to dance and sing. I love adventure and excitement. Life is always a challenge, an opportunity. I always find the bright and hopeful side to a challenge.

I love peace and harmony in my home. I have an excellent relationship with Judy because I actively listen to her. At mealtime we always discuss her day; at bedtime I take time to listen to her prayers, and then I softly scratch her back to relax her. I am sensitive to her feelings. Bedtime is a special time for us to talk and listen to each other and review the day's events.

Judy is a joy to me, an inspiration. I ask Judy how I can be a better mom and I listen. I give wise counsel to my daughter. I have infinite patience. I respond to frustrating situations with calmness and serenity. I express my concerns with love.

I create an atmosphere of love and acceptance in my home. My child and her friends feel unconditional love and freedom to grow and develop their individual unique gifts and personalities. Because I am nonjudgmental and see the good in individuals, and because I use my sense of humor, my home often rings with laughter, abounding in warmth and love.

I create an atmosphere where Judy is taught and encouraged by example and word to have good manners and consideration for others' feelings. My actions always demand respect. I tolerate only loving and kind behavior. Everyone's space is of equal importance in my home.

I am consistent. I have the strength and ability to accomplish my goals. I am not alone. I need and accept God's help and love, and also the friendship and advice from those persons whose wisdom and experience exceed my own. Because I am intelligent and successful, I welcome and appreciate the counsel of positive and successful people. I seek constant and continual encouragement and give the same. I align myself with the loving, positive, good powers and energies of the universe.

I am good and I respond to love—love of God, love for myself, and love for my fellowman. I am committed to my course.

I choose to do right and worship God in deed and thought. I give thanks for my blessings. I acknowledge the power and the authority of God and His servants. I am in His service and in His debt. I thank Him always, day and night.

My Relationship with Self

Sample Creed 1: Emotional/Intellectual

I know that it is okay to say "no" or to say "I'm tired" or to even say "I don't want to" when someone asks me to do something. I stay in control of my time so that I am always stress-free and in full control of my emotions. I schedule my time carefully and keep the commitments which I have made. Doing this brings great peace into my life.

I listen to Charles Beckett's tape on communication between men and women in order to stay focused on the different methods of communicating and in order to deal objectively with other's responses to my requests or suggestions. I listen to these tapes on my drive to work and on my way home. I am improving my communication skills more each day and my family and co-workers are amazed at how effective I am. I create an atmosphere where people can feel comfortable and enjoy talking with me.

I schedule my time so that I have proper rest. I retire before 10:00 p.m. Sunday through Thursday and I arise rejuvenated and excited at 6:00 a.m. Monday through Friday mornings. I carefully monitor my medications and take my vitamins on a daily basis so that I have the physical reserves I need to maintain proper health.

I discuss problems promptly so that I do not harbor bad feelings toward others which could create emotional and spiritual stress on me. Others appreciate my openness and gentle honesty and this improves my relationships with those around me.

I remind myself daily that faith and fear cannot exist at the same time and that with proper communication with my Heavenly Father I do not *react* to fear as I make my decisions, but *act* out of knowledge and faith. Doing this increases my self-confidence and my confidence in God, knowing that together we can do anything!

I always remember the plaque in our bedroom that says "Lord, help me to remember today that nothing is going to happen that You and I together can't handle." This is one of the first things I see each morning and it gives me a gentle reminder as to the power of prayer in my life and the blessing of peace to my soul.

I read articles on good mental health as I become aware of them, and I attend classes and workshops on stress and burnout at each convention I attend so that I am always alert to the need for emotional and mental fitness. When I learn something that is meaningful and important in my life, I put it in my LifeCreed where it becomes part of who I am.

Sample Creed 2: Emotional/Intellectual

I thrive on gaining new knowledge and learning new marketing ideas in my chosen career. I always learn one new idea each day that improves my skills and effectiveness and I record that idea in my idea book. I review these ideas every Monday morning at 8:00 a.m. to refresh myself in all the new knowledge I have gained. I take the most important things I learn and put them in my creed so I can listen to them everyday. After awhile they become automatic habits. By doing this I am constantly moving to a higher level in my career.

Every night at 9:30 p.m., I love reading from books of fiction and motivation. I am so excited to learn that I stay wide awake and alert while reading. I have to pry myself away from books in order to go on to other important events. I always listen to motivational tapes on Tuesdays and Thursdays while eating my lunch. When I hear something that really stands out, I make a note of it and put it in my creed. I am becoming more and more positive and balanced with each passing day.

I demonstrate my positive attitude about learning to my children, and I create an atmosphere where they can develop the same enthusiasm for learning that I have.

Sample Creed #3: Emotional/Intellectual

My mind is focused! Every morning during my prayer and meditation period I plan my day, emphasizing the goals and objectives of my Creed. Then, throughout the day, as interruptions occur I handle them graciously and immediately return to the priority at hand. The intensity of my concentration impresses all who come in contact with me. I maintain focus!

I sense my capacity to remember things growing every day. As I meet a new person I find myself repeating his name over and over during the conversation and associating it with something unique about him. I am also using this tremendous skill to memorize one new poem or quote each week and find this is one of the most rewarding mental exercises I am involved in. People are amazed at my remarkable memory.

I always sing in the church choir, taking other opportunities to sing solo or with groups. I love seeing the happiness on people's faces when they listen to my music. This is a wonderfully fulfilling part of my life.

My love for music has also expanded to instruments. Each evening at 9:00 p.m. before we retire, uplifting music from the piano and French horn fills our home. I constantly work to create the atmosphere and give encouragement so that our family can sing and play instruments together often. My love for and involvement in music touches all the family for good.

I am a terrific speller. What used to be a weakness has become a great strength. I am amazed at how I use the spell-check less and less when I write letters and business documents.

I love reading! Truth expanding in the soul is one of life's most sublime experiences. As I read each morning during exercise, and on Tuesday and Thursday evenings at 8:00 p.m. during study time, my soul expands and it becomes an uplifting experience for me.

My Relationship with My Body

Sample Creed 1: Health/Fitness

I am a healthy person. Others can tell because I look great. I always have abundant energy because my body is extremely conditioned and very well maintained. I have so much stamina that others are amazed and have difficulty keeping up.

My physique is slender and well proportioned. I maintain my ideal weight of 190 pounds by exercising six times a week (Monday to Saturday from 6:00 to 6:30 a.m.). My resting heart rate is 60 BPM. I ride my stationary bicycle for 18 minutes, perform flexibility and stretching exercises, and work out with light weights to keep my body firm and well conditioned. I make certain that I maintain a heart rate of 150 for at least twelve minutes during my exercise period so aerobically my heart stays in perfect condition. I always use the stairs and take them two at a time when there are only two or three flights, and I walk at least a mile Monday, Wednesday, and Friday. I encourage my sweetheart to walk with me. For short trips the car stays in the garage and I use my bicycle.

I enjoy life. And to ensure that I continue enjoying life, I take extreme care to eat well-prepared and nourishing meals. I always eat three meals a day and delight in a variety of vegetables and grains, along with small amounts of meat. I always get seven hours of sleep at night, because I go to bed at 11:00 p.m. I am up at 6:00 a.m. and I feel fabulous!

Sample Creed 2: Health/Fitness

I weigh 199 pounds and I look and feel like a million. My waist is 35 inches and my chest is as solid as a rock.

I am always up at 5:30 a.m. to enjoy the most beautiful part of the day. I always walk three miles every morning in forty-one minutes which makes me feel like I am on top of the world. I know that I am in control.

I eat three well-balanced meals every day that consist of the right amount from each of the food groups. I have tons of energy and enough vitality to tackle all the activities of the day. I always eat legal snacks in the evening and always drink eight full glasses of water every day.

Weekly, I do fifteen minutes of stretch exercises on Monday, Wednesday, and Friday, and Saturdays at 5:50 in the morning, just prior to my three-mile walk. In addition, I do sit-ups and pushups which make me feel like I'm Arnold Schwartzenegger.

I swim a mile every week on Tuesdays at 6:00 a.m. and I play racquetball every Saturday, where I run Mike and Bill into the ground. I love the way I look and the incredible feeling of being in top shape.

Sample Creed 3: Health/Fitness

I am as regular as the rising sun in the exercise and care of my physical body. My healthy body is a gift from God and I show my love for Him in the way I care for my body. For this reason I retire each night by 10:00 p.m. and arise at 6:00 a.m. I am refreshed and invigorated as I greet the day while it is still young. I feel a great surge of power and confidence by this expression of self-control.

Every weekday morning at 7:15 I follow a regular routine that includes thirty minutes of exercising the large muscle groups of my body aerobically and rhythmically (running, walking, biking, or swimming) and challenging my body to become stronger and more fit. Monday, Wednesday, and Friday I exercise at 140 beats per minute for a minimum of twenty minutes (with an appropriate warm-up and cool-down). Lifting weights every Wednesday at 6:00 p.m. and Saturday at 10:00 a.m. provides my body with excellent body tone and muscle definition.

Eating the right foods is also a habit for me. I savor the natural flavor of foods. I particularly enjoy fresh vegetables and fruits and the whole grains. I love these high-fiber, low-fat, complex carbohydrates and find myself using no salt in my diet. Reading labels has become second nature to me and I treat items that are high in refined carbohydrates or fats as if they had a skull and crossbones on them. Taking three vitamins with each meal and three Omega-3 fatty acid capsules with dinner is also a habit that helps me feel terrific.

My thirty-inch waist and moderate tan make me feel comfortable in any group, and my wife drools over how good-looking I have become.

My Relationship with My Family

Sample Creed 1: Family

Because my family is important to me, I find at least five minutes to talk to each member of the family every day. With my hands empty I make direct eye contact and my eyes and facial expression say "I love you." Each day I tell each member how much I love them. I always look for the positive aspects of their lives and compliment them.

I always know what is happening in the lives of my family because I talk with them, and when we talk I really listen to what they are saying. I always say kind and pleasant words because I am in control. Even when I am angry, I can show my displeasure while at the same time communicating my love and concern.

The center of my affection is my wife, Sue. Even though I love all members of the family, I always let her know every day that she is the center of my love and that she is the source of happiness for me. I let her know that her smiles, cheerfulness, intelligence, and wit make life joyful. Every day for fifteen minutes at bedtime, I share with her the occurrences of the day, and I tell her of at least one of her positive qualities and at least one thing she has done that I appreciate.

Every Friday my sweetheart and I have a date. During the date I continually court Sue's affection and seek counsel and guidance from her as to how to be a better father, a better husband, and a better person. I listen to her answers, especially when she has criticism. I respect her so much that when she has suggestions for improving my life, I begin implementing the suggestions immediately and put them in my LifeCreed. Because she is my love, I share my innermost desires, fears, and dreams with her.

Because I love and respect each member of my family, I want them to grow emotionally, intellectually, spiritually, and physically. I provide opportunities for individual growth regardless of the obstacles that come up. I strive to provide opportunities for each child to be challenged and to actually crystallize what he or she believes.

I reserve every Saturday for family activities, and we have an activity night every Monday evening. The last Sunday of each month we have a family meeting to plan our Saturday activities and our vacations. We plan in detail for the next month and lay outlines for the entire year. Each month we update the master schedule. When an activity is scheduled, we follow through and complete that activity. These activities are so much fun that everyone can look forward to the planning meeting just for a chance to discuss them.

We always have Family Council on Sunday evening at 7:00. Even when I am not teaching the lesson, I am prepared with stories, object lessons, or other material to help whoever is giving the lesson and to reinforce the things that Sue and I are teaching the family.

Sue and I always take eight weekends each year (scheduled in our twelve-month calendar) away from our family and spend them together. We always go to some romantic place and get to know each other again as we gain perspective on our lives, our marriage, and our family. The children enjoy the weekends when we are away too because we always employ such excellent babysitters.

Sample Creed 2: Family

Because I am so happy with myself, I'm happy with those around me, especially my family. I am always easy to get along with—tolerant and pleasant. I realize that I cannot change my wife, so I work on improving myself. I treasure the time I spend with my family. I look forward to getting home and being with them. As I get closer to home I put my business cares aside and think about how much my wife and the kids need my strength and great attitude.

I have been blessed with the greatest family in the world.

I have a special day set aside every week for each of my children when I think about how much I love and appreciate them. I concentrate on the worth of each one as a child of God and on the talents and special gifts they have been blessed with. On their special day I always spend a minimum of twenty minutes, one on one, seeking for ways I can serve them better. I always ask how I can be a better father and person, and I listen on their special day. Bill's day is Monday. I am grateful for his striving to do what's right and for his obedience. I look for ways to help him share his feelings more.

Brad is Tuesday. I appreciate his fun-loving nature and the way he makes us all laugh and feel good. I work hard to help him appreciate the value of schooling and the importance of his desire to get good grades.

Steve is Wednesday. He is a hard worker when he's able, and he has a tender heart underneath. By my example, I teach him the value of life without drugs and alcohol.

Thursday is Susie's day. She is so tender and concerned about others and has great sensitivity to their needs. I constantly teach her to assert herself more and stand up for what she believes. I want each of the children to know that they are unique and that they have special gifts.

I love taking my beautiful wife on a date every Friday. I am absolutely committed to this special time with my precious companion, and nothing comes before her. I always ask her how I can be a better husband, father, and person, and I listen without defense. I put her suggestions in my creed so I can start implementing them immediately.

I strive to lead my family in being creative in the activities we do together. My goal for our family is to see that we go camping once a month in the summer, hiking in the mountains twice a month, and skiing twice a month in the winter. I see to it that we swim once a week in the summer. We plan all of these activities the first Thursday of each month at 7:30 p.m. We go over the events of the coming month and schedule the coming year in advance.

Without fail I always support my children by being at their school activities and sporting events.

My wife always comes first, then the kids, in my priorities. Church and business come next.

Everyone knows by my actions how important my family is to me, including my family themselves.

I tell everyone in my family I love them every day. I hug them at least once a day and kiss them as I leave each morning. I give my wife an extra long hug and a big kiss every morning as we depart and every afternoon as we meet again. I show her by word or deed every day how glad I am that I married her.

My positive example and loving manner with my family creates an atmosphere of love and harmony in our home. My wife and children know they can come to me no matter how they feel and can count on me being a good listener and having lots of understanding. I always ask them how they are doing and I listen.

Sample Creed 3: Family

I am a great dad and a terrific husband. I create a feeling of peace, trust, harmony, happiness, and love in our home. It is indeed a heaven on earth! Through my efforts, I create the atmosphere in our home where my wife and children can feel that our home is a safe haven—an oasis—from all worldly influence. This is due to the fantastic communication I have with each member of the family.

Every Friday night is date night with Diane. This time is for entertainment and relaxation and, most importantly, for open communication about our relationship. I always express gratitude and love for Diane as my wife and best friend. I specifically point out the things I appreciate about her during the week. I continually let her know of my confidence in her as mother and teacher of our children. During date night I always ask how I can be a better husband, father, and person—and I listen. My ability to accept and immediately act upon her suggestions is one of my strongest traits. I keep Diane constantly aware of my business activities and our financial situation. I convey my innermost feelings to her so that she understands me completely and knows I need her.

My children also benefit from my excellent communication skills. Every week I spend a minimum of twenty minutes in an individual session with Karen, Mark, and Erin. Monday is Karen's day, Tuesday Mark, and Wednesday Erin. In these sessions I ask each of them how I might be a better dad. Then I listen carefully with undivided interest to whatever they want to talk about, whether it's seeking fatherly counsel and advice or just shooting the breeze. I use this time for positive communication. Discipline or reproving is saved for another time, and even then it is done in a manner of loving concern. On their day I focus on talking about their gifts and blessings and only address one area of concern I might have. Each Thursday, on rotating basis, I take each of the kids on a daddy-date-night. These dates are always scheduled in advance on our twelve-month calendar. My total focus is on them and how I can assist them in developing their gifts and easing their fears.

I let Karen know what a joy she is to be around with her subtle sense of humor. I tell her how blessed she is that God gave her creative a hand for art. Along with her physical beauty she has a very sensitive and caring nature; I express this to her often.

Mark is intelligent and bright—also very coordinated and skillful in athletics for his age. I tell him every day how proud I am to be his father, because of his willingness to always do what is right and honest.

Erin is extremely bubbly and fun-loving. She makes friends easily. I thank her often for coming to our home, for we need her constant reminding to have prayer and family time together.

I am blessed to have such heavenly spirits in my home. I express unconditional love to each child often—individually and collectively so they know their dad loves all of them. I show no favoritism. Through my words and actions, my children know of their worth and importance to their family and friends.

The consistency of our date nights and communication sessions draws us closer together as a family. I am the greatest source of earthly love that Diane and the children receive.

While at home I schedule my activities very carefully so I maximize the quality time I spend with the family. I enjoy playing with the kids and helping Diane with household duties in the evening. I read the newspaper only when it doesn't infringe on time which should be spent with members of my family or tasks that I am asked to do.

I take time every evening to discuss the day's events with Diane. This is done after the kids are in bed or when working together cleaning up the kitchen and dinner dishes.

Through my actions my wife and children know I love and care for them more than anything or anyone else in this world and they know I need them as much as they need me. I look for ways to let them serve me. Every family member is reminded by me of his importance to the whole family which helps to maintain their own self-worth and individualism.

My Relationship with Others

Sample Creed 1: Social

I love people and I am thankful for my opportunities to interact with those around me. I enjoy talking with others and being able to help them by giving wise counsel when they come to me for help. I look for the good qualities in others and make a special point of giving honest compliments and praise. I am tolerant of values and backgrounds which are different from my own. I see each person as a son or daughter of God and allow that person his or her weaknesses.

I am a fantastic conversationalist. I keep myself well informed and am able to discuss current events and issues intelligently. I do this by reading the newspaper and my magazine subscriptions every day during my lunch hour. People are amazed at how conversant and knowledgeable I am. My favorite practice is to "interview" whomever I am talking to. I am fascinated by people's stories. I am a warm and loving person. I create an atmosphere of comfort and safety when others are confiding in me. I have a great sense of humor and am able to use that talent to put others at ease and relieve tension when appropriate.

I have a talent for putting my thoughts into words. When I am having a conversation with someone, I am assertive and able to say what I am thinking and feeling in a concise and interesting way, being tactful and diplomatic. I listen empathetically and actively while the other person is talking, concentrating on what he or she is saying and the feelings behind the words.

I feel comfortable entertaining friends and colleagues in my home or attending social functions. I am a gracious ambassador on behalf of my husband and always speak well of him to others. In the community I am active in voicing my opinions and encourage others to do so. I attend PTA meetings and parent/teacher conferences because I believe it is important for me to know what my children are being taught and what sort of environment they are being taught in. I research political issues and learn the views of candidates, actively supporting those with whom I agree and opposing those candidates or issues I am against.

Sample Creed 2: Social

I have the most fantastic and enjoyable life imaginable. I love every minute of it because I am proud of what and who I am. Even though I am very satisfied with my life, I am doing more so that it is getting even better.

I care about everyone I meet, and so I'm anxious to make new acquaintances. I make it easy for people to like me because they can tell I care; I listen to what they say by looking them in the eye and giving them my undivided attention. I observe a good point about each person I meet and mention it when appropriate. I use it to remember that person. I love being where people are and getting to know them.

I express my opinions but am very careful to understand the opinions and feelings of others. I strive to keep my opinions based on sound facts and change them only when better information shows my errors.

I like laughter and have good times but never at the expense of others. I am the first to laugh at my own mistakes but work hard to help others not feel self-conscious or ill at ease when they make mistakes.

I am a good and loyal friend. I work to keep informed of my friends' successes and trials. I am there when I'm needed but quickly disappear when I am in the way.

I work hard to help all people know how fragile and delicate our environment is. I work to stimulate people's minds so that they realize their lives are greatly improved by working to clean the air, purify the water, and avoid unnecessary waste.

I show people by example that an individual can make a significant contribution toward improving life by reducing consumption and preserving resources. I conserve resources by developing energy-saving programs for my home, business, and community.

Sample Creed 3: Social

I love to share my thoughts and feelings when I am in a group of people. I constantly look for ways to share ideas and experiences that uplift others around me.

I am blessed with great insight and wisdom in the area of human relations. People feel at ease in my presence and are in awe of my many special talents and abilities.

I am a fantastic listener. I have mastered the ability to zero in on what people are thinking and feeling. I always listen for five minutes for what someone is feeling before I speak. This great skill allows me to become intimately involved in people's lives in a very short time. People trust me with their innermost feelings and know that I do not violate that trust.

I am a very active listener, especially with my wife and my wonderful children. They are in awe of how well I listen to them without defensive rebuff.

People love being around me, not only because I am very outgoing, but because they can talk to me on their own level knowing that I listen attentively and give them honest feedback. They realize that I am a man of high moral conduct and that I am totally honest in my dealings.

I feel good about myself. I am 100 percent in control of my life and know that my conduct is the epitome of what my God expects of me.

My Relationship with Job and Money

Sample Creed 1: Career/Financial

I am a true professional in the life insurance business: I look sharp and I am highly organized.

I always begin my workday knowing exactly where I am headed. I have a well-developed system that maximizes the use of my time and energies. A color-coded weekly chart is the key to this system. I keep it before me all during my workday, and it shows me at all times what my ideal work-week consists of. I constantly strive to fill my week with the activities that are recorded on the chart. By keeping a written record of my activities I am always aware of where I am in relation to where I should be. This makes me stretch and grow each week as I strive to have my actual week match up with my ideal week. I have eight priorities I am committed to accomplish each day. As I accomplish each priority I color code it with green, indicating that it has been done. I know that this system gives me a slight edge and magnifies my results tenfold.

I always set up a minimum of fifteen interviews per week. Of these at least five are new interviews. This assures me I'll end up with consistent results each week.

One of my greatest assets is my enthusiasm and self-discipline. I am always in my office by 7:45 a.m. and I leave at 6:00 p.m. I always remember to record my activity and pinpoint the areas where I am improving my effectiveness. I always have my prospects and clients meet me in my office during the daytime. This gives me the feeling of being a true professional.

When I set a goal I always achieve it because I clearly define it and know the amount and type of activity that is required to achieve it.

Over the next twelve-month period I am writing $72,000 in commissions. This breaks down to $1,500 per week for 48 working weeks.

On October 1 of this year I am debt free and have $10,000 in the bank. We move into our new home on October 2. This new home is in the Cedar Breaks area, which allows my children to remain in the school they are accustomed to.

My wife is shouting for joy because she no longer works outside the home as she finishes her degree.

On July 7 of this year I have a new Cadillac Coupe de Ville. It is white with a beautiful red interior, cruise control, air-conditioning, and power windows and seats. This beautiful machine makes me feel secure and powerful.

I really love this business and love what it does for my family. I know that there is no other business in the world that gives more personal freedom and financial independence. I am 100 percent committed to excellence in my career and am grateful that my God has blessed me so abundantly.

Sample Creed 2: Career/Financial

Financially I have the ideal life. In two years I earn $160,000 per year, which allows me to take care of all the temporal needs of my family. I meet all of my financial obligations with ease. I have extraordinary money-handling capabilities and have mastered the budgeting for both my personal and family financial affairs.

I automatically set aside 40 percent of my earnings in a separate account earmarked for all taxes and church obligations. I am free from all debt (including the mortgage on our primary residence). I give Cheryl $2,000 each month for basic monthly expenditures on home and family needs. In addition, she receives $500 each month which is allocated for gifts, kids' clothing, Christmas fund, and her personal savings. This leaves me with $65,000 to fund the following areas:

Children's Trusts. I have set up a trust fund for each of my kids. Every year I place $5,000 into separate trust accounts for Susan, Tom, and Monica. These funds are only used for education and emergencies, plus a future resource to help springboard them in starting up a business or to begin financial plans for their own kids' education, or so forth.

Personal Planning for Cheryl and Myself. I use $20,000 each year for funding our own savings, insurance, retirement, and estate plans. This includes fees associated with creating and maintaining sound and proper estate-planning documents (will, trust, and agreements).

The "Fun Fund." This is my reward for all the blood, sweat, and tears used in generating this income and religiously sticking to my financial plan. The remaining $30,000 in the annual budget are discretionary dollars used for special business opportunities or charitable projects. I have a keen sense for recognizing honest and profitable business ideas. I am full of charity toward all men, women, and children and give willingly to charities which serve to benefit the youth—particularly the abused and homeless. I love to give!

I use the "Fun Fund" to purchase a new car every three years. I also invest in rare sports cars and collect them. Every year I plan two major vacations which are financed from this fund. I plan one with the entire family. The other is a vacation and annual planning retreat with Cheryl only. These trips are planned in advance and scheduled on the twelve-month calendar. In addition, I take Cheryl on a spur-of-the-moment getaway for two or three days. During the next eight years, Cheryl and I have visited Hawaii, Western Europe, Israel, Australia, New Zealand, and the Orient.

In eight years on January 1, I have $100,000 in liquid and semi-liquid resources for any emergency or opportunity which may come along. This is formed from the "Fun Fund," and if it is ever dipped into it is my main priority to build it back up as quickly as possible, even if it requires using all of the "Fun Fund" for the year, or more.

Above all, I use the utmost prudence and sensibility when spending money. I always exercise total honesty and integrity when investing.

Some Additional Sample LifeCreed Statements

Over the years my female clients have offered sample creed statements regarding improving their relationship with their husbands.

NOTE TO MEN: *As you review the following statements, convert them into the masculine and use them in your own LifeCreed.*

- I feel extremely honored to be a wife. Because I am always supportive, understanding, and caring, my husband feels it an honor and a blessing to be married to me.

- The highlight of my day is the time we spend together. No matter what I'm doing, it's more fun with John. We joke and laugh; we find a zillion ways to do little things for each other.

- I keep a list of all his favorite things and another list of all the things I admire in him, so I'm always armed with warm fuzzies. I have an unlimited supply of hugs and kisses to keep his reservoir filled. Not a day passes without my sharing my intense love for him.

- I am competent, self-assured, well-groomed, easy to be with, and approving of him. I make him feel competent, attractive, masculine, romantic, young, intelligent, appreciated, wanted, needed, cherished, and loved.

- I'm adept at resolving differences that may stand between our oneness.

- He loves my back rubs, foot rubs, or body rubs, which help relax both of us and sends a message to him that his pleasure is worth my time.

- I make it my business to be aware of his needs and desires. I find out what he likes and how he likes it, and I give love to him just that way, sharing with him my undiluted, undivided attention.

- I also communicate to him my needs and preferences, my pleasure, and my enjoyment of being close to him.

- Romance is alive in me and I bring it to life in him!

- I am the bride he always dreamed of, the sweetheart he continues dreaming of, the lover he'll never tire of.

More Sample LifeCreed Statements

Here are some wonderful sample LifeCreed statements submitted by women for improving peace and love in the home and harmony in life. (Again, men, convert these to the masculine and use them in your Life-Creed.)

- When my priorities are challenged, my husband is first, then my children.

- I treat my husband and children with courtesy and respect. I always think the best of them, saying only good about them to others.

- I treat my husband and children with unconditional love. When my children do something good, I feel like telling everyone. They know how proud I am and that I'm always here for them.

- I want the best for my fine husband and my beautiful children. I make the atmosphere in our home a comfortable place for my family to learn, grow, and retreat to.

- When people walk into my home, they immediately feel a sense of excitement, a zest for life, as if the sun were going to burst right into their arms.

- I am the happiest, brightest woman in the world.

- Sunshine is my trademark. Next to my smile, even the sun takes a back seat!

- I am always smiling, always laughing, always ready for a good time. I have a spring in my step that makes others think I'm going to take off and fly.

- I am enthusiastic. I am excited about life and spontaneous in my actions.

- I'm always positive and excited about new ideas and suggestions.

- Positive Mental Attitude is my middle name.

- I am easy to please. Even the smallest pleasures make my day. I am easy to be with, fun-loving, easy-going, and flexible.

- I warmly welcome visitors and make them feel glad they came. When my schedule can't accommodate lengthy visits, I always make them want to return.

- When those burdened with sorrow knock on my door, they leave with lifted hearts and brighter spirits, having greater faith in tomorrow.

- I radiate love, virtue, goodness, and nobility.

- I am so happy when the children awake each morning. I eagerly convey to them my love and delight in being their mother.

- I am especially delighted in being able to help members of my family.

- I am a peacemaker. I offer solutions, not problems.

- I am teachable. I enjoy learning from others and make changes when a change is for the best.

- I always think for five minutes before talking about an emotionally upsetting subject.

- I strive to have childlike qualities—quick to love, quick to forgive, and quick to forget.

- I show frequent signs of affection daily to my family and express my love and gratitude for them many times each day.

- I honestly listen to my husband and children and am sensitive to their need for a listening ear.

- I maintain a 9-1 ratio of positive-negative comments with my children. I genuinely praise every effort they make and give special praise whenever they make good choices. I ensure that good choices get more attention than wrong choices.

- Each disciplinary session is a positive learning experience. I always discipline with love and gentleness.

- I feel exhilarated when my home is clean. Keeping it in order is so second nature to me I hardly realize I'm doing it.

- I take time to help my children learn how to care for our home. We always have a great time working together.

- I teach my children to love work and take pride in doing their best.

- I include good music in every area of my family's life. I teach my children to enjoy uplifting, beautiful music.

- I take twenty minutes each weekday just to play with and talk to my children—Monday and Friday at 9:00 a.m. with Carson; Tuesday and Thursday with Tiffany; and Wednesday and Saturday at noon with Amber.

- I include our parents in our lives by making them a vital part of our children's lives. I express frequently my love and appreciation for all they do. We spend at least two evenings a month visiting or writing them.

- I spend a fun evening with my husband each Friday night, when we just relax, enjoy each other, and have a great time.

- I say "I'm sorry" whenever unkind feelings arise, regardless of whose fault it is. I readily admit when I'm wrong.

- I have a family planning session with Steve every second Sunday at 6:30 p.m.

- I frequently ask how I can be a better wife and mother.

- I am constantly striving to be better.

- When I make a mistake, I realize tomorrow's a new day and that I'm still a great person. I am strong and wise enough to forgive myself and refocus on the things that matter.

- I have a special affinity for and talent with the youth. I make it a point to search them out when they're around. I always try to build their confidence and self-esteem.

- I am a leader among women. Many look to me as a role model for strength and courage.

- People love to be around me because I only say positive and uplifting things about others.

- I have a unique ability to put my thoughts and feelings into appropriate words and always have something meaningful to talk about.

- I practice and teach my children to have good manners. I provide opportunities for them to learn social skills by inviting guests to our home and allowing the children to participate in formal visiting.

- Family priorities take precedence over time conflicts. I have the courage to graciously bow out of social responsibilities when they conflict by saying, "I'd love to but I have a prior commitment."

- I retire at 10:30 p.m. and arise at 6:00 a.m. sharp to greet each beautiful new day!

- I cannot blame my genes, but I am the one who must wear my jeans. Therefore, I keep my body strong, gorgeous, and desirable. I exercise five days a week—Monday to Friday from 6:45–7:30 a.m. I bike or jog, keeping my exercise heart rate at 134 BPM for thirty minutes on Monday, Wednesday, and Friday. I have Pritikin-type eating habits that keep me in the best of health. All I ever want of treats or desserts is a taste.

- I think, act, feel, and look young. People who don't know me think, "What a cool lady."

- I always maintain the youthful, vigorous body of a twenty-year-old. I am totally committed to my exercise program and proper nutrition.

- I am able to function at peak performance and physically do anything I want to.

- My mind functions with a keenness and clarity not possible without physical exercise and good nutrition. I feel great about myself.

- When Steve sees my lean, tan, 120-pound body with my perfect dimensions and beautiful blonde hair, it mesmerizes him.

- I am well-read and love to delve into the intellectual reservoirs of this life. I choose from the best reading materials.

- I've been blessed with many talents and don't hide them. I share them with others for their benefit and mine.

- I support and encourage my husband in his work. By showing interest in his work and spending time discussing business, I let him know that I also place importance on how he spends much of his time. When he comes home late from work or needs to spend home-time doing business, I always assume that he is doing what he feels is best for our family.

- I have the courage and skills to tactfully discuss priorities if they seem to get out of balance.

- I maintain good professional habits by (1) improving public relations skills; (2) always keeping myself well-groomed and attractive; (3) occasionally taking classes relating to my professional interests; (4) frequently using my secretarial skills for others and for my personal needs; and (5) keeping my eyes open for other effective ways of earning money.

- One of my current responsibilities is to help secure our financial future. I do that by thinking not what I can buy, but what I can do without and how I can save. I am frugal and provident in the purchasing of food, clothing, gifts, and the like.

- I admire so much the generosity of my husband and know we'll both find much happiness as we create financial stability for our family, using what we gain to bless the lives of others.

Complete LifeCreed Samples

The following completed LifeCreeds reflect each individual's perception of his or her ideal self and ideal life. Many of these ideals were not yet realized when the LifeCreeds were written.

As you study them, look for ideas you may have missed in your own LifeCreed. Some of the areas emphasized may not reflect your hopes, dreams, and aspirations, while others may. These are private and important for these individuals, so please respect them.

Putting It All Together For Men

Young Father

I love my life. I have outstanding potential, and I am accomplishing great things.

I have the most wonderful family, and I love them very much. Debbie is terrific. I am so blessed to have her for my companion. I constantly work at keeping my relationship with her fantastic. She knows how much I love her because I always consider her feelings and place her first in my life. I demonstrate my affection and respect for her by always treating her like a true gentleman does, opening doors for her and getting up when she enters a room of guests. I constantly look for ways to serve her and make her happy. I ask her how I can best help her at home and promptly follow through with her requests.

I love Debbie very much. She is my best friend, and I enjoy being with her. I know I can't change my wife, so I work on improving myself. I know the love and respect I show to her in the presence of our children increases the love and harmony in our home. I create an atmosphere of peace, trust, happiness, harmony, and love in our home. In times of tension and stress in our home I am calm and control my voice and temper. My wife and children are in awe of how cool I am.

Debbie comes first in my life, then my children, then church and business. The center of my affection is Debbie. Even though I love all the children, I always let Debbie know every day that she is the center of my love and that she is the source of my greatest happiness. I let her know how much her thoughtfulness, kindness, and caring for me, the kids, and others means to me. Every evening at bedtime I look forward to talking to her for fifteen minutes, finding out about the occurrences in her day, and asking questions that will help to pull out the feelings she wants to share.

I reserve every Friday night for Debbie. It is our date night. During the date I give her affection and seek counsel and guidance from her in how to be a better father, husband, and person. I put her suggestions in my Creed and immediately start implementing them. I continually court her each day of the week. I show her how much I love her through my actions and by telling her I love her each day. I find a warm fuzzy each day to do for her. I kiss her each night and tell her I love her. Because she is my love, I share my innermost desires, fears, and dreams with her.

Debbie and I discipline the children together in a joint effort. We discuss problems each evening and jointly decide on the solutions.

I am a great dad. Through my efforts I create an atmosphere in our home where my wife and children can feel that our home is heaven on earth, a safe place to return from all worldly influence. This is created by the love I demonstrate toward Debbie.

Everyone, including my family members, knows by my actions how important my family is to me. I tell everyone in my family I love them every day. I know what is happening in the lives of my family members because I communicate with them and really listen to what they are saying. I look them in the eye and give them my total attention.

As I drive home after work each day, I concentrate on unwinding and releasing the daily stress before the garage door opens. After I enter the garage I sit in the car for three minutes and spend quiet time alone before I enter the house. Then when I enter our home, I greet my wife and children with joy; I am happy to be with them.

Debbie and I have a planning session once each week on Sunday at 9:00 p.m. when we plan our upcoming activities. We discuss our goals and dreams, and we spend time talking about and planning our future.

Because my family is important, I always look for the positive aspects in their lives and compliment them. I love my kids and I always relate to them in a kind and loving manner. I influence them "only by persuasion, by long-suffering, by gentleness and meekness, and by love unfeigned. By kindness and pure knowledge . . . without hypocrisy and without guile." Each week I have a special day set aside for my sons and I focus on each one on his day. I show my love by concentrating on helping him to reach his potential.

Monday is for Brett. He has such a unique spirit. I always remember the inspiration I received the day he was born. I encourage his creativity, compliment his kindness, and especially set a good spiritual example for him.

Tuesday is for Billy. I love the way his face lights up when he smiles. I encourage him in his athletics and spend time playing with him. I pay particular attention to his need for positive recognition and always look for ways to compliment him.

Wednesday is for Bobby. I love him for the joy he brings into my life. I take time to be affectionate with him and to enjoy his tender years.

The spiritual progress and development of my family are important. I always lead out so we have family council every Sunday at 7:00 p.m. We pray and sing together; then we have a spiritual lesson, which I prepare. I always ask my family how I can improve and I listen to what they say.

I feel comfortable entertaining friends and colleagues in my home or attending social functions. I am a great conversationalist. People love to talk to me. I keep myself well informed on current issues and am able to discuss them intelligently. I am approachable and have a great sense of humor. I use my talents to entertain and put others at ease.

When I am having a conversation with someone, I am assertive and say what I think in a clear, concise, and interesting way. I am an active listener, concentrating on what others say and the feelings behind their words.

I have a fantastic memory, especially for people's names. When meeting someone new I always use his or her name three times in the first conversation. I create a name association and hook which enables me to instantly recall the name the next time we meet. I have great ability to recall information about finance, current events, and other items of interest. I love to learn and am hungry for information. Because of my excellent memory, friends and associates come to me for the wealth of information I am able to recall.

I have complete control of my thoughts and actions because I always act as if the Lord were here with me. Whenever inappropriate thoughts enter my mind I replace them by singing "Come Unto Jesus." The most important part of my day is the time I spend with my Lord. I search the scriptures every evening before going to bed and spend ten minutes in mighty prayer. I pray earnestly each morning and again at noon and always carry a prayer in my heart.

I gather my family together for family prayer before we leave the house each day and upon retiring each night. I receive inspiration in all my activities because I always counsel with the Lord about all I do and I listen for his direction.

I confide in those I serve and seek their advice as to how I can serve them better. I listen without defense and make specific commitments for improvement. I love the opportunities I have to serve others.

My office is located in Charleston Square and is tastefully appointed in the traditional decor of rich walnuts with accenting furnishings. My associates and clients are impressed with its subtle elegance. It exhibits an air of sophistication and success, yet is warm and inviting. People feel at ease and are comfortable when visiting.

The key to my success is commitment: first, to the success of my clients; second, to my goals; and third, to effective planning. I always begin my week with eight planning and four introduction appointments scheduled, because I follow my Ideal Week plan and have it in front of me continually. I know that the law of averages works in my favor, and as a result, I earn $3,000 weekly, $156,000 annually by June four years from now.

In two years on January 1, I have $25,000 in the bank. On July 1 in three years, we are completely out of debt. On January 1 four years from now, we purchase with cash our wooded building lot. By January 1 in five years, I have saved $50,000 and we begin construction on our new home. On August 1 in five years, we move in. Debbie has designed it beautifully. I particularly enjoy sitting on the back deck looking out into the yard and listening to the river passing by. I can feel the cool breeze rustling through the trees. From my bedroom window I love to listen to the song of birds in the distance.

I save $750 per month, putting $500 into permanent life insurance and the balance into investments. We have no debts outside of our home mortgage, which is paid off in ten years. We use credit cards as a convenience and pay all our bills on or before their due dates.

I am proud of my body. I work very hard to build it into perfect proportions. My chest measures 44 inches, my waist 32, my biceps 16, my thighs 23, and my calves 16. I weigh 195 lbs and my body fat is less than 10 percent. I measure myself on the first Monday of each month. At 6:00 a.m. on Monday, Tuesday, Thursday, and Friday I exercise for sixty minutes. I get my heartbeat up to its training rate of 140 and maintain it for twenty minutes. I follow a healthy diet consisting of fruits, vegetables, and quality proteins. This gives me tremendous energy and stamina and I feel great!

I listen to my Creed in the morning while driving to work and again while driving home. I carry a copy with me in my day planner and read it when I am waiting for appointments. This continually reminds me of who I am and keeps in focus my blessings, my talents, and my goals. I am an incredible success and I thank God for my success.

Middle-Aged Father with Younger Children

I really have a great life. I am a good person to know. I am respected by the people who know me because of my reputation for being a professional. People trust me because I care about them, and I help them get the things they want. I am respected by my peers as someone who is successful and willing to serve in professional organizations.

I am a successful manager. My office is tastefully decorated in mauve and grey, and some of my original photographs are expertly displayed. When people enter the office they notice the new carpet and wallpaper, the floral arrangements, and the new furniture. Many people comment on how professional the office looks. I am particular about the standards of cleanliness in my office and the image that is reflected as people enter.

I create an atmosphere that helps the people who work in this office feel that they are part of a professional team. I always wear professional-looking suits in dark, tasteful colors, solid-colored newly pressed shirts, and clean, sharp ties. I carry myself with authority and my manner is always calm, befitting my position. I inspire confidence in my ability by the way I speak slowly and confidently. I always look people straight in the eye and I always listen carefully to what they say. I am relaxed in my manner and careful in my speech.

I have the uncanny ability to find and attract quality people who become self-motivated achievers because I am always aware of each employee. Each week I hold a personal performance review with each employee to let them know of my support for them and to help them identify and achieve their goals.

I have a nice home that is comfortable to be in and well-suited for having good times with friends. I enjoy having people over for swimming parties; they enjoy the pool area and the play yard, which I keep neatly trimmed and landscaped. The house is freshly painted and in good repair.

In the family room my friends and family enjoy the dynamic sound that comes from the JVC stereo system; we enjoy good movies on the Mitsubishi big-screen video monitor. It feels good to come home each day. My friends and associates always enjoy coming to my house because they feel comfortable there.

I am proud that I am able to give Nancy $3,000 each month for household expenses and that I have $1,000 each month to use as I please. I am proud of our home and our swimming pool and that we live in such a nice area.

I am married to a beautiful, dynamic woman. I am proud of Nancy and I encourage her to reach her best potential by developing her talents and abilities.

Nancy is action oriented; she has a good sense of her goals and what she wants to accomplish in her life, and she is working steadily toward them. She is overcoming her former feelings of low self-image by being fiercely competitive. She is respected by her peers and is gaining recognition in the community for her accomplishments.

Each day as I drive home from work, I think of something that I can say to compliment her. I get excited thinking how my kind words will make her feel, and I can't wait to get home to give her a loving hug, a tender kiss, and tell her that I love her.

I tell Nancy of my love for her each day. We are partners together in running the household and in raising the children. I reserve each Friday to spend with Nancy. This is our date night, and we always do something by ourselves to bring us closer together. During these times I seek feedback on how I am doing as a husband and father.

I am always a gentleman, constantly courting her with thoughtful etiquette and good manners. Even when I am provoked I speak in low tones. I am fiercely loyal to her, both in her presence and when I am away from her. In public and in private I only say those things which build her esteem. I flirt with her and her alone. My behavior provokes no jealousy. I bring variety and tenderness into our sexual relations and feel my greatest satisfaction when Nancy is fulfilled.

I create an atmosphere where Nancy can be proud of my accomplishments and eager to share them with other people. I conduct myself around my family in a way that Nancy is inspired to tell my children how proud she is of me, encouraging them to be like me. I am calm and self-assured at home.

As I drive toward my home, I also begin to think of my children and how I can reinforce their individual strengths. I have a special day set aside every week for each of my children where I always spend twenty minutes, one on one, listening and sharing with them, asking how I can be a better father and person.

Monday is for Susan. I am proud that she is playing on the basketball team and that she is doing well in her classes. I enjoy being around her—she is my friend. My concern is that she develops a sense of urgency about her life, and that she will challenge herself to reach a greater potential, never satisfied with average performance.

Tuesday is for Shana. She is much like her mother, and I am excited to think of the potential for achievement she has. I am proud of the growth I have seen in her these past two years. She is a compassionate person and is kind to people who may not have many friends. My concern is that she will be strong enough to lift others, but will not lower her own standards, even though her friends may exhibit lower standards of behavior. I am also concerned that she will be able to control her emotions as she begins to explore the world of boys.

Wednesday is for Robert. He is tender, sensitive, and good-looking. He is popular with his friends, yet is learning to be a leader in doing what he knows is right. I am proud of his accomplishments in the Boy Scouts, and I am committed to being with him for most of his activities. I am concerned that he will gain a strong character and sense of right behavior so that he will not be swayed when his friends tempt him to do something that is popular, yet wrong. I am also concerned about his health since he does not want to eat vegetables.

Thursday is for Tom, my athlete. He is feisty, physical, and very creative. He is emotional and enjoys all the physical attention I give him. I encourage his creative talents and help him with his soccer games. My concern for him is that I give him the affection and attention he needs to build a strong self-image. I also encourage him to keep his creative talent active and channel it into productive areas as he progresses in school.

Friday is for George, my most interesting challenge. He is very sensitive and needs lots of affection and attention. Of all the children he has the greatest need for individual attention. My commitment is to continually have the patience and wisdom to give him the individual attention he needs so that he may improve his reading and social skills. It appears that he will not be good at athletics and will likely be attracted to dramatic arts or music. I am excited to think of the great potential he has as he grows up.

Saturday is for Liz, my pride and joy. I am constantly pleased with the cute things she says and does. It is fun to watch her grow up, and it's great to have a little girl around the house. My concern is to teach her good social skills and to be a responsible member of the family. I try to avoid giving her everything she wants, which could spoil her.

I write a letter to each member of my family every six months and share my feelings with them. Susan in January and July; Sharon in February and August; Robert in March and September; Tom in April and October; George in May and November; Liz in June and December. I write to Nancy at least every January and July.

I create an atmosphere where my children can develop self-confidence and discover their talents. I do this by being supportive and by showing my love for them constantly so that they can recognize the power within them to become anything they want to become.

I help my children learn common sense by using it in my own actions; wisdom by allowing them to make mistakes; and high moral values by being honest in my own dealings.

I pray for guidance in knowing how to better serve them.

I have a monthly planning session every first Sunday at 4:00 p.m. with my family. I conduct these meetings, and we discuss the things we want to accomplish in the coming month and in the coming year. I record these things on a twelve-month planning calendar that is kept in the office at home where everyone can look at it.

Quarterly we create a new tradition for our family, which I identify, and record in our family history book.

With my family I plan for the acquisition of everything we decide we want. This includes the vacations we will take and the time we spend together, and it is written down in our yearly planning calendar.

I set an example of spirituality in my family by reading the Bible and other inspirational books each day for fifteen minutes before going to bed, always striving to know what Heavenly Father would have me do. I discuss my reading with my family when the opportunity presents itself.

I always get up before 6:30 a.m. and go through my exercise routine. I think of my flat stomach and my narrow waist as I do four sets of pushups, three sets of sit-ups, then ride the exercycle or jog in place. I get my heart rate up to 140 BPM for at least twenty minutes each day and I check it regularly. This keeps my heart strong and my waist trim. Because of my highly conditioned, energetic body, Nancy can't resist coaxing me to quit working and to come to her at night.

I go biking twice each week and climb each of the major peaks around the valley every year. I know that doing this maintains my weight at 160 pounds and my waist at 33 inches. People often comment on how good I look because I keep my abdomen flat and always have a smile. I always have energy to play with my children. My body feels better than it ever has and I am glad to be alive!

In my relationships I zero in on what others feel, think, and want—if I am confused I always check it out. I go beyond the superficial surface. I am an interpersonal explorer. I realize that anger is a defensive emotion and covers up either hurt or fear, so I am patient with angry people and try to discover what it is that is truly bothering them. I don't blame; I problem solve. I listen to understand and talk to be understood using feelings, thoughts, and wants. I then try to identify the problem, brainstorm alternatives, and seek solutions and alternatives for a win/win solution. I allow others their freedom. I forgive others and myself. I allow us to be human and have our weaknesses and mistakes in life. I am very patient and tolerant. I believe that I and others like me are trying to do our best and need support, love, understanding, recognition, praise, and forgiveness. I am a skilled communicator and teach others by my own example how to be intimate and loving. I consistently do a role-check with significant others I ask, "How can I be a better boss, father, son, business man, psychologist, and so forth?" I in turn am very disclosive. I allow myself to be interpersonally vulnerable.

I address people's needs: I try to provide a safe, secure environment where people feel valued and respected and where they can grow and have variety. I ask what a person's vision and dreams are, what they want and need, and why they want it. Then I ask how I can help them achieve those goals.

I recognize that all good, positive, faithful, hopeful, charitable thoughts are inspired of God and that all negative, discouraging, hateful thoughts come from the adversary. I encourage and nurture the positive in myself and others and discourage in myself and others the negative by replacing it with the positive. I actively support and encourage faith, hope, and charity. I have a positive mental attitude.

I am curious and fascinated with life—a kid at heart. I play, joke, tease, and love life and its challenges and humor. I am successful in the truest sense of the word. I live life to its fullest, savoring every experience. I am sensual. I stop to see, taste, feel, smell, and listen to the world around me. I am an adventurer. I jump in with both feet and get involved. Sometimes I choose to just sit back and observe, savor, enjoy and be fascinated with life and my experience of it. I value and love my sense of humor and playfulness, my enthusiasm and zest for life and all its experiences. I realize that I am at my best when I am happy, having fun, and making a game of what I am doing. I make sure I'm not too darn serious and I don't sweat the small stuff.

I am a leader who is as wise as a serpent but harmless as a dove. I take initiative and responsibility for being successful and leading others. I lead, teach, and show others how to be successful by (1) giving others a detailed vision of what the success will look like when we get there; (2) outlining goals based upon our vision; (3) establishing motives by asking "why" we want a certain thing; and (4) outlining a detailed plan of how to accomplish our goals. I present this rough draft of our visions, goals, motives, and plans to the group and refine our program, enlist their support, and receive feedback.

I am in total control of my thoughts and actions. If thoughts enter my mind that would otherwise detract from my purpose, I immediately begin to recite the song "Amazing Grace," which reminds me of my need to be worthy of inspiration from God in Heaven. As I go throughout my day I am confident because I know that I am doing the things that I have planned to do. I am flexible enough to adapt, as circumstances require changes in my plans.

I am aware of my divine origin, and I always strive for improved communication with my God by having a running dialogue in my mind, thanking him when things go well, and asking advice on what to do next. I think of him during the day and ask his advice constantly as I make decisions. I am eager each night to share my day with God, and I always begin each day by thanking him for his blessings and pleading for his constant companionship.

Sunday is a special day for me. I always wake up with the determination to be especially patient with my children and to set an example of Christian living for them.

I am excited about my LifeCreed; I know that by listening each day and incorporating these principles into action, I am constantly improving myself.

I feel each day that I am better than the day before and I am excited at my progress. I love to feel the joy that comes from living in total harmony with my beliefs.

Middle-Aged Father with Older Children

My role in life is to perfect myself. This entails daily personal growth through acting more Christlike each day. The most valued of all experiences are those involving giving and receiving love. By this I mean the development of a closer relationship with my wife and each of my sons and daughters. I exemplify Christ's attitudes and actions in every involvement that I have with them. These actions bring me closer to my Heavenly Father and influence my wife and children to seek that same end.

I serve the Lord as husband and father. I am a close personal friend to my wife. By this I mean that I affirm her in all she does through active listening and by valuing the things that are important to her. I create an atmosphere that encourages my sweetheart to succeed in the things she desires. I am a great confidant because I always listen to her thoughts and feelings without rebuff or defensiveness.

I grow closer to my Lord through scripture study each day at 6:30 a.m., always searching for what He would have me know and do to serve Him better. I love discussing my life with Him every night and morning, and I listen carefully to His promptings and instructions to increase our relationship to a deeper and more meaningful level. Through scripture study, meditation, and prayer I learn about the lives of great men and find examples of exemplary love. Heavenly Father has blessed me with a reasonable mind and a pleasing personality which help me to give love. I focus on Betty each Friday, Timmy on Monday, Robert each Tuesday, Marci each Wednesday, Sandi on Thursday, and Erin on Saturday. On their special day I mention to each one the joy I feel as I review their unique gifts and talents. I set aside twenty minutes on their special day, creating an environment of love and acceptance. I focus on my deep feelings of love for them and express my gratitude and thankfulness that they are part of my family. I always take Betty out each Friday night on a date to court her. I schedule time for a monthly daddy/daughter, father/son date with each of my children on the twelve-month calendar. These dates are unique and memorable as my no-limit attitude encourages their sharing of dreams and aspirations with me.

I love my mother and father. I feel great strength and joy in my family association as I have forgiven them of all the real or imagined injustices of my younger years. I view my parents and grandparents, as well as my children and their future children, as part of an unbroken line of God's children who are privileged to associate closely in earth's school.

I am a sensitive person who understands the feelings behind what people say to me. I am an active listener, listening for five minutes before I speak. I then respond to the emotion as well as the words. I question the speaker until I understand both. I am up-front and positively assertive, demonstrating my personal regard for everyone with whom I speak.

I have great friendships in my life because I value friends highly and seek constantly to find ways to serve them. By this I mean that I consciously and subconsciously seek and follow up on things that I can do to show others that they are valuable and worthy persons.

I help each of my children to understand and value close friendships and help each to interact in a positive way with people their own age—and, in fact, with people of all ages—through active listening. I am a great example for my children to pattern their lives after as a friend.

I look for the good in everyone I meet and allow all people their weaknesses. I am, therefore, a "safe haven" to those around me as I am able to see and express their strengths through compliments and sincere praise as an automatic and entirely natural act on my part. This draws people to me and helps them to be their best selves.

I am a man of action. By this I mean I get things done and follow good ideas to their completion. I am also thoughtful and wise and consider all possibilities of each issue before committing to a course of action.

I am totally self-disciplined. I focus all my mental powers and creativity and analytically examine all aspects of each challenge and decision that I am blessed to encounter. The tougher the challenge, the more focused I am. My confidence in my own ability and my faith in God's help enable me to be comfortable with upcoming decisions without worry or fear because I relate all decisions to my Creed. I know I always make the best choices because I have all the information that I need.

I value spiritual moments of meditation and prayer, remembering with fondness and awe the deep feeling of peace beyond words which filled my soul when the Lord gave me the spiritual confirmation of my decision to move to this town.

I remember the spiritual experiences I felt up on Weaver Mountain, in Madison and Rock Canyons, and at Yellowstone Lake.

I enjoy the weekly opportunity to share my special experiences with my family and to plan our lives together in family council. I encourage all the family to attend this important meeting; we always schedule it in our planning meeting on the first Sunday of each month at 4:30 p.m.

I am absolutely delighted with our new home and now have it completely furnished. Betty is really proud of it and loves showing it to our family and friends. I put her first in my life and have rewarded her for her strong support and help for the last twenty-eight years. She no longer feels like she has to "make do" and hope for better times. I feel like I have provided her with a home and lifestyle that she deserves. I appreciate her making our home more attractive and enjoyable and always tell her so.

The atmosphere in my home is constantly improving because I compliment and positively affirm my loved ones continually. Because I am happy with myself, I am happy with those around me. I am easy to get along with, tolerant, and pleasant. As I return from work each day, I put my business cares aside and think about how much my wife and children need my strength and good attitude. I find something specific to compliment my wife on and do all I can to create an atmosphere in which she can grow and bloom into the choice woman she wants to be. I include her in my life, both business and personal. I talk with her and seek her advice. I trust her, feel close to her, and am strengthened by her. I constantly search for ways to show her affection. I let her know my feelings and I am sensitive to her feelings. I enjoy giving her the things she desires. She is unique and important to me and I express this to her every day. I help with the housework and look for ways to lighten her load. I compliment her on her appearance and keep myself in shape to inspire her to stay in shape. I am her friend and confidant, someone she can lean on, trust, and depend on for support. I laugh with her and enjoy sharing those little humorous anecdotes that happen every day. Nothing comes before my wife.

I investigate and broadcast the successes of each family member. We celebrate those victories and revel in the unique strengths of each other. When adversity or defeat come, I am supportive, strong, and understanding. I respond to their feelings because I respond to my own feelings. I acknowledge the validity of the other person's feelings without judgment or denial.

Our most relaxed times at home come during quiet evenings when we warm ourselves before the fire in the fireplace. There is time then for one-on-one interaction, which I actively seek.

Our favorite winter family activity is skiing. I enjoy those excursions together into the mountains where we can appreciate the fabulous beauty of the winter landscape. I find great happiness in seeing my family enjoy the interaction and the activity, as well as the beauty. We ski together eight days each season and schedule these in our yearly planner so they are not neglected. We similarly enjoy water skiing in the summer for many of the same reasons and schedule eight days annually in our family planner.

My perfect physical body has tremendous endurance and stamina. I possess amazing reserves of energy and have the capacity to accomplish tremendous work at a high level of activity. I have very powerful leg and back muscles and a flat stomach. My upper body is well muscled and firm. I weigh 177 pounds and I am a hunk.

Aerobic exercise keeps my body in good shape and gives me a feeling of well-being. I always start my day at 6:00 a.m. with twenty minutes of exercise on the Nordic track at a heart rate of 145; then I do ten minutes of strength-building exercise.

I render community service through my church and as a parent who is actively involved in the affairs of the schools. I always attend parent-teacher conferences and go prepared to discuss specific issues of concern to me and to my children. Each teacher knows who I am. I always share my deep concern for quality education for each of my children.

I am so grateful for this wonderful life I have. Life is really beautiful.

Putting It All Together for Women

Young Working Mother—Married

I have a wonderful life. I am the one who determines what I do each day, and I am the only one who determines how I react to people and the situations around me. Therefore, I am always happy because I choose to be happy. I listen to this magnificent Creed at least three times every day because it keeps me focused on the wonderful goals and priorities I have set for myself.

I am well organized because I have the greatest daily schedule. It really helps me keep my life in order! Each morning at 6:30 a.m. I jump from my bed filled with enthusiasm for a new day. I love my special exercise time from 6:45 to 7:15 a.m. It really invigorates me physically and it makes me feel so great about my gorgeous body! I love taking care of myself and I always look fantastic and well put together. My elegant, classic wardrobe is such a delight to wear. I really enjoy acquiring one new coordinate to add to it each month. I take care of myself so that my husband's eyes constantly reflect the pride he feels in having such a great-looking wife. I set aside time each morning from 8:00 to 9:00 to keep our beautiful, large custom-built home neat and clean.

I love my family more than anything else in this world and I love being a great example to them. I have an aura about me that draws my husband and children to me. It says to them, "You are important to me. I love you. I support you. I actively listen to what you are thinking and saying. How do you feel? What can I do to make life better for you?"

I am a fantastic companion to my husband. I am constantly aware of his needs and I create circumstances where great communication takes place between us. My husband knows he is first in my life because of the way I treat him in word and action. I look forward to our weekly date night because it gives me another chance to be together with my best friend. We especially enjoy going out to eat and attending concerts together. As part of our special night, I always ask Richard how I can be a better wife, companion for him, and mother to our children. I put his suggestions in this life creed.

Richard and I love to travel. We spend one month each year traveling. We especially enjoy traveling around our beautiful country, but we also consider ourselves to be citizens of the world. I am anxiously anticipating our exciting trips to Europe, Canada, New Zealand, and the South Sea Islands that are coming up as scheduled in our ten-year planner.

I love each one of my five beautiful children. I treasure the time I spend with them! I like my children as people and I enjoy talking to them. I go to all their activities and I support them with my presence and with my enthusiasm. I am absolutely committed to keeping a scrapbook for each of my children. To that end I set aside the first Friday morning of each month to work on these special records.

I am committed to taking one formal class each school year to feed my curiosity about the world around me. I discover one new thing about the world each day and I pass along those insights to my children every day as I help them with their homework from 7:00 to 7:30 p.m. I am also a voracious reader and spend twenty minutes every evening at 9:00 p.m. reading a good book.

I am so very thankful for the gifts of an understanding heart, compassion, and intelligence that I have been blessed with. I relish the opportunity I have each Sunday from 4:00 to 5:00 p.m. to reflect on the things I am doing well, to set new goals for myself, and to prepare myself for the things that are going to happen in the coming weeks and months. I am absolutely committed to keeping a journal of my life for me and for my children. I write in it every Sunday night during my reflection time.

Family Council on Sunday night is sacred in our home. I carefully prepare each week so that I am ready to support and participate in this choice family activity. I am committed to making birthdays and holidays around our house something special. I actively work to find and implement or develop new traditions that help us enjoy these times together even more.

I treasure the opportunity I have to attend church each week with my family. I am always prepared to partake of the Spirit that is there and I learn something new about our Lord every time I go to church. I love taking my family to church with me. I am so excited about it that I am able to motivate them to leave early enough so that we can be in our seats five minutes before church starts.

I have been blessed with so many wonderful things: I am healthy and strong, I have a Heavenly Father who loves me, a family that idolizes me, and a husband who thinks the world revolves around me because I work so hard at deserving these blessings. Because I know there are many who do not have these same blessings, I reach out to them through the service I perform for my community. I spend several hours each month helping those who are less fortunate than I am. My favorite charities are public radio and TV, the Red Cross, and shelters for abused women and children. It's so nice to be able to share my financial resources, as well as my time, with these great causes.

People are awed by my ability to remember their names. I am a great listener and I always find out what the other person is thinking before I speak. People come to me with their problems because they can tell by my actions and attitudes that I am a person who really cares about them.

I enjoy the professional work that I do. My work place is a fantastic, interesting, and intellectually stimulating place. There are so many exciting, financially viable projects being developed by our company! I know I make a valuable contribution to this company with my honed organizational skills.

My motto is "Do it now." I always do what I commit to and I make every deadline. I am always honest and straightforward in my dealings with my colleagues and I communicate with them openly and truthfully at all times.

I finish my PhD in October two years from now, and I stay up to date in my field by reading professional magazines and journals from 4:30 to 5:00 p.m. every weekday. I love my part-time job teaching undergraduate and graduate students at the university and am so grateful to have the greatest research project imaginable.

All in all, I think I have a wonderful life and I wouldn't trade places with anyone in the world!

Working Mother—Single

I am so happy to be alive. I love my life and the opportunities that I have for growth and success.

I am organized. I am always on time to every appointment. I arise at 6:00 a.m. every morning, pray, and write in my journal. I awake excited for another day, and I feel great because I always get the needed rest for my body and mind. During the weekdays I always go to bed at 11:00 p.m.

Because my life is organized I have plenty of time for all areas of my life: social, mental, physical, spiritual, and family. I am creative and very successful at earning a living. I am financially secure. I always have ideas for creating an income for myself and my family.

In January six years from now, my income is $100,000 per year. I have $50,000 in a life's savings account. I am in total control of my spending and live by a budget. I have a comfortable life as my needs for clothing, food, and shelter are always met. I am able to travel to Europe once a year, and I always pay cash. I have no debt. I am free to completely enjoy the challenge of free enterprise.

I am admired and respected by my family and peers. My brothers often ask for my opinion and advice on financial matters, and I have been able to lend them money on occasion at an interest rate below the bank's current lending rate. When they speak to me, the look in their eyes and the tone of their voices communicate admiration and respect, and even a bit of reverence. They are appreciative of my help because I give good, sound financial advice.

I love my work. I am excited to see each client. I have the highest regard for every person. They are unique and I am always happy to have the opportunity to use my talents. My creative juices really flow in my workplace. I have endless ideas and inspiration. My workspace is always clean and organized. I love being there because I always have the necessary tools and supplies to do whatever my client's desire.

I often travel to shows and classes. I attend a weeklong seminar at least once a year. Because I do well and am financially secure, I am able to pay for travel expenses and maintain my home and business while I am away.

My expertise in my field is sought after by my peers because I am well versed in the latest methods of (my business). I am grateful for my talents, always excited to improve them and share my knowledge and skills with others.

I always finish what I start. Whatever project I start gets completed with the same enthusiasm and integrity that it was started. I complete art projects, home improvements, business, and family commitments. I always keep my word to friends, family, and business associates, and especially to myself. I am reliable and constant.

I only commit to those projects I know I can finish and I do quality work. I give my best effort. I have a tremendous amount of energy and talent and I am absolutely dependable.

I bike every morning at 7:00 a.m. I ride seven to ten miles per day. I also work out at the spa three times a week on Monday, Wednesday, and Friday from 10:00 to 11:00 a.m. I love to exercise because it makes me feel great. My lung capacity is constantly improving, my body is cleansing itself of toxins, my muscles are getting stronger and tighter. I am feeling better as I grow older. My skin is getting tighter as well, and it glows with health and vitality. I have the look of an athlete. I feel the dedication and competitive spirit of an individual who wins. My body is lean, muscles well defined. When I walk into the gym guys stare. They are both intimidated and admiring. I am a winner. I work hard and I achieve my goals. I push my muscles to the limit. I thank God for my strong, healthy body. I am graceful as well as strong. I am a dancer. I feel rhythm and movement. I am a combination of femininity and strength, of softness and courage.

I am at peace with my body. I treat it with love and respect. I eat only good foods. I eat fruits and vegetables, grains and pasta. I eat smaller amounts of lean meats, fish, and dairy products. I love to drink water—cool, refreshing, wonderful, water. When I drink water I feel it flushing the toxins and fats out of my body. I feel it moisturizing my body, my skin. I drink at least two quarts of water per day. I am young, healthy, and happy. I am complete. I am proud of my body and my face. I am gifted in body and mind. I overcome any obstacle. I am alive and aware. I am in control. Life is wonderful!

I am a caring person. I am sensitive and responsive to people's needs. I am expressive and loving. I create great friendships and loyalties because I give great love and loyalty. I am intelligent and sensitive and love a good time. I have the ability to see humor and use my wit to soften life's stressful times. I am resilient and strong.

I love to dance and sing. I love adventure and excitement. Life is always a challenge, an opportunity. I always find the bright and hopeful side to a challenge.

I love peace and harmony in my home. I have an excellent relationship with my daughter, Judy, because I actively listen to her. At mealtime we always discuss her day; at bedtime I take time to listen to her prayers, and then I softly scratch her back to relax her. I am sensitive to her feelings. Bedtime is a special time for us to talk and listen to each other and review the day's events.

Judy is a joy to me, an inspiration. I ask Judy how I can be a better mom and I listen. I give wise counsel to my daughter. I have infinite patience. I respond to frustrating situations with calmness and serenity. I express my concerns with love.

I create an atmosphere of love and acceptance in my home. My child and her friends feel unconditional love and freedom to grow and develop their individual, unique gifts and personalities. Because I am nonjudgmental and see the good in individuals, and because I use my sense of humor, my home often rings with laughter, abounding in warmth and love.

I create an atmosphere where Judy is taught and encouraged by example and word to have good manners and consideration for others' feelings. My actions always demand respect. I tolerate only loving and kind behavior. Everyone's space is of equal importance in my home.

I am consistent. I have the strength and ability to accomplish my goals. I am not alone. I need and accept God's help and love, and also the friendship and advice from those persons whose wisdom and experience exceed my own. Because I am intelligent and successful I welcome and appreciate the counsel of positive and successful people. I seek constant and continual encouragement and give the same. I align myself with the loving, positive, good powers and energies of the universe.

I am good and I respond to love—love of God, love for myself, and love for my fellowman. I am committed to my course.

I choose to do right and worship God in deed and thought. I give thanks for my blessings. I acknowledge the power and the authority of God and His servants. I am in His service and in His debt. I thank Him always, day and night.

Single Woman

I awake and arise at 6:00 a.m., joyful at facing a day full of opportunity. I look forward to beginning the day. I feel rested and alert and excited to see what the day will bring. I exercise for forty-five minutes with my heart rate at

132 for twenty minutes. I choose walking, aerobics, or the ski machine. When I am walking I feel myself in tune with the trees and breeze; my soul renews as I walk. I happily search for opportunities to walk alone or with Sarah. I enjoy the exercise, feeling my muscles stretching, growing taut, relaxing, and my body growing lean and healthy. My body reacts to exercise by increasing circulation, metabolizing food well, ridding itself of toxins, balancing hormones, and using oxygen well. With each exercise session I feel stronger, healthier, and the exercise becomes easier.

I stand tall, with good posture, moving gracefully and with poise. I have energy. My body is firm and well-shaped and I have confidence in how I look. My hair and nails are healthy and well groomed. My body is clean and sweet smelling. I am 5 foot 6 inches and weigh 125 pounds. My eye-hand coordination is excellent and I enjoy playing volleyball, tennis, softball, and group sports. I particularly love to dance. My body responds well to the demands made by my mind as it expresses my feelings and responds to the music. I dance jazz, Latin, and ballroom style. I attract partners in partner dancing because I keep myself well practiced in various dances. I delight in body control and my ability to express myself well through dance. I am in harmony with my body and appreciate its added dimension to my soul. I take good care of my body, giving it 12 glasses of water each day, which efficiently serves my body's needs.

I eat grains, fruits, and vegetables. My body accepts the food easily, using it effectively. I enjoy eating and eat until filled. My body burns the excess fat quickly so that it remains lean and trim. My stomach is flat, my legs strong and slim, my buns tight, my back straight. My body is limber, lively, strong, and works well. It never lets me down.

I enjoy feeling the clothes fall on my lean body and slither down. I have abundant energy because my body is extremely well conditioned and very well maintained. Every day I feel an increase in stamina. To ensure that I enjoy life to its fullest, I take extreme care to eat well prepared, nourishing meals. I plan them ahead, always eating three meals a day. I make sure that I always eat them at a regular time. I savor the flavor of good foods. I make sure that each meal includes several vegetables and grains. I eat slowly and chew carefully. I enjoy the preparation and anticipation of the coming meal.

I obtain power from righteous living. The ever-growing strength in my spirit causes me to eschew evil. I love being a daughter of Heavenly Father; I have a glow and warmth from that love. I open my heart to feel His approval and appreciation. My high self-esteem comes from my relationship with Him and I tenderly protect that relationship. Each morning at 7:15 I have an hour of meditation and planning time right after I have dressed for the day. I read the scriptures and study guides as I seek for greater understanding. I thoughtfully prepare and then speak with the Lord. I respectfully approach Him and carefully listen to His direction and teachings to me. I tune into His strength and power and add to my own. I speak with the Lord honestly and openly. My prayers are purposeful and meaningful. I have confidence that I understand His directions and trust my ability to respond to His promptings.

I am optimistic. I expect the best.

I recognize the value of my time, resources, and energy and wisely make decisions on spending them. I see what steps need to be taken and what resources are needed. I effectively judge the energy required from me and make allocations of my time and resources for that which I want most in life. I master my time so that I handle stress easily. I schedule time carefully and keep the commitments I have made. I choose uplifting and enlightening books, movies, and television programs. I choose to be with people who uplift and enlighten, but learn from everyone I am around. I relax well, even as I go about my daily routine. I am slow to jump to conclusions and calm in a crisis. If I feel stress I recognize it, take time to stretch and rid my body of its effects, close my eyes for a moment, and calm myself.

I am fun to be around—spontaneous, creative, and exciting. I am positive and happy and have an uncanny ability to attract quality people. I enjoy life. That joy is contagious to those around me. I have a rewarding time establishing and maintaining relationships and look forward to spending time with friends, both men and women. People seek to be with me. They sense there are wonderful things in my soul and our bonds grow.

When I meet people I look them in the eyes. I observe good points about each person, mention it when appropriate, and use it to remember that person. I notice their eyes—the color, expression, and physical features around them. I key in on their eyes the next time I see them and it reminds me of their names. I use their names at least three times in the conversation. I have a great memory for names. I always key my memory by saying, "What is that person's name? It will come to me in a minute."

I sense my capacity to remember growing each day. I use this skill to memorize a scripture, quote, or poem each week. The mental exercise is very rewarding. I am so excited to learn that I stay wide-awake and alert while reading. My mind is focused. I study things and people around me. I notice changes in people, and I take note of my environment. I read magazines, books, and newspapers. I read religious information, current events, self-improvement topics, the classics, and much more. I particularly enjoy reading on Sunday when I have time to concentrate and relax. I remember what I read with excellent recall.

I easily grasp new concepts and am stimulated when using my brain to understand, memorize, and find solutions.

I am gracious and appreciative. When others are giving or kind I am responsive and grateful. I graciously accept others' giving to me, but judge well before asking too much of anyone. I acknowledge those who have a part of my life and my personality.

I am generous. I constantly surprise people anonymously, receiving great joy from doing so. I am the first to laugh at my own mistakes, trying to help others not to feel self-conscious or ill at ease when they make mistakes.

I make a point of giving honest compliments and praise. I am a good conversationalist. I keep myself well-informed on current events and issues and am able to discuss them intelligently. I have a talent for putting my thoughts into words that express my feelings and ideas. I say what I am thinking and feeling in a concise and interesting way, being diplomatic and tactful. I am honest and real. I tell people how I feel and am true to myself without feeling guilty. I am gentle and kind, but firm when necessary. I recognize when it is important to share from myself. I remember stories and incidents and clean jokes and bring lightness and laughter into conversations. I am entertaining at appropriate times.

I am an active listener. When I am with others, I look them in the eyes. Each person has my undivided attention until other priorities enter in. Then I kindly extricate myself. I invite others to share in such a way that they are comfortable and at ease. They know they can trust me and that I keep confidences.

I give others space to make their own decisions, control their own lives, and encourage them to reach their potential. I am happy to be a sounding board and like the role of cheerleader for their lives. I also allow them to work out their own problems in the way they choose—expressing confidence in their ability to do so. I give others the benefit of the doubt and realize they may have other perspectives. I allow others their weaknesses, focusing instead on their strengths. I expect the best of others but accept what they give. I am appropriately confrontive. If I feel tension in a relationship, I work for resolution so the lines of affection are kept open. I seek feedback from those I respect and avoid being defensive. I am aware of actions that make others feel uncomfortable and clearly evaluate the necessity of those actions in my happiness. When someone offends me I deal with the emotions at that time with the person from whom I took offense.

I feel each day that I am better than the day before, and I am excited at my progress. I love to feel the joy that comes in living in total harmony with my beliefs.

I sing well. My voice is clear and full. It's easy to breathe correctly. My diaphragm moves properly to support the tone and I easily reach notes in a broad range.

I like learning new ideas. I like deep thinking and problem solving. I am creative in my thinking. I am good at brainstorming and finding options and possibilities. I have vision and good imagination.

I tole paint with confidence and decisiveness. I visualize the final project, quickly and decisively painting each item, and finding great pleasure in my talent. I also arrange flowers beautifully and finish all crafts well. Whatever I put my hand to I complete, and I learn in the process. I challenge myself and enjoy stretching my abilities.

I am comfortable before a crowd. I enjoy singing, dancing, delivering a speech, or teaching a class. I always prepare well and have confidence because I am ready.

I love working with youth. I enjoy being their cheerleader and aiding in their search for their souls and personalities. I savor their growth and point out their strengths. I teach them by example and personal contact. I spend time with them, listen to them, and encourage them. When we are together their souls are warmed and they are inspired to believe in themselves.

I thoroughly enjoy my work. I love my clients. When clients meet me, they feel that they can trust me and that I have a great deal of knowledge about my field. They sense respect and warmth from me. I have great insight and understanding of those I meet. I am cordial when clients come in and think empathetically about their needs and feelings. Our relationship is always a positive experience for them. I explain well the information I give and they feel that they can ask questions. I am patient with their need for information and reassurance. They feel comfortable with me. I keep in mind the importance of customer satisfaction. I am wise when deciding which clients to take on and which ones will tax our resources too much. On their return visits to the office, I call them by name, often touch them on the shoulder, and acknowledge their importance to our office.

I arrive at the office at 8:30 a.m. The first hour is spent in studying, filing, and preparing for the day. At 9:30 I focus on the files that need my attention the most. I organize my priorities well and stay focused as the other demands of the day present themselves. I use my time effectively, choosing each hour the most effective and important things to do. I approach my clientele with positive expectations. I am committed to excellence in my career, always mindful that my personal life comes before the demands of work. I quickly return phone calls and always follow through on assignments that I take on. Deadlines are always met because I plan so well ahead. I wrap up my paperwork by 5:00 p.m. I work hard to be a positive part of our team. I work on ideas until we come together on our desires and are not competing with each other.

I enjoy the office staff. I watch closely for their accomplishments and compliment them specifically. I enlist their help in establishing office rules and expect them to conduct themselves accordingly. They appreciate my leadership and follow easily. We have fun and laughter in the office at appropriate times. They know from my actions and attitude that their happiness is a priority to me. I have an efficient office system and strive to continually improve to meet our clients' needs. I am open to ideas from the staff and enlist their suggestions and feedback. Staff members know that they can approach me for counsel, that I am wise and fair in making decisions. I approach them in an open, easy, happy, grateful manner. I am generous with praise. I pitch in whenever necessary to take action in resolving conflicts and problems. I speak well of them to others. I am favorably viewed by upper management and, when I am with them, I converse easily.

I have a keen sense for recognizing honest and profitable business ideas. In four years my earnings are $85,000; in six years my earnings are $100,000; and in eight years my carnings are $120,000. I save ten percent of my income and keep a savings account of $25,000 for emergencies for myself or my family. I seldom use credit, using cash for most purchases. I have mastered the discipline of budgeting. I use the utmost prudence and sensibility when spending money. I save $40.00 monthly for "The Sisters" reunion. In one year we are flying to Boston for a vacation. My savings allows us to schedule other vacations together every other year. I enjoy my home and furnishings and the wardrobe that my income produces. I receive satisfaction and joy by performing anonymous acts of giving to those in need. My income allows me to send money, flowers, gift certificates, or food when I recognize a way I can help.

Giving of my time and efforts is always more important than money. I am descriptively precise in writing my Creed. I listen to it daily and my subconscious mind recommits to the values and expectations I have for myself.

On the first Sunday of each month I review my goals and my Creed and make changes as warranted. I anticipate these reviews and enjoy the growth and planning. I record my feelings in my journal daily, especially noting spiritual insight, growth, understanding, and accomplishments.

My strong, well-directed inner drive and brilliant imagination allow me to visualize myself reaching my goals. My mind, heart, and spirit are united and congruent, creating a power and force that gives me all I desire.

Appendix C:
Mindbody Science Empowers
LifeBalance Principles

While it is not critical to understand how your watch operates in order to tell the time accurately, some of us just need to know how things work to be comfortable using them. And while we use our brain each day with no thought to how it functions, when we are discussing changing it, there are many who want to know what is going on behind the scenes that makes this possible. This appendix will assist those who need to know, and those who are just curious. I should also say, that for many of you this is not just idle curiosity, but an absolute prerequisite to begin the process of implanting the LifeBalance Tools I have presented in this book. The concepts presented here will give you the confidence to try out the tools they validate.

It is also important for me to point out that the science presented here supports the authenticity of what over forty years of personal experience has already proven to me: motive is power!

With tremendous admiration and gratitude, I wish to give special recognition to my dear friends, Mark Kastleman and Dr. Page Bailey. A world-renowned neuropsychologist, Bailey dedicated his life to helping people understand and implement original methods and processes through which they can consciously direct their **mindbody** to overcome addiction, chronic illness, chronic pain, negative habits, and achieve success in every aspect of life. The results—Bailey helped people around the world—are nothing short of miraculous. His influence, tutelage, and mentoring have had a profound effect on me.

Why Is It So Difficult to Change?

Have you ever been introduced to a great self-improvement idea from a book, tape, radio or TV program, or seminar and excitedly thought to yourself, "If I could just find a way to integrate that into my life, it would make such a positive difference." You write the idea down and set a goal to start living it. Perhaps it's a strategy to lose weight, improve your marriage, reduce your stress, make more money, or communicate better with your children. The point is, when you first hear the idea you're excited, and you really want to do it! But after a few days or weeks your enthusiasm wanes, and you end up right back in the same old rut and routine. Why? Why is it so difficult to make a change? The answer is the enormous power of habits.

The reason people have such a difficult time changing is due to the enormous power of habits. From the moment of your birth, your mindbody seeks to turn every important activity and tendency into a habit. (The term *mindbody* may be unfamiliar to you. Dr. Page Bailey created it. This term and others like it, such as *bodymind*, are used by a growing number of leading neuroscientists and psychologists to refer to the mind, brain, and body as one completely connected and integrated system of constant communication and modification.) Your mindbody seeks to automate everything you do. Once something is mastered and becomes automatic, the mindbody can direct its resources and energies to learning new skills. This is called the principle of efficiency, and it is the mindbody's number one goal. Think of all the things you learned as a child that you now do automatically: tying your shoes, writing your name, riding a bike. Imagine what would happen if every time you wanted to perform a common task your mindbody had to master it all over again?

In his book *A Universe of Consciousness*, Dr. Gerald Edelman quotes Henry Maudsley: "If an act became no easier after being done several times, if the careful direction of consciousness were necessary to its accomplishments in each occasion, it is evident that the whole activity of a lifetime might be confined to one or two deeds."

Were it not for the power and efficiency of habits, we would accomplish little in life.

Change is difficult because the mindbody expends enormous time and energy to develop habits. Asking the mindbody to go back and change a habit—something it has worked so hard to make automatic—is asking a lot; it goes against the mindbody's natural and dominant goal of efficiency. The mindbody jealously guards its habits and doesn't change them quickly or easily.

You already have natural built-in habit-forming mechanisms and skills you have been using since the day you were born. You are amazingly effective and efficient at forming habits. Unfortunately, most of your habits have been formed subconsciously, without you being aware of the process. What if you could learn how to consciously and purposely direct your natural habit-forming processes to eliminate your negative behaviors and attain the life, success, and relationships you desire?

In order to harness and direct your powerful habit-formation abilities, you must first learn how these processes operate in your mindbody.

The Power of Mental Models

Through your genetic make-up you have inherited the tendency to form what are known as totalities. From the day of your birth, and perhaps even in the womb, your mindbody has been taking everything you experience and using it to build a vast network of connections that Nobel Prize recipient Dr. Gerald M. Edelman calls a Dynamic Core. Within this dynamic core, your mindbody builds specific groups of connections known as mental models. It is through these mental models that everything you experience is interpreted and given meaning.

To illustrate the operation of mental models, Bailey has created the following exercise

If I ask you to connect these three dots, how would you do it?

●

● ●

If you're like most people, you immediately visualized a triangle. How did you get a triangle from three dots? You've just experienced the result of a mental model. As the three dots were processed through the appropriate mental model, you instantly perceived a triangle. For you, the meaning of the three dots is a triangle.

This mental model process can be illustrated as follows:

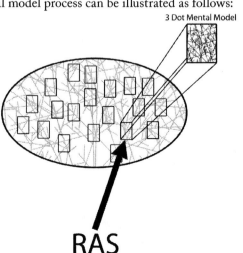

3 Dot Mental Model

RAS

Connections = Mental Models

Within your mindbody are virtually limitless connections linked to everything you've ever experienced, and these connections are constantly expanding. Specific groups of these connections form mental models.

The RAS: Your Air Traffic Controller

At the base of your brain is the Reticular Activating System or RAS. Your RAS is like an air traffic controller. In any given situation it decides which of all the vast number of your mental models to activate. Unless you force it to do otherwise, your RAS will always choose the mental model that is the most dominant for the given situation. When you see the three dots, the image is routed through your eyes to your RAS and then to the most dominant mental model—the one you have accessed most in the past to interpret what the three dots mean.

When you first saw the three dots, why didn't you immediately visualize the following:

The reason you didn't choose this option for connecting the dots is that you have never seen it before; you don't have a mental model for interpreting the three dots in this manner. However, now that you have seen this new way of connecting the three dots, you will never be fooled by this exercise again. Your "Three Dot Mental Model" has been forever altered. If you see this exercise in the future, you will respond to it differently. From now on, the meaning of the three dots will be different for you.

In Your Mindbody, *Meaning* Is Everything

The meaning of everything in your life is the result of mental models. Your mental models control your beliefs, attitudes, and perceptions. They control the expectations you have for certain outcomes in your life and your response or reaction in any given situation. The way you're sitting right now, your posture, your reading speed and style, the way you're dressed, the style of your hair—all of these are the result of mental models. And perhaps most important to our discussion in this appendix, all of your habits flow from the mental models you have repeatedly activated during your lifetime.

Whether you are conscious of it or not, mental models are always active in your mindbody, dictating your perceptions and determining the content and quality of every aspect of your life. The meaning of everything around you is determined by the mental models you have formed over your lifetime.

Learning to Drive a Stick Shift

The various connections in a mental model determine the meaning that is triggered when that mental model is accessed. For example, imagine learning to drive a stick shift and the connections your mindbody forms in that mental model: coordinating the right hand on the gearshift, left hand on the steering wheel, left foot on the clutch, right foot on the brake and gas pedal. Add to this feelings of embarrassment and awkwardness, and you have some of the initial connections in your mental model for "driving a stick shift." The mental model might look something like this:

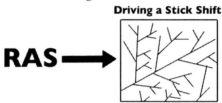

Now imagine while trying to coordinate the shifting procedure, you take your eyes off the road resulting in a horrible accident. You nearly die and you're in the hospital for six months. Imagine the vast number of connections added to your mental model for driving a stick-shift! Your transformed mental model would look something like this:

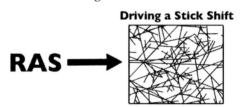

Imagine after your recovery, you get into a car with a manual transmission. As you take hold of the gearshift, imagine the mental model your RAS accesses and the vast array of connections that switch on. What does taking hold of that gearshift mean to you now? How is the meaning different from what it was before your accident?

Mental models with connections to powerful feelings, emotions, and memories can create powerful thoughts, reactions, attitudes, and habits. These mental models create powerful meaning.

Repetition and Mental Models

In addition to meaning, repetition also plays a major role in the power of mental models. The more a mental model is accessed and activated over time, the more powerful it becomes—its connections increase in number and strength. In addition, the pathway from the RAS to the mental model becomes increasingly rutted. This is akin to the saying practice makes perfect. Doing the same thing over and over again forms powerful habits, bringing the activity or behavior to the point where you don't have to consciously think about it any more. Remember, your mindbody's number one goal is efficiency. As soon as an activity becomes automatic, your mindbody can move on and direct its energies and resources to learning and mastering something new.

When you first form a mental model, the pathway from your RAS is shallow and faint. It looks something like this:

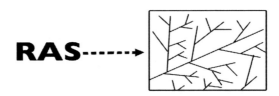

However, when you repeatedly access a specific mental model over time, an exaggerated pathway from your RAS to that mental model is formed, like a set of deeply rutted tire tracks on a muddy mountain road that has been traveled over and over again. In addition, each time a mental model is accessed, it expand—its connections increase in number and in strength.

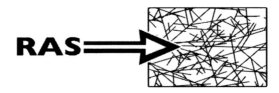

When these dominant connections and deeply rutted pathway are present, your RAS will automatically select this mental model in the applicable situation.

Combining Meaning and Repetition = Powerful Habits

While meaning or repetition alone can form strong habits, putting the two together is a powerful combination. Consider the following real-life examples:

The Dentist and Vomit

I know a dentist whose greatest fear in life is throwing up—he fears it worse than death. (Imagine the vast connections in his mental model and the rutted pathway leading to it!) Early one morning as he approached his first patient of the day, he noticed something in the sink next to her. You guessed it—vomit! He thought, "Oh no, she got up late, ate too fast, and was nervous about the visit. She's gone and thrown up in my sink!"

Even though he was twenty feet from the sink, he could smell it. Immediately he began to feel nauseated, his head started to hurt, and he was just about to stagger off to the restroom, when his assistant took the vomit from the sink and threw it across the room, bouncing it off his chest. It was rubber!

Knowing of his phobia, his assistant had purchased fake vomit at a gag shop and in collaboration with the patient, played a joke on him.

How is it that a grown man, an intelligent, successful professional, could smell plastic vomit? The answer: meaning!

When the image of that vomit was routed through his RAS, where did the RAS instantly send it? Right down the rutted pathway to his dominant mental model for vomit. All of the connections in that mental model, including those linked to his childhood flu memories; his smell, his stomach, and his head were instantly switched on like Las Vegas at night!

The Swastika

When Ruth was a child, she was separated from her parents and confined to a Nazi concentration camp. Although she survived the experience, the mental model (meaning) she formed through the horror and atrocities was vast and deep, expanded and accessed (repetition) thousands of times during her years of imprisonment.

Over sixty years later, as Ruth was walking down an American street, she instantly recognized the symbol on a flag hanging from an apartment balcony; it was the Swastika! When that image entered through her eyes and reached her RAS, it was immediately routed to its mental model. Imagine the deeply rutted pathway leading to the dominant mental model associated with that symbol and the meaning it had for Ruth!

Instantly Ruth experienced an overwhelming response in her mindbody. Her heart rate spiked. Her breathing became heavy. All of the horror, fear, anger, and myriad other emotions boiled up inside her. She started to cry as she felt panic racing through her. She felt an overwhelming urge to run! She was reliving the childhood trauma. As a result of the mental model, her mindbody repeated the same physiological and biological responses it had produced countless times in the concentration camps.

A moment later, a child on a tricycle rode past her and looked up at the same flag. He showed no response to the image.

Why the extreme contrast in their reactions? The information they received through their eyes was identical. It was the meaning the image held for each one, the pre-existing mental models, that were radically different. In the concentration camps Ruth had developed a powerful Swastika mental model and through accessing that mental model thousands of times, she had etched vast connections and a deeply rutted pathway leading to it. The habit (mental model) was still with her sixty years later.

Giving Blood

During his teenage years, Dave became addicted to heroine. After tremendous struggle through several recovery programs, he was finally able to continue on and lead a normal life. However, there was one thing Dave would never be able to do: give blood.

Just seeing the needle moving toward his vein caused a chemical and physiological reaction so powerful, it was as if heroine had just been injected into Dave's body! Frequent repetition of his earlier heroine habit had created a dominant mental model, meaning, and rutted pathway that made the routine act of giving blood unbearable.

Reality versus Memory

In the three examples above, you will notice that each of the individuals responded, not based on reality, but according to their perception of that reality, their memories, and their pre-existing dominant mental models: The dentist could smell plastic vomit; Ruth saw the Nazi flag and reacted as if she were in immediate and terrible danger; Dave saw the needle and responded as if he had just injected heroine.

Every day we react to people, situations, and stimuli in ways that don't agree with reality. Why? Carefully consider the following principle: when meaning is powerful, your mindbody cannot distinguish between what is real and what your mental models tell you is real.

When a specific mental model is accessed over and over again in response to a certain stimulus or event, the response becomes habitual—it generates a habit. When confronted with the same circumstance or stimulus in the future, your mindbody accesses the same mental model, producing the same response. Your mindbody doesn't stop to ask, "Is this real or imagined?" As Bailey so eloquently states, "The mindbody is always engaged in the process of bringing our experience into a state of agreement with the expectations that are produced by our mental models."

With dominant mental models and their resulting habits, history continually repeats itself in your mindbody.

Are there automatic negative behaviors you keep repeating in your life that prevent you from attaining all the success, fulfillment, and happiness you desire? Do you sometimes react in ways that aren't logical or based on reality? Do you have certain negative mental models with deeply rutted pathways that dominant your life? For example:

- Poor eating habits
- Addictions
- Negative thinking
- Critical or judgemental
- Temper
- Fears or phobias
- Closed-minded, stubborn
- Harboring a grudge or resentment

- Negative financial habits
- Poor physical condition
- Unhappy marriage
- Unsatisfied with career
- Stressed out
- Stuck in a rut
- Childhood trauma
- Cynical, pessimistic

If any of the above, or other negative patterns apply to you, it probably isn't for lack of effort. You probably have set numerous goals and tried many times to change negative habits and behaviors, sometimes succeeding and many times not. Why not? Because it's an unfair competition.

Habits versus Goals: A Competition

Whenever you pursue a goal to behave differently than you have in the past, you immediately create a competition between your new goal and your existing dominant mental model. Consider the following illustration:

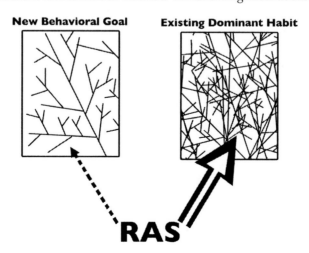

New Behavioral Goal   **Existing Dominant Habit**

RAS

Notice the connections in the new mental model are few, while the connections in the dominant mental model are vast—the power of emotion and meaning in each mental model is very different. Notice the pathway leading to the mental model for the new behavioral goal is faint, while the pathway to the existing mental model/habit is deeply rutted.

Imagine each mental model is a magnet and your RAS is a compass arrow. The more powerful the connections in the mental model (feelings, emotions, memories, meaning) the more powerful the magnetic force pulling your RAS toward that mental model. And the more deeply rutted and well-traveled the pathway to that mental model, the more easily your RAS goes there.

What chance is there that your RAS will select the faint path to the mental model with few connections over the deeply rutted path to the dominant mental model containing vast connections and powerful meaning? Without your conscious intervention, there's no chance. If you don't know how to use specific intervention tools in this automatic mindbody process, expecting the new behavioral goal to win out is like facing a fire hose with a squirt gun.

In any given situation, the time it takes your RAS to select a mental model is a fraction of a second. And the entire selection process typically takes place at the unconscious level. You don't fully realize what's happening until the heat of the moment passes. Frustration and disappointment set in. You can't believe you've repeated the negative behavior again.

Based on what you now know about mental models and habits, and how they become dominant, is it reasonable to expect that just because you read a few books and attended a seminar, you can derail a lifetime of mental model and habit formation?

Every day people pit new behavioral goals against existing dominant habits. Not understanding that the mindbody jealously guards its habits and doesn't change them quickly or easily, people attempt to change years of habitual behavior by reading a book, listening to a CD, or attending a seminar. They attempt to reverse poor financial habits, get out of debt, reduce stress, improve a struggling marriage, lose weight, break out of depression, balance a hectic life, or overcome addictions. But aside from occasional victories, old habits seem to win out most of the time.

Are You Free to Choose?

You may be wondering, "Do I truly have the freedom to choose my own destiny or am I more or less subject to my negative habits and the dominant mental models that drive them?"

For centuries the debate of free will versus a product of my past has raged in the scientific and philosophical communities.

My Past Made Me Do It

Many neuroscientists and psychologists insist that the concept of mind can be fully explained as "neurons doing their electrochemical thing in the brain." Feelings, memory, attention, and free will are nothing more than neurochemical reactions over which we have no control. They claim there is no such thing as free will or independent thought, that these ideas are romantic illusions. Everything we have experienced over a lifetime is stored in the brain, thus their reasoning that every conscious thought we have can only be the result of that stored past. This group believes there is a specific place in the brain that directs every state of consciousness. If you apply a mild electrical shock to a particular location in the brain, the individual feels hunger, another spot and he feels fear, and another conjures up memories of family. Once every brain location and matching function/emotion is traced, this group believes the mystery of the mind will be solved once and for all. As one neuroscientist involved in mapping all of the brain's functions put it, "The mind is obsolete."

Sigmund Freud supported this theory. In his view, your present experience is fully determined by your past. The popular comedian Flip Wilson summarized many of Freud's theories with his mantra, "The devil made me do it." If you replace the words "the devil" with "my past" then you are in one of the primary fields of Freud's speculative psychology. It is fascinating to note that in all of Freud's vast collected works—his books, papers, and written lectures—there is not one use of the word *responsibility* or any other word that represents the concept of a person having true independent free will or the ability to respond in any way they choose.

The Power of Your Mindbody and Your Will

The opposing view of many prominent neuroscientists and neuropsychologists is that we have a mindbody that can exert a literal force over the creation and transformation of presently active mental models, and the habits that their repeated use has created. This group readily acknowledges that while many of the mindbody's functions are automatic and unconscious, we do have the power to consciously direct the things that truly matter in our lives. If we choose to, we can be the captain of our ship and determine our own destiny. This group believes that we can use the power of our will to override old dominant habits, and create new ones. Through the power of your will you can choose to modify the effects of your past and create the future you desire. You are not a slave or a victim to any aspect of your past life.

Which group is right? Are you simply a product of your past or can you exercise your free will to truly change your life? Are you responsible? Do you have the ability to respond as you choose?

You Do Have Free Will and Choice!

Fortunately, those who claim our future can only be dictated by our past, and the brain controls everything in the body, have been and are continuing to be proven wrong by cutting-edge mindbody science. You do have free will. You can break out of old habits! You can modify the effects of your past and create a future that you desire.

In the 1970s and '80s, the brilliant and courageous research and work of professionals like Candace Pert, Antonio Damasio, Jeffrey Schwartz, John Hughes, Hans Kosterlitz, Page Bailey, Francis Schmitt, Gerald Edelman, and others began to shatter many of the cherished beliefs held by Western scientists and psychologists for more than three centuries. These pioneers proved that the body is not a mindless machine, simply obeying the dictates of the brain. There is a mind and it directs both the brain and the body. Each of us can use the power of our mind to direct and improve our future, without fear of our past habits, environments, or family history.

Yet there are many in our society who choose to live their lives on autopilot, allowing existing mental models, dominant habits, and their past to dictate their future. For these individuals, the claim that "the power of the mind is a romantic illusion" holds true. Concerning these individuals, Dr. Jeffrey Schwartz in his ground-breaking book, *The Mind and the Brain,* states, "For if we truly believe, when the day is done, that our mind and all that term entails—the choices we make, the reactions we have, the emotions we feel—are nothing but the expressions of a machine governed by the rules of classical physics and chemistry, and that our behavior follows ineluctably from the working of our neurons, then we're forced to conclude that the subjective sense of freedom is a 'user illusion.' "[1]

The bottom line is you get to choose! You can live your life on autopilot at the unconscious level, or you can learn to consciously exercise the power of your mind to overcome your past and direct your future.

Your Conscious and Subconscious Experience

If you truly desire to overcome past negative habits and dominant mental models, and form new ones leading to the realization of your highest goals and aspirations, then you must learn to bring your habit formation process to the conscious level.

Your mind operates in your body at two levels: the level of which you are aware (conscious) and that of which you are not aware (subconscious).

Most of the activity in your mindbody takes place at the subconscious level with billions of cellular processes taking place continuously. However, subconscious activity is not limited to functions such as digestion, immune system processes, blood flow, and breathing. Many of your behaviors, beliefs, and attitudes have become so habitual, their mental models so dominant, that you are no longer aware of the process. You can remain stuck in your day-to-day ruts, repeating the same behaviors over and over again, unaware of the processes going on below the surface.

Compared to all the subconscious activity going on inside of us, that of which we become consciously aware is small. Bailey uses an analogy of the vast ocean to represent our unconscious experience, and a tiny teacup of salt water as our conscious experience.

But here is the grand key: You can use the power of your will at the conscious level to dictate much of what goes on at the unconscious level—the tiny teacup can influence the vast ocean! Your mindbody is designed to give you a choice!

Consider what Candace Pert said about this reality in her revolutionary book, *Molecules of Emotion*: "While much of the activity of the body, according to the new information model, does take place at the automatic, unconscious level, what makes this model so different is that it can explain how it is also possible for our conscious mind to enter the network and play a deliberate part."[2]

Of all the billions of activities going on in your mindbody, when one suddenly reaches your awareness, your consciousness, it is so special and unique that Page Bailey refers to it as privileged information—information that has reached the Privileged Place. It is only in the Privileged Place that you can exercise your will to eliminate past negative habits and develop new positive behaviors.

The Power of the Privileged Place

To better understand the Privileged Place, consider the following expansion of Bailey's analogy of the ocean:

Imagine you're standing on the shore looking out over the vast ocean. You can't see the billions of activities going on under the surface; they are invisible to you. This represents your unconscious experience or that of which you are not aware. Many people live significant portions of their lives at very low levels of conscious awareness, "below the surface of the water," allowing themselves to be driven by their past: family background, childhood traumas, negative habits, attitudes, and routines like passive backseat passengers in a car forever traveling down the same deeply rutted road. Unknowingly, they continually add to this cycle through self-talk, TV and other media, and input from family and friends, repeating unproductive behaviors again and again.

A few years ago, a news article stated the following:

> Recent studies conducted by a Stanford University research team have revealed that "what we watch" does have an effect on our imaginations, our learning patterns, and our behaviors. First, we are exposed to new behaviors and characters. Next, we learn or acquire these new behaviors [from mental models]. The last and most crucial step is that we adopt these behaviors as our own [they become a habit]. One of the most critical aspects of human development that we need to understand is the influence of "repeated viewing" and "repeated verbalizing" [repetition] in shaping our [mental models]. The information goes in, "harmlessly, almost unnoticed," on a daily basis, but we don't react to it until later, when we aren't able to realize the basis for our reactions [a habit has formed at the unconscious level]. In other words, our value system is being formed without any conscious awareness on our part of what is happening.

People who allow themselves to passively form mental models and habits in this way, repeat sayings such as "You can't change the past," "That's just the way I am," and "Learn to live with it. We're too old to change things now."

For these individuals, much of life is an unconscious experience driven by habitual mindbody processes they are unaware of. Their RAS activates the same mental models over and over again. They are stuck in the same old behavioral cycle or rut. Bailey calls this living a circular life.

In a circular life, you live as a slave to existing dominant habits and unproductive behaviors, a product of your past. In the confines of the circle, your options are extremely limited.

Now imagine as you're looking out over the ocean, your attention is suddenly drawn to an object breaking through the surface like a shark fin. This represents mindbody activity that has appeared at the conscious level. It is clearly visible and you are focused on it. Page calls this experience privileged. He describes people having conscious experience (like listening to your creed or journaling) and learning how to use that conscious experience as entering the Privileged Place. Conscious experience is privileged experience because you can do something with it, something about it, and something to it. Only privileged information—that of which we become aware—is information we can use to build habits with acts of our will that enable us to achieve the new goals that bring us to a place of greater success and happiness.

The grand key to getting what you want in your life and your relationships is learning how to bring your habit formation process into this Privileged Place where you can direct it. It is only in this Privileged Place where you can permanently form the positive habits you desire and eliminate the negative habits that you no longer desire to be present in your life. You can learn how to take something you're already great at—forming habits—and in the Privileged Place use this process to purposefully and consciously sit in the driver's seat on your journey to your ideal self and your ideal life.

Direct the Formation of Mental Models and Habits

While you genetically inherit your tendency to build mental models and habits, you do not inherit the specific mental models and habits themselves. You can choose and direct the mental models you build and the habits that flow from them. This is what my LifeBalance System teaches you. You have been building mental models your entire life. Most of the time you have been doing this at the unconscious level. Many of your mental models were built as a result of the environment you grew up in and your family of origin. Many came from experiences you had no control over, while others you purposely directed. Now with my help in this book, you are learning how to build new mental models to replace old ones.

The point is, you are already amazingly effective and efficient at forming mental models and habits; this is the built-in natural tendency of your mindbody. While most self-improvement programs, marriage handbooks, weight-loss regimes, and money-making strategies contain valuable information and great ideas, they fail to give people easy-to-implement tools they can use daily to enter the Privileged Place and consciously direct the natural mental model and habit-forming processes already built into the mindbody.

The definition of insanity is often stated as doing the same thing over and over again while expecting a different result. You can't form new habits and achieve the successes you desire while continuing to access and utilize your existing negative mental models. You must build and access new mental models that match your goals for the future. You must break out of your circular life.

You can only do this in the Privileged Place. Consider the wonderful example of Dr. Jeffrey Schwartz and his OCD patients.

The Remarkable Success of OCD Patients

If there is any example of individuals living lives dominated by what goes on under the surface, by automatic behaviors, it is those who suffer from Obsessive Compulsive Disorder, or OCD. OCD is a neuropsychiatric disease marked by distressing, intrusive, unwanted thoughts (the obsessive part) that trigger intensive urges to perform ritualistic behaviors (the compulsive part). OCD patients describe their obsessive thoughts as coming from a part of their mind that is not their true self, like a highjacker taking over their brain's controls. Thus the urge to wash their hands for the fortieth time, fully realizing that their hands aren't dirty, or ritualistically dialing a friend's phone number twenty-seven times before finally letting the number ring through, knowing full well—despite the nagging in their gut—that failing to do so will not doom their friend to instant death.

Because the obsessive thoughts can't be silenced, the resulting compulsive behavior can't be resisted. OCD sufferers feel like puppets on the end of a string, manipulated and jerked around by a cruel puppeteer—their own brain. These individuals are the ultimate example of someone enslaved by powerful mental models and automatic behaviors, individuals dominated by negative habits.

In the 1990s a brilliant and courageous psychiatrist, Dr. Jeffrey M. Schwartz, began developing a revolutionary treatment for OCD that has forever changed the way we view our abilities to overcome negative habits—to change the effects of our past. For over a decade Dr. Schwartz worked with OCD patients, helping them achieve miraculous results, far beyond traditional methods and what was believed possible. Dr. Schwartz made the amazing discovery that willfully directing one's conscious thoughts (in the Privileged Place) produces a mental energy, a force that causes the mindbody to literally shrink existing dominant mental models and build and expand new healthy ones! This mental force actually vetoes the RAS's natural tendency to select the dominant mental model and literally moves it to access the newly desired mental model!

Dr. Schwartz refers to this as "Free Will" vs. "Free Won't"—I will cause my RAS to direct energy to new healthy mental models, and I won't allow the old negative mental models to rule my life. By bringing their automatic OCD behaviors above the surface into the conscious Privileged Place, his patients were able to use their own mental force to literally change the physical structure and circuitry of their brains and attain a whole new life! These remarkable results, and similar success with Taurette's Syndrome, Chronic Depression and other disorders are documented in Jeffrey's astonishing book, *The Mind and the Brain: Neuroplasticity and the Power of Mental Force.*

Consider the "before and after" mindbody processes and brain structure/circuitry of the OCD patients:

Illustration 1: Before working with Dr. Schwartz, the OCD patients' mental model process took place at the unconscious level where they were helpless to do anything about it. The RAS followed its natural tendency and selected the dominant OCD mental model every time. The OCD patients remained stuck in their rut, in their circular life.

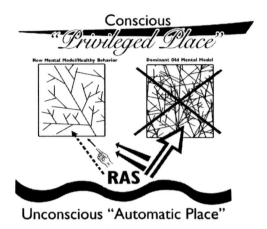

Illustration 2: Under Dr. Schwartz's program, OCD patients were taught to bring the mental model process above the surface into the Privileged Place where they could direct it. Through the exercise of their free will, the patients held an image of their new behavioral goal in their conscious thoughts until the mental force needed to move their RAS to the new mental model was created. Even though the pathway to the new mental model was faint and the connections few, they actually vetoed their RAS's natural tendency to select the dominant mental model. Mental energy created a tangible force that made the RAS switch to the new mental model for healthy behavior.

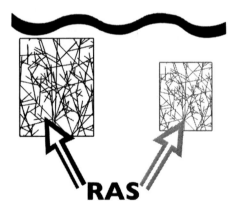

Illustration 3: With practice and repetition over time, the new mental model became dominant while the old OCD mental model faded. Eventually, the entire process became automatic, the new healthy behavior a habit, and was moved under the surface where the OCD patients no longer had to think about it. They were free to move on and accomplish higher goals and aspirations in their lives!

In parallel but separate professional work, Bailey has developed his own unique neuropsychological and mindbody therapy programs. For nearly twenty years Bailey has been using his powerful techniques to help his clients recover from chronic illnesses, chronic pain, addictions of all types, depression, sleep disorders, and many other kinds of mental and physical disorders.

This Program Is for Everyone

You may be wondering, "What do OCD sufferers and people with serious disorders have to do with my current situation and goals for the future?" The purpose in citing these examples is not to suggest that the LifeBalance System is only designed for people with serious disorders and challenges. Absolutely not! The work of Schwartz, Bailey, and others is sited to illustrate the enormous power of this program for everyone, regardless of their situation, needs or goals for the future. I have used the LifeBalance System to help thousands of individuals achieve success in every area of their lives. With amazing results being experienced by people with extreme challenges, imagine what you can do to overcome your own negative habits and move forward to attain the success, joy, and fulfillment you desire!

Attention! Entering the Privileged Place

As Schwartz, Bailey, and others have clearly shown, the Privileged Place is a place of power! Thoughts are things—tangible, traceable, producing a mental force that acts on the physical brain and body. What this means in real-life application is that you get what you think about; you get what you expect. The thoughts you allow to play on the stage of your mind create a self-fulfilling prophecy; good or bad—you choose the mental models that are activated by the thoughts you entertain.

Many people allow whatever thoughts happen to enter the Privileged Place to dwell there, generating a mental force and the resulting consequences. Too often, these thoughts are negative, based on years of habit. They rise up from below the surface and enter the Privileged Place, generating the same negative behaviors they always have. Most of us become preoccupied with what does not go well rather than what does.

Guard well the gates to your Privileged Place, the place of your conscious thoughts. It is a place of incredible power. Whatever you allow to enter and dwell in this sacred place will fully determine the quality and success of every aspect of your life.

Harnessing and Directing Your Habit Formation Powers

As already mentioned, each of us is incredibly effective and efficient at forming habits—we've been doing it since the day of our birth. Most of our habits are formed at the unconscious level, without our being aware of the process. Unfortunately, some of these habits, beliefs, thoughts, and behavior patterns are negative, disruptive, and keep us from all the success and happiness we desire in our lives and relationships. But here is the good news: The same steps you have followed to form your negative habits can be used to form positive habits and achieve the success and happiness you desire in your life and relationships. The process is the same. You're already great at it! All you need are a few simple rules and basic tools to bring the process in the Privileged Place and direct it.

The process of combining forty-plus years of coaching individuals, with the cutting-edge work in neuropsychology and clinical psychology carried out by Schwartz, Bailey, and others provides for us the daily system for entering the Privileged Place and using the power of your will to create the mental force necessary to direct the creation and transformation of your mental models and habits.

The LifeBalance System will allow you to create what I call Consciously-Directed Goals: goals you bring into the privileged place on a daily basis where you can direct their progress and fulfillment. Consciously-Directed Goals shine in stark contrast to their distant cousins: the written goal in the day planner; the New Year's Resolution; and the "this is finally it" declaration of a determination to change. These good intentions often fail, because they fail to incorporate the Three Rules of Mental Model and Habit Creation and Transformation that are essential to creating Consciously-Directed Goals.

The Three Rules of Mental Model and Habit Creation and Transformation

Each of the Three Rules that follow are preceded by their equivalent negative habit-formation principle. Compare the automatic unconscious habit-formation process you've been engaged in all your life, with the Privileged Place process of Consciously-Directed Goals.

Negative Habit-Formation Principle 1: Over your lifetime you have formed negative mental models with vast connections to feelings, emotions, and memories, producing deep and powerful meaning. These connections are like a magnetic force attracting the compass needle of your RAS. It's no surprise that these dominant mental models are easily and automatically selected by your RAS.

Rule 1: Discover and articulate your goals in a way that builds and accesses mental models with powerful meaning.

The negative habits, beliefs, and behaviors in our lives stem from mental models with powerful meaning. In order to form new positive habits, you must first build mental models with equally powerful connections, emotions, and meaning. Control meaning and you control your future. The most effective way to do this is to incorporate four basic elements into the description of each of your Consciously-Directed Goals:

1. Clearly state your goal. This may appear to be obvious—scarcely worth mentioning, but many people are far too broad and generic in describing their goals. Common statements like "I want to make more money," "I want to improve my marriage," "I want to get into shape," or "I want to lose weight" make it difficult for the mindbody to build a specific mental model to match the desired goal.

Imagine you have written down your goal and a complete stranger reads it. From your written description alone, would the person understand the specifics of your goal? Look at your goal statement and ask yourself, "What do I mean by that?" Keep refining and asking that question until you can refine no further. Now you have a clearly stated goal.

2. Identify and clearly state your motive—why you want to achieve the specific goal. Describe its positive benefits, rewards, and outcomes. Doing this creates three critical results in the mental model formation process: a) A powerful motive forms powerful connections and meaning in the desired mental model; b) Focusing on motive initiates and magnifies the mental force that moves your RAS to select the new mental model over the old dominant one; and c) When faced with obstacles and the temptation to fall back into your old habit, turning your attention to your motive will instantly activate the desired mental model.

3. Act as if you've achieved your goal. Visualize yourself already having achieved your goal. Describe in great detail how you feel. Describe what it has done for the quality of your life, relationships, your successes, and so forth. Describe how those you care about respond positively to the achievement of your goal. Imagine the vast connections this forms in the mental model you are building.

In a recent lecture, Dr. Antonio Damasio, one of the world's leading neuroscientists, taught that the mindbody forms memories, not only based on past experiences, but also based on the future that we expect. Thus, as we expect and visualize the achievement of a specific goal, we build mental models with memories of that expected future—connections to all of the images, feelings, and emotions associated with that future. Thus, you can build powerful new mental models with vast connections based on your desired future—as if it were already a reality! Remember, when meaning is powerful, your mindbody cannot distinguish between what is real and what your mental models tell you is real. We literally attract what we think about.

4. Use present tense. One of the most effective ways to create powerful meaning in your mindbody is to express an expectation. The final element under Rule 1 is to state your goal, your motive, and your visualization of its realization in the present tense—as if all of it is already taking place, already a reality. Rather than using statements like, "I will," "I want," or "I try to," put everything in the present tense: "I am," "I do," "I deserve," "I am becoming," or "I feel."

Remember, your mindbody is always in the process of bringing your experience into a state of agreement with your expectation. Based on what you expect or believe, your mindbody activates the mental model most suited to making that expectation a reality.

Negative Habit-Formation Principle 2: Negative thought patterns, behaviors, and habits are repeated and practiced thousands of times—expanding and reinforcing the mental models they flow from. This is why the pathways leading to these mental models become so deeply rutted.

Rule 2: Engage in daily practice and repetition in the Privileged Place

Many of your dominant mental models and habits have been created, accessed, and expanded over many years of daily practice and repetition. You must find a simple, easy way to generate the same type of daily practice and repetition if your new mental models and habits are to become dominant. On a consistent daily basis, you need to bring your Consciously-Directed Goals into the Privileged Place and begin forming increasingly rutted pathways to new mental models. Your LifeCreed, listened to daily, is the perfect tool to accomplish this. Through this daily repetition, your RAS will begin activating your desired mental models automatically—you will form new habits. Each time the desired mental model is accessed, it expands; its connections grow in number and strength. Each time the old dominant mental model is not selected, it shrinks and the pathway to it becomes increasingly faint.

In *The Mind and the Brain,* Schwartz sites a study directed by neuroscientist Alvaro Pascual-Leone. Pascual-Leone had one group of volunteers practice a five-finger piano exercise, and a comparable group merely think about practicing it. They visualized each finger movement, playing the piece in their heads one note at a time. Brain scans of the physical practice group showed changes in brain structure as expected. But, amazingly, the same level of brain change was noted in the mental rehearsal group! Merely thinking about moving one's fingers produced brain changes comparable to actually moving them.

Simply visualizing or mentally practicing your desired goals by listening to your LifeCreed begins creating mental models and habits leading to their fulfillment.

Eventually you can move the process to the unconscious level where you don't have to think about it any more and you can shift your willful attention to other Consciously-Directed Goals you want to achieve. Your life becomes one of success building on success, a perpetual upward spiral.

Negative Habit-Formation Principle 3: Unfortunately, negative habits don't require any accountability to form and continue progressing. Because these habits are typically created and reinforced at the unconscious level, the process is automatic.

Rule 3: Give yourself and others permission to hold you accountable

In the hectic busyness and stress of everyday life it's very easy to lose conscious awareness of your Consciously-Directed Goals and slip below the surface, back into old habits. You need to give yourself and the special people in your life permission to remind you and hold you accountable to consistently implement daily tools for the creation, transformation, and continual development of new habits.

NOTE: *In this book you were introduced to the basic tools and other resources that make it easy for you to fully implement into your daily life all components of the three essential rules described above. You can take full control of the mental model and habit formation processes and begin your journey toward your ideal self and life.*

Moving to Ever Higher Levels

Through the daily implementation of the LifeBalance System, you can continuously bring the areas of your life that you want to change, or the goals you want to achieve, into the Privileged Place. Here you can use your natural built-in habit formation skills to make your desired behaviors automatic and your goals a reality. You can then move on to the next level and do the same thing. Your life will look something like this:

Dr. Page Bailey
The Brain-Mind Dialogue

"The mind is the modified history of that which the brain has experienced. The history of brain experience is a living and active record of our lives. The brain in its dialogue with the mind does not give us a personal history that is written in stone. That dialogue provides us with a malleable history that has been and that is being continually remade by both our dominant present purposes and the specific behavioral goals toward which our creative energies are now being directed."

NOTE: *Does all the information in this appendix mean to suggest that the mentally ill, the addict, the violent husband, or the suicidal teenager only need to exercise their will to correct the problem—they only remain sick because of a lack of will power? To approach these challenges as an all or nothing—choice or no choice—is far too simplistic.*

There are situations where years of dominant mental model access and reinforcement at the unconscious level creates a habit so powerful, it can become overwhelming. Sometimes unwanted negative processes at the unconscious and conscious levels are too great for mental force to overcome. Sometimes will power alone isn't enough, but must be accompanied by knowledge, training, support from loved ones and the community, and appropriate medical, psychological, and therapeutic interventions. The LifeBalance System, its rules and tools, are designed to work in harmony with and support higher level interventions when needed.

NOTES

1. Jeffrey Schwartz, *The Mind and the Brain: Neuroplasticity and the Power of Mental Force* (New York: HarperCollins, 2002), 19.
2. Candice Pert, *Molecules of Emotion: The Science behind Mind-Body Science* (New York: Touchstone, 1997), 186.

Index

About the Author

Leo Weidner is probably the country's first Personal Coach. He has spent over forty years personally coaching over 2,000 mostly successful individuals to have a more balanced life. Leo's primary role is that of an implementer. Clients are shown how to balance and structure their lives between personal and career-oriented goals. Leo's focus on journaling enables a client to weigh what is important in his or her life and why. The client and coach then create a LifeCreed, which is a written visualization of the ideal balanced life they want to live without the horrible stress. They then record this Creed and listen to it every day.

Working through only one-on-one phone sessions, Leo has clients locally and internationally. Clients are coached for twelve months, forty-five minutes every week for four months and then every other week for eight months. Half of his clients are in the financial services industry. Most earn well over one hundred thousand a year, and some are even in the million dollar plus range and lead their companies.

Leo started developing his unique system when he worked with the grandfather of goal setting and motivation, Napoleon Hill, in 1966.

Leo helped Dr. Hill develop the Napoleon Hill Academy. From there, Leo worked both in the field and the home office, for Success Motivation Institute in Waco, Texas for over five years.

While Leo graduated from Brigham Young University with a BS in business, it's what he has learned from his clients that has provided him his greatest treasure of knowledge, which he loves to share.

Leo draws on a rich background of having helped develop or lead five national and three international sales organizations. He was founder and past president of the Utah Speaker's Association. Leo and his wife, Shirley, have nine children and twenty-one grandchildren.